CONSERVING CULTURES

CONSERVING CULTURES

TECHNOLOGY, GLOBALIZATION, AND THE FUTURE OF LOCAL CULTURES

Harry Redner

ROWMAN & LITTLEFIELD PUBLISHERS, INC.
Lanham • Boulder • New York • Toronto • Oxford

ROWMAN & LITTLEFIELD PUBLISHERS, INC.

Published in the United States of America
by Rowman & Littlefield Publishers, Inc.
A wholly owned subsidiary of The Rowman & Littlefield Publishing Group, Inc.
4501 Forbes Boulevard, Suite 200, Lanham, Maryland 20706
www.rowmanlittlefield.com

PO Box 317
Oxford
OX2 9RU, UK

British Library Cataloguing in Publication Information Available

Library of Congress Cataloging-in-Publication Data

Redner, Harry.
    Conserving cultures : technology, globalization, and the future of
local cultures / Harry Redner.
        p. cm.
Includes bibliographical references and index.
    ISBN 0-7425-2733-6 (cloth : alk. paper) — ISBN 0-7425-2734-4 (pbk. :
alk. paper)
    1. Culture. 2. Technology and civilization. 3. Globalization—Social
aspects. 4. Information technology—Social aspects. 5. Culture
diffusion. 6. International relations and culture. 7. Civilization,
Modern—21st century. I. Title.

HM621.R426 2004
306—dc22   2003020111

Printed in the United States of America

∞™ The paper used in this publication meets the minimum requirements of
American National Standard for Information Sciences—Permanence of Paper
for Printed Library Materials, ANSI/NISO Z39.48-1992.

CONTENTS

INTRODUCTION

Eons of time formerly passed without producing such changes as are now produced by a few years. The fundamental cause is the triumph of modern high–technical society, which is transforming the whole world—its crust, its oceans, its biosphere and atmosphere—in ways that were formerly unimaginable. . . . The primary effect has been a mass massacre of independent art traditions in every inhabited region of the globe. . . . In many regions, the process no doubt began in the nineteenth century heyday of Western imperialism. Yet the essence of the process has been something never seen before, in fact worldwide cultural homogenization. Because of the power of high-technical society, homogenization has actually gained momentum since the twentieth-century retreat of Western imperial powers. Right around the globe, just about all the surviving independent art traditions, whether nourished by little tribes or great races of men, have been destroyed by the impact of high-technical society. Or at best they have been debased to market production of new kinds of art, often for airport shops for tourists.[1]

In just a few passing sentences in the midst of a book on art, Joseph Alsop, once an internationally renowned American journalist, has astutely summed up most of what is wrong with the cultural state of the world, and, fortuitously, what are also the key themes of this book. He has perceptively linked the problems of ecology with those of art and referred both back to their root cause, which he calls "the triumph of modern high-technical society" and which we shall call the triumph of technics. He has noted that the effect has been "worldwide cultural homogenization." This has become even more evident since these lines were penned in the early 1980s, for at about that time an increased tendency toward cultural homogenization ensued, which we now describe by that ominous term "globalization." This development has enlarged and speeded up the destructive effects of our technological civilization on both nature and culture.

With the onset of globalization in general, culture has assumed an unprecedented form, identical in all parts of the world—global culture. This is also a kind of monoculture which, like its analogous manifestation in ecology, is threatening to wipe out all species diversity. In both its forms, monoculture is diffused throughout the world by multinational corporations that represent a new stage of capitalist development. These impose on all societies their more or less homogeneous products, allowing for very little local variety. As a result, the still extant local cultures, some of them going back thousands of years, are being rapidly subverted and overwhelmed by the constant flood of such imports. This invasion seems impossible to stem in an era of globalization, with its open markets and porous borders and satellite communications. If this trend is allowed to continue for much longer there will soon be nothing left but the one pervasive global culture, the ultimate in homogenization.

Such an outcome would be an unmitigated disaster for mankind, one falling little short of the concurrently threatening ecological catastrophe. The human creative spirit, which is invariably individual and local, would be crushed in a uniform world of global culture where even personal identity would be severely restricted in the forms it could assume. If all people became nothing better than cultural consumers, and if all that were available for them to choose from were the same range of products, they would eventually become as alike as these products themselves, at best only distinguished as upmarket or down-market buyers. In the cultural supermarkets of the future choice will be limited to brand-name labels as little different as Coke and Pepsi or *Time* and *Newsweek*.

The only course open at present in attempting to counter this horrendous outcome is, at the least, to conserve both traditional and modern local cultures in a holding operation to prevent them disappearing forever and to check the unresisted sweep of global culture. This is a cultural conservation effort akin to nature conservation; both seek to preserve environments or milieus and the "species" that inhabit them. Cultural "species"—distinct ways of life and the forms that govern them—are disappearing at as great a rate as natural species. And just as many breeds of animals will only survive in zoos, so many cultures will only be remembered in museums and ethnographic collections. A simple example of this is the rapid loss of spoken languages, many of which will soon only be preserved in textbooks.

To retain anything of what is left a new movement needs to be launched to uphold local and oppose global culture. But such a culturalist movement will have to distinguish itself from the antiglobalization movements current at present. The strident and sometimes violent opposition to trade liberalization and other such purely economic measures, which often is a disguise for a visceral anticapitalism, is doomed to failure, for it is seeking to reverse the whole course of global development. Like a latter-day Canute, it is trying to hold back the tide of history. Nevertheless, there are specific issues raised by the antiglobalizers that are worthy of support, such as the exploitative and inhumane labor conditions in some developing countries, Third World debt and poverty, and the grossly uneven distribution of wealth in most societies. However, the activists, as well as their opponents, confuse the economic and cultural impact of globalization, and are unable to grasp that the greater danger lies in the latter. For it is well possible that mankind will, overall, enrich itself economically from globalization, yet in the process become culturally destitute. Much the same argument applies against the capitalist advocates of globalization who only see the economic benefits and fail to note the cultural losses that these entail.

In short, to be averse to global culture is not necessarily to be opposed to all other aspects of globalization, which is the culmination of a long-extended historical process that encompasses so much more than culture. Such a total opposition is bound to be futile, for globalization in some form or other is inevitable. It is but the latest manifestation of the changes that humanity has been undergoing for the last two centuries and which gave rise to our present technological civilization. These began in Western Europe with the industrial revolution, but have by now extended to the rest of the world. This has been a momentous historical event that can only be compared with a few others in the whole of human history. In its scope, immensity, and likely consequences it is comparable to only two other such transformations that totally changed humanity and its relation to the natural environment: the Neolithic revolution starting about twelve thousand years ago, and the rise of cities and civilizations starting about five thousand years ago.

Like these previous epochal changes, the rise of a global technological civilization opens up unprecedented opportunities for mankind; but, unlike them, it also involves unprecedented dangers. Whether mankind can overcome these dangers to its own existence and capitalize on the opportunities is now unpredictable and will only become apparent in the centuries to come. We can only think and act as if we expect that these dangers and opportunities will become apparent, for that is the necessary expression of faith in ourselves—that is, in humanity as such; without it, we could not confront the overwhelming problems that present themselves to us now, above all those of culture and nature.

The problems of ecology are now the most obvious and the ones best understood. They mostly arise out of the application of a whole range of technologies to agriculture. This has brought about the most drastic change in our relation to nature since the Neolithic revolution, when hunting and gathering gave way to agriculture and animal husbandry. These traditional ways of farming only began to change radically a few centuries ago in Western Europe and then even more decisively in North America. From these beginnings derive the present fully industrialized methods of working the land, to agribusinesses and factory farming, and eventually to the genetic modification of plants and animals. Due to these technological changes our whole relation to nature has been transformed. It has given rise to both tremendous achievements and commensurate failures. Food production has expanded almost geometrically to feed a constantly rising population, against all Malthusian expectations. But at the same time this very success is creating all the environmental disasters with which we now have to learn to cope. How to sustain food productivity and yet undo the environmental damage is the unsolved ecological problem for mankind.

The cultural problem is strictly analogous. The effects of our technological civilization on culture have been no less decisive than those on nature. One could put this in brief by saying that just as nature has been devastated, so has human nature—namely, the quality of human life and the character of human beings—been adversely affected. The change in the quality of life is most visible in the transformation of cities, which have grown from the poleis of tens of thousands of inhabitants or at most the metropolises of a few hundreds of thousands, whose sizes more or less remained constant throughout history, to the present megalopolises of tens of millions joining each other in whole regional conurbations. The cause of this urban congestion is once more bound up with technology: as fewer people are now required to till the land, the excess rural population drifts to the cities where industrial and service work is available and where life seems easier, thanks to the technologies of transport, communication, water and sewerage, sanitation, and so on.

Once again we can only compare the scope of this change in the quality of human life with the original rise of cities that led to the early civilizations. The current urbanization is also a civilizational change, one that began in Western Europe and North America a few centuries ago and is now extending to the rest of the world, especially so in the heavily populated regions of Asia. This change, too, has had its good and bad consequences. On the positive side it has undoubtedly improved the material conditions of life as measured by quantitative factors such as longevity, infant mortality, access to facilities, housing, schooling, and so on, and in most societies it has eventually led to rising standards of living. But on the negative side it has brought about huge deficits in the qualitative aspects of living, especially so in its cultural forms. Communities have been uprooted and destroyed, family life and personal relations have been damaged, individuals have been left alienated and isolated in the midst of anonymous urban masses. People might eat better, live longer, become more literate, and have greater access to the media, but they suffer a loss of identity and value-orientation that brings with it anxiety, depression, and a lack of meaning and purpose in life, which they try to drown out with sex, sport, alcohol, drugs, and television.

Thus the dilemmas we now face in relation to nature and culture are both interconnected and analogous to each other. One the one hand, there is the dilemma of how to maintain productivity in order to feed a huge global population without poisoning the earth—the source of all nourishment—and eradicating all wildlife. On the other hand, there is the equally great difficulty of how to increase living standards for most people on earth without compromising completely the cultural quality of their lives. Both of these supreme problems are bound up with our historical transition from the various civilizations of the past to the one global technological civilization that is common to all of mankind. Both are, therefore, linked to each other to constitute a conjoined crisis of humanity. How this overwhelming crisis is resolved will determine the fate of human life on earth.

It might seem as if the present prevalence of global culture is merely a small matter in such momentous circumstances. It might be contended that the cultural homogenization of humanity—the fact that tastes, activities, aspirations, and lifestyles are becoming everywhere the same—is simply a necessary and inevitable by-product of our technological civilization. It might be assumed in a positive spirit that these uniformities are the cultural manifestations of the newfound unity of all of mankind. For the first time ever since hominids emerged out of Africa, human beings all over the earth have finally been reunited and brought together—also thanks to technology. We now live in a global electronic village, we are told. So, it is assumed, as humans all over the world become interconnected—by ties of communication, transportation, organization, migration, tourism, etc.—they inevitably become more alike culturally. Whereas previously throughout history human groups were separated by distance and other geographical barriers, and divided by race, language, religion, nationality, culture, and so on for all the other divisive factors, now, for the very first time, such differences are disappearing and being replaced by unifying conditions.

It might seem, then, that cultural homogeneity is but a small price to pay for these newfound unities and the benefits they bring. The old grounds of conflict and contention are eroding. People who share a common culture have less to bicker about or battle over. When nations compete on the football field rather than the battlefield people cannot do each other much harm. What is the point of chivalry when there is no need of cavalry? Giving up our ethical traditions of honor does not seem much of a loss under these circumstances. Giving up our many old cultures for the sake of the one global culture seems a gain when that global culture can act as the basis for a unified and pacified world freed of conflicts and wars.

Unfortunately, it is not so clear that global culture is the harbinger of perfect peace. It is not only cultural differences that make for contention; any kind of differential in power and property can lead to rivalry, competition, and war. And the technologies of weaponry we now possess make even minor wars a threat to the whole world. By contrast, it does not always follow that cultural differences make for conflict. History has provided many instances of empires, such as the Persian and Roman, where peoples of different cultures coexisted in peace for long periods. There is no inherent reason that this could not happen on a global level, as it were, in an "empire of the world." A technological civilization could organize itself to maintain effective peace through one or another type of community of nations.

Hence it might be argued, to the contrary, that the world would be less stable with no cultural differences than with them. A world pervaded by the one global culture might give rise to all kinds of social pathologies leading to disturbances and upheavals that could assume global dimensions. Global culture, which is a consumer culture, satisfies no basic needs, either psychological or existential, for it is incapable of establishing identity or endowing meaning. It nourishes the soul just as little as fast food nourishes the body; it provides ephemeral satisfactions that soon revert to the hunger for something more substantial. It produces masses of disgruntled people all over the globe who wander about as nomadic hordes in times of trouble or vacation times. Such people are the tinder that can easily be set alight to cause a global conflagration.

It is only local or traditional culture that makes for identity and meaning through communities of belonging that give a purpose for living, that establish personal relations, that confer worth and standing, that inculcate morals and manners, that give faith and hope, and so on. It is true that such things make for differences, but where people do not have much to differ about they do not have anything they can call their own. This does not mean that we must strive for a return to the old divided world, or that this is possible under the conditions of a technological civilization. Of course the newfound unity of mankind must be maintained but without forfeiting cultural diversity. How this is to be achieved is at the heart of our endeavor.

If it is to be achieved at all then global culture must be opposed. This is the first step—and a most difficult one it will be, for global culture is in keeping with the major forces and power centers of our present world. It is produced and upheld by powerful economic interests, above all by the multinational media and advertising conglomerates. It serves the prestige needs of the leading nations, above all of the United States. It is the preferred choice of people in a mass society as expressed through the open market. It carries the aura of progress through expertise, utilizing the most advanced methods and instruments of technology. Thus it is the culture expressive of the triumph of technics that is the hallmark of our technological civilization.

Such a triumph of technics is peculiar to this civilization and to none other. Techniques of various kinds are an inherent component of every cultural activity in any civilization, for every culture has its own technical methods, instruments, media, skills and practical ways of proceeding. But in no previous culture were such techniques pursued for their own sake or for the sake of sheer efficiency and allowed to become preponderant over the meaning-giving and value-endowing functions of culture—that is, over representation and ethos. Representation, in all its possible senses, refers to those symbolic modes that enable discourse, equations, pictures and all other such depictive forms to stand for or reflect a given reality, and thereby to express all that a culture upholds as true. Ethos refers to the normative and evaluative dimensions, those which govern ethical, artistic, and other creative activities. Technics, our third major term, refers to the ensemble of techniques and media that are also necessarily present in any given culture. Usually in all previous cultures the means of technics served the ends of representation and ethos. It is only in our technological civilization, with the triumph of technics, that this relation has been reversed, for it is the means of technics that now determine the ends to be pursued. If we have the means to do something, if in Robert Oppenheimer's phrase it has become "technically sweet," then almost inevitably it will be done, whether it be building an A-bomb or cloning a human being.

This triumph of technics is also the present culmination of a long historical process going on for many centuries in the West. Various authors have described and explained its different aspects. Its domination of culture has been neatly summed up in a recent publication by Richard Stivers: "Until the nineteenth century technology developed at a pace that allowed it to be integrated into culture. Because of an unbounded faith in technology and a conscious intention to experiment with technology and find a diversity of uses for a single technique, technology came to dominate culture."[2] As Stivers, following the earlier work of Jacques Ellul, makes amply apparent, technology in this context is no longer a mere matter of tools and machines, it has become a system of technics: "as technology proliferates, has generalized application and becomes co-ordinated (through the computer), it tends to form a system. Techniques relate to one another before they are adjusted to human use and need."[3]

It is in these ways that techniques invade and take over our ways of representing, and so insert themselves into our symbolic system. A technically superior method or medium of representing can impose itself and determine what can be represented, even though it might be far more limited symbolically than previous more traditional ways of representation. Thus in this way the technically advanced media of mechanical image and voice recording and manipulation are gaining supremacy over the older verbal and written discursive forms. Films and television are now the preferred media for narration, and all the older ways of storytelling are becoming antiquated. Storytelling has suffered considerable losses in expression, as is obvious when one compares a good novel with the film based on it. The gains in visual vividness and dramatic enactment seem minor by comparison to the losses in meaning content, form, and style.

Something analogous is happening with the technification of the ethos. Newly developed techniques for behavior control and human management displace the ethical norms and values that were in force before. As Stivers puts it, "[H]uman techniques (techniques for the manipulation of human beings) tend to supplant morality, manners and social institutions. Bureaucracy (a technique of organization), propaganda, advertising, public relations, psychological techniques (such as how-to books on child rearing or becoming successful or having a positive outlook), and expert systems are only some of the most obvious examples."[4] Other examples are the law and order enforcement techniques that rely on an intricate network of rules, regulations, bylaws, and restrictions of all kinds designed to keep people in check in every conceivable situation. With these comes the whole apparatus of policing and punishing to enforce compliance. These are the technics that dominate the ethos to the detriment of traditional methods of autonomous self-control.

But is it possible for such traditional nontechnified measures to endure in a technological civilization? Can a technological civilization be compatible with any culture other than a technified global culture? That is the supreme question of our time and of the future. To give a negative answer seems both obvious and preordained. It seems obvious because on most theories of culture everything about a technological civilization points to a technified culture. If culture is seen in the Hegelian manner as the spirit of the times, then how can a technological age produce anything other than an *ésprit technicien*?

If culture is seen in the Marxist manner as the reflection of underlying material conditions, then how can a technological base give rise to a nontechnical superstructure? If the matter is considered sociologically, no better response is forthcoming, for how can a society structured around a technological system not promote a technically mediated and organized culture? In whatever way the question is approached the answer seems negative and despairing.

Yet, theoretically considered, there must be some room for hope, since a technological system cannot be coextensive with the whole of society. There is much more to social life than technology, and part of that is culture. Culture can be technified to a considerable degree, but never completely. There will always remain a nonreducible residue that cannot be rendered technical. Hence there are limits to the technification of representation and ethos, beyond which it cannot be pushed short of destroying the culture altogether and debasing human beings along with it. But if that makes for hope, then it only does so in the last resort.

However, there is another consideration that is more positive and that lies in arguing for the relative autonomy of culture and its partial independence from other major social spheres. On this view, the degree of technification of a culture is not determined by the prevalence of technics in the rest of society. An industrialized society does not necessarily produce an industrialized culture. If that were so, then a Gothic revival, or in general, a Romantic movement, would not have been possible in Victorian England. Even now, in the midst of a technological civilization, it is still possible to resist the excessive technification of culture. All kinds of means can be employed to prevent this happening. A deliberate countermovement can be launched against it.

In fact this is the very movement against global culture we are here advocating, for global culture and technified culture are in effect the same thing. Global culture tries to reduce to a technique every cultural activity it touches. It aims for procedures in which everything is, as far as possible routinized, planned, and prescribed. As little as possible is to be left to the discretion of individuals or their creative talents. The dream factories of Hollywood worked to a production schedule and employed a division of labor among specialized teams of workers on set formats. Now much is left to computer simulation in filmmaking. Advertising firms work in much the same way. Record producers are mainly concerned with the engineering of sound. The dispensers of culinary products have taken these technical processes to their logical conclusion where most of what is done can be automated or performed by unskilled labor. Moves are in fact underfoot to automate other forms of cultural production. Perhaps one day pop music will be composed by computers, though that day is still far off.

In opposition to such a highly technified global culture we must seek recourse to every cultural form that has remained untechnified. Invariably these are the still-surviving forms of local culture. It is in these that there remain openings for the personal touch and for unregulated creativity, because symbolic meanings and values have not been perverted or repressed through technical controls usually serving commercial ends. In such cultural forms it is not yet the case that the medium is the message. In these the content of what is represented, its basic truth and reality, takes precedence over the media and means of representation. The values expressed are not a function of the mode of expression. In general, representation and ethos are not subservient to technics.

Local culture is the all-embracing term for all that stands in opposition to global culture. The term covers everything that is still left, so to speak, in a humanly natural state, that has not been expropriated and converted to a cultural product for the global market. Many such local cultures still exist at an elite or popular level, among the wealthy or the poor, in town or country, or wherever else something autonomous has survived that retains its own integrity and has not bargained away its soul for the fleshpots of globalization. Some of these are the cultures of so-called primitive or native peoples, others are the cultures of the former great civilizations and universal religions. Where there is an identifiable group of people, big or small, sharing a common cultural life, there a local culture will be found. Hence it is not possible to give an exhaustive list of all local cultures short of a very exhausting catalogue that nobody will want to read. Nor is it possible to provide an exact definition of the *genus proximum differentia specifica* type, for local cultures cannot be neatly categorized.

Local cultures differ vastly not only in type but in value as well. Not all are worthy of admiration and respect, or even of preservation. The cultures of headhunters or of fanatical fundamentalists are clearly not to be encouraged. It is always necessary to exercise value judgments and deem some cultures more worthwhile than others. Some are so bad that even global culture is preferable to them. We must not fall into an undifferentiating value relativism for the sake of some superenlightened tolerance and universalist good will. All cultures cannot be ranked equal; perforce, invidious comparisons have to be made. It is, of course, a very difficult matter to make cultural comparisons, and one must allow room for fundamental differences and irresolvable disputes. Cultures cannot be ranked in a simple hierarchy of value. But none of these difficulties should preclude value judgments where these are called for.

Such judgments should not always be in favor of the authentic and traditional. Intelligent and creative adaptations or modernizing tendencies should be given their due regard. It is no use trying to keep local cultures fixed and unchanging. Cultures are not like museum exhibits that must be preserved intact and not tampered with; they are living forms that must be allowed to grow with the changing ebb and flow of human life. Conserving culture does not mean keeping it unaltered. Particularly in a world of rapid globalization with all its associated transformations, it is all the more necessary that local cultures develop ways of adjusting to these new pressures, for otherwise they will not survive. What matters is in what spirit this is done, and that it should not lead to selling out. Those cultures that refuse to change in any way whatsoever become like living fossils condemned to a state of artificial preservation. Paradoxically, as tourist attractions, such cultures themselves become part of global culture.

It is in this way that global culture threatens to absorb all others—by treating them as exotic specimens useful for providing local color. Those who advocate multiculturalism as a panacea sometimes have no more in mind than that. They speak as if all that was called for is the preservation of quaint local customs, ethnic habits, some of the ancient lore of tradition, the repertoire of old skills, and their associated songs and stories—select fragments of the past. Unwittingly these multiculturalists play into the hands of the exponents and entrepreneurs of global culture who can make good use of such flotsam and jetsam in tourist attractions, theme parks, restored villages, renewed neighborhoods, and multiethnic festivals in which people put on show their inherited cultural heirlooms. But this is a trivialization of local culture that will inevitably destroy it all the quicker.

All surviving local cultures are thus faced with a double imperative: to retain their identity and essential traditions, but at the same time to transform themselves in such a way as to be able to cope with the changing pace of a global technological civilization. This seems like a contradiction, which is a measure of the difficulty involved, but it is not so difficult as to be impossible, for it can be achieved. How a local culture negotiates these intricate difficulties will determine its chances of survival and its worth. Any one that does manage to maintain its essential character and, at the same time, to prove itself compatible with technological civilization will provide a model for a future cultural life. The more such models are developed, the less the chance of the cultural homogenization of humanity in the triumph of technics.

The remainder of this book consists of four chapters and an epilogue. A brief summary follows to indicate the contents of each of these.

The first chapter, "What Is Global Culture?" is a general presentation of the main issues to be discussed and a descriptive definition of the terms invoked. Thus global culture is specified by being distinguished both from popular culture and from national mass culture. The recent origin of global culture, largely from American mass culture, is traced historically over a number of preceding stages. However, it will be contended that the spread of global culture is not simply a matter of Americanization since elements from other cultures also play a key role, as, for example, English football, Japanese judo, and Indian yoga. Adherence to local culture is advocated as a counter to this cultural "imperialism." It will be argued that this does not have to go against sensible forms of multiculturalism.

The second chapter, "Why Is Global Culture So Successful?" is an attempt to provide a comprehensive set of explanations of the very rapid spread of global culture and its capacity to overcome the opposition of local cultures all over the world. The initial reasons considered are economic: global culture has the full weight of an expanding global capitalism behind it. Directly through advertising and indirectly through other forms of publicity, vast sums have been expended to provide free or very cheap cultural products against which no other culture can compete on the market. This money can also buy the very latest in technological equipment and expert manpower. A culture that employs technological media to carry its messages attracts larger audiences than any other and, in becoming addictive, acquires a surer grip on its public. There are also historical reasons why high-technology media have overcome more traditional cultural media. Chapter 2 will continue this study in following the transition from popular culture of the period 1850–1950 to mass culture of the period 1900–2000, then from mass culture to global culture from around 1980 onward. The main focus in this chapter will be on the European experience, especially of Britain and France. The key importance of youth culture in effecting the various transitions will be stressed.

The third chapter, "How Does Global Culture Differ from All Other Cultures?" is a slightly more theoretical excursus. All cultures are analyzed according to three constitutive aspects: representation, ethos, and technics. The nature of each of these and its relative importance in relation to the others varies from culture to culture and from style to style, providing a ready basis of comparison between cultures. Thus it can be shown that global culture differs from all others because it is the only one that favors technics over representation and ethos. This means that symbolic meanings and values matter less than techniques. Chapter 3 will explore the kinds of techniques that operate in global culture and how these are enlarging their scope by invading the spheres of representation and ethos. What consequences this has in ordinary life contexts will also be detailed.

The fourth and last chapter, "What Are the Alternatives to Global Culture?" is a defense of local cultures as the only possible counter to global culture. To argue this case involves making numerous value judgments, something that itself has to be defended at a time when value judgments are eschewed on many grounds. There are those who on economistic grounds refuse to distinguish between commodities and goods of cultural value. Then there are the so-called postmodernists who treat cultural styles as mere fashions or lifestyles that are all relative to each other, and maintain that no one is intrinsically superior or inferior. New academic exponents of cultural studies, or media and communication studies, have made such views the basis of their educational practices, which in effect promote global culture. Upholding standards is thus a necessary first step if anything is to be achieved in countering the cultural debasements taking place in education throughout the world. But only a determined culturalist movement, one that is popular and powerful enough to take its place next to the environmentalist one, has any prospect of succeeding in holding back global culture. The joint action of both of these movements is essential in establishing the eco–cultural balance necessary to restrict the inroads of technology into nature and culture.

This book is a small step in the direction of an ideal vision of a future multicultural humanity, one capable of living with itself in peace and in harmony with nature. But it is only a guiding assumption, one which is neither a prediction nor a prophecy, as the epilogue makes clear. Nevertheless, it is the first step on a long journey to a goal different from that of the incessant march of progress toward the triumph of technics. And as the old Chinese proverb puts it: even a journey of a thousand miles must begin with a single step.

In conclusion it is perhaps worth mentioning for those readers who wish to pursue further a theoretical and historical study of culture that this book belongs with three others that together provide a comprehensive theory covering all historical periods. Each of these works focuses on one or other of the key aspects of culture: representation, ethos, and technics. The first book deals extensively with representation. The second book concerns itself with the ethical and moral aspects of the ethos. The third book, which has not yet appeared, will deal with the aesthetic side of the ethos. This, the fourth book, is a more limited treatment of technics because it is mainly focused on its relation to global culture.

A New Science of Representation: Towards an Integrated Theory of Representation in Science, Politics and Art (1994) is a comprehensive theory of every type of representation in every cultural field. The echo of Vico in the main title indicates something of the scope of this work and the kind of extensive historical study it undertakes. It distinguishes four main stages in the cultural evolution of representation: the fetishistic, iconic, mimetic, and representational. Each of these is dominant in a particular epoch of history, the first in primitive societies, the second in the early civilizations, the third after the so-called axial age of universalist philosophies and religions, and the fourth in the age of modernity following the Reformation and the scientific revolution. The close interaction between the various representational practices in each of these, and especially so in science, politics, and art in modernity, is closely examined. The book ends by considering the contemporary crisis of representation due to the dominance of the image. This last part might be profitably read in conjunction with this book.

Ethical Life: The Past and Present of Ethical Cultures (2001) is also a wide-ranging historical study of the major ethical traditions. It distinguishes four main types: morality, civic ethics, ethics of duty, and ethics of honor. Moralities are to be encountered historically in two main forms, Judeo-Christian and Buddhist. Civic ethics is that of the Greek polis and its later incarnations throughout the classical tradition in the West. Ethics of duty arose three times independently of each other: as Confucianism in China, Krishnaism in India, and late Stoicism in the Roman Empire. The ethics of honor is that which emerged in the West as medieval chivalry, but it had earlier antecedents stretching back to ancient Persia. The development of ethics in the West involves a syncretic interaction among a number of these fundamental types. The rise of modern secularized ethics from the Age of Enlightenment onward is due to different kinds of transformatory processes, such as revolutionary puritanisms and rationalization. All this historical background studied in the first part of the work is followed, in the second part, by an analysis of the ethical problems that have arisen in the course of the calamitous twentieth century. Among these the main ones are the dominance of law over ethics and the onset of demoralization or, literally, the breakdown of morality. This second part might also be profitably read in conjunction with the present book.

Aesthetic Life: The Past and Present of Artistic Cultures is the provisional title of a book that has not yet appeared but which is substantially complete. It is a companion volume to the previous work on ethics. It deals with all the arts and other aesthetic phenomena in all cultures and historical periods. Its relevance to the situation of the arts in a global culture will be readily apparent. It will develop further and in greater depth criticisms and suggestions concerning the arts that could only be mentioned in the present work. In particular the theme of style in the arts, what it means and how it is judged, will be taken up and studied in relation to the great styles of art history.

The present work could have been much larger had it attempted the extended historical treatment that is a feature of all the others. There already exist, of course, excellent histories of technics, so it might seem as if there is nothing more to be said on the subject. But that is not the main reason for not attempting another survey from a different point of view. The subject is by no means closed. Yet to have done so in this book would have detracted from its main thrust, which is to focus on the problematic role of technics in relation to contemporary culture. Any extended historical excursus might have taken attention away from this contemporary problem and confused the issue. Hence it is necessary to alert the reader that some very basic historical knowledge of technics is here presupposed. Apart from that no knowledge of any specialist kind is assumed. This book is very much intended for the general reader—that is, anyone who is interested in the subject and believes it to be of some importance.

1

WHAT IS
GLOBAL CULTURE?

Like a stumbling drunkard, mankind lurches from crisis to crisis. No sooner has one potential collapse been avoided than another appears in its wake. With the lessening of the danger of imminent nuclear annihilation and the ending of the Cold War, it seemed that humanity could breathe easily for a while. But there really has been no respite, for that deadly crisis has been followed by another, one more insidious but no less dangerous.

Now in a liberated and open world a new threat is looming—that of ecological and cultural catastrophe. Paradoxically, this is itself the partial product of the very freedom and openness that was striven and fought for during the long era of totalitarian domination. It is the culminating outcome of the new globalization that has swept the world with the downfall of the totalitarian tyrannies.

Globalization might be welcomed on many grounds—the economic, political, communicational, and even linguistic ones come readily to mind—but it also has some unfortunate side effects that might prove deadly to the very future of mankind. This is no mere surmise of congenital misanthropes, but the expressed fear of some who are otherwise well disposed to it. Thus Thomas Friedman, in an otherwise optimistically minded book,[1] nevertheless, writes as follows:

> The more I observed the system of globalization at work, the more obvious it was that it had unleashed forest-crushing forces of development, which if left unchecked had the potential to destroy the environment and uproot culture.

. . . And because globalization as a culturally homogenizing and environment-devouring force is coming on so fast, there is real danger that in just a few decades it will wipe out the ecological and cultural diversity that took millions of years of human and biological forces to produce.

Something as ominous as all that is a real threat indeed. And yet, despite such apprehensions, Friedman and others who think like him believe that effects of this magnitude can somehow be sidestepped without interfering with the technicizing sweep of globalization. Is that merely wishful thinking or an inability to take in the full import of his own words?

As Friedman points out, the globalization threat is at once to nature and to culture: to the environment and the whole ecological variety of plants and animals, as well as to the quality of human life and the cultural diversity on which it depends. Damage to nature eventually translates itself as damage to culture, and vice versa. The fate of many ancient civilizations that collapsed because they outgrew their natural resources is historical proof of that fact. Our modern civilization is subject to the same self-limiting conditions. Thus, if all agriculture is reduced to an agribusiness industry, then the diversified countryside landscape that humans have created since the Neolithic revolution will become a monocultural ecological desert, for with it will disappear a host of animal and plant species as well as a whole rural way of life with its myriad varieties of folk cultures that have been carried on for millennia.

The loss of natural species through the destruction of their natural habitat is paralleled step by step by the loss of cultural "species" through the elimination of their social habitat, which is rooted in a natural environment. The clearing of jungles does not merely exterminate the animals living there, but also the native people whose homes have been there for countless generations. An exact numerical measure of this cultural loss can be partially established by calculating the rate of extinction of languages. Of the six thousand or so languages once spoken on earth, barely half that number now remain, some of these represented solely by a single speaker. Of the remainder only a few hundred have more than a million speakers, and eight have emerged as giants with over one hundred million speakers; of these, Chinese, Hindi, and English are the most numerous. Though language and culture are not identical, the loss of a language almost invariably brings with it the elimination of distinct cultural forms, if not a whole way of life. Eventually when the speech of the world is completely dominated by an international version of English, its culture, too, will have been reduced to the one stultified global form.

Nature and culture are in these and in many other more subtle ways intertwined: loss to the one brings with it debilitation to the other; both are threatened by forms of monoculture. To avert this threat—to save the environment and to maintain the quality of human life—calls for establishing an eco-cultural balance such as some traditional societies managed to maintain, albeit on a much lower technological level than now is possible. How to achieve such a balance on our level of technology is the major unsolved problem for mankind. However, it is clearly apparent that maintaining diversity in natural and cultural species must be a key part of the solution. This diversity—and with it any hope of an eco-cultural balance—is now being so drastically and rapidly upset by globalization and its associated technological, industrial, economic, social, and communications revolutions.

The ecological damage wrought by globalization has already been well studied and understood. Some decisive organized steps have also already been taken both by voluntary bodies and international agencies to reduce the harm. But, unfortunately, the cultural damage of globalization has not as yet been equally appreciated, and few measures, if any, have been taken to counter it. By some tragic irony of history, those who are most intent on averting the coming ecological catastrophe are often also the very ones who are unthinkingly contributing to the potential cultural one. Thus young people, those who are most dedicated to ecology and active in conservation movements, are also often the ones most addicted to a commercialized global culture and display most markedly its homogenizing propensities. Rock concerts to save endangered species are a very worthwhile ecological endeavor, but culturally they play into the hands of the very multinational media conglomerates and recording companies that in their overall activities are furthering cultural destruction and thus harming the very environment, both human and natural, on which the endangered species depend. Those who initiate and direct such one-sided ecological movements tend to have little understanding of the broader picture of eco-cultural balance and its interrelationships. They do not appreciate how much ecological conservation depends on cultural preservation.

By a parallel contrast, those most intent on cultural preservation, such as members of national trust societies, who tend to be not so young, have little awareness of nature conservation and how any viable culture must depend on a sound relation to the environment, one that is capable of maintaining a sustainable mode of social life, especially so in agriculture. Often the very funds they rely on to pursue their cultural endeavors—the sponsorships and subventions—come from firms that garner their profits from misusing the natural and cultural heritage of countries other than their own. In this respect they are like the temperance advocates of another age who relied on donations from the liquor distillers, as George Bernard Shaw so wittily satirized in his play *Major Barbara*. If Shaw were alive today he would have endless scope for such satires, for ours is a time when, as Juvenal once put it, *difficile est saturam non scribere*.

This work, too, ought to be a satire to measure up to the perverse realities that its subject affords. Unfortunately, we now lack a classical Juvenalian temper or even a biting Shavian wit. The last time anyone approached such a subject in that bitter spirit was when Aldous Huxley wrote his now distopian classic, *Brave New World*, many of whose apparently poetic fantasies have now become prosaic truths. To deal with such realities this work can only muster the duller prose of contemporary scholarship and polemic.

What Huxley perceived *in nuce* seventy years ago, taking place in the Los Angeles of his time, has now become commonplace in all the metropolises of the world. Globalization has been everywhere followed by its spectral cultural doppelgänger: global culture, as it is now called. To combat this growing menace, the young and the not-so-young must join hands and work together. The latter will have to learn something about ecology; the former will most likely have even more to learn about culture, for many of them are held spellbound by the siren songs of the global bands. Though concentrating mainly on the cultural side of the eco–cultural equation, this book is dedicated to bringing the two sides together in a joint effort to address the common danger of globalization.

A. THE CULTURAL IMPACT OF GLOBALIZATION

Globalization in general is a recent event, but no longer a new subject—a voluminous amount has been written about it already. However, its cultural consequences have not been so well documented. As we have already indicated, globalization is a gigantic process of integration of all human societies that takes place in all the spheres of social existence—above all, the economic, technological, scientific, communicational, political, linguistic, and even demographic, through tourism and immigration. Though the beginnings of this process have been under way at least since the first great period of European expansion during the nineteenth century, its culminating development occurred very recently, no earlier than ten to twenty years ago. It was only then that major economic, social, and technological changes took place in the advanced Western societies which coincided with—and perhaps even contributed to—the collapse of most communist totalitarian regimes, the ending of the Cold War, and the emergence of the United States as the sole superpower or hyperpower, as the French dub it. During this same period there also took place a number of crucial technological developments, above all those touching on communication and computing in conjunction with each other. This brought about a level of global interconnection that made it possible to transform and vastly enlarge the capitalist mode of production, distribution, and finance. The free market system became omnipresent and so global; now almost no country can stand out against it. So the whole world has become one open market for the almost free circulation of investments, production facilities, products, and to some degree, labor as well. Much of this productive power is now concentrated in the hands of a small number of giant multinational conglomerates.

The tendency of globalization to bring about a concentration of ownership is clearly apparent in the market for cultural commodities. For just as the production of motor cars will eventually be controlled by a dozen or so major firms, so, too, the production of cultural goods might eventually be reduced to a similar number. Already at present most of global media culture is controlled and owned by about a dozen major conglomerates: Time Warner, Disney, Vivendi-Universal, Sony, News Corporation, Bertelsmann, Viacom, AT&T, and a few others—it is difficult to be precise and up-to-date about this as the lineup changes every few years. The merger of Time Warner and AOL, which resulted in the world's biggest media empire for a time, gave an early foretaste of the trend ahead, which is toward ever-tighter integration. Already just four of the above conglomerates dominate the music industry of the world, one with a yearly global turnover of $210 billion:

Bertelsmann, Sony, Seagram, and Time Warner; this also changes rapidly. As Norman Lebrecht, the author of a book on the corporatization of classical music, has observed: "the totalitarian reality of restricted cultural ownership by a handful of shifting global entities was taking on Orwellian dimensions."[2] Eventually, when not just music but everything else in culture has merged into four such global giants, a point of no return will have been reached with potentially catastrophic consequences for humanity, for it will totally transform what it means to be a human being insofar as this is culturally determined. In other words, as a historical formation human nature will change.

The aim of such mergers is to achieve an integration within the one firm of all the major aspects of cultural production, as Rupert Murdoch put it in his September 1993 speech in London, in which he laid down the policy lines of News Corporation, the media company with the widest global reach: "five of the world's biggest industries—computing, communication, consumer electronics, publishing and entertainment—are converging into one dynamic whole." The new technology behind this project is the digitalization of all information. The upshot of this policy of synergy is that any media product or "message" must be utilizable in all the media sectors of the company. As a result, books are published that can furnish scripts for films; films are made that can be developed into television series; or alternatively, television shows are reprogrammed as scripts for films or as books and further adapted for videos and computer games; alternately, computer games are turned into films with computer-generated "actors" and "settings" in a version of virtual reality; background music and songs are routinely reutilized to become hit tunes, or, vice versa; characters—either humans or monsters or cartoon figures—are so constituted as to be able to furnish faces and logos for the brand-name recognition of a wide range of consumer goods, especially games and toys for children, and the actors who play them become stars and so act as the arbiters elegantiarum for branded goods—above all, for clothes, accessories, and other fashion accoutrements; and so on for all possible translations of the one "message" into all other commercial spin-offs. All this integrated product-marketing drive is lubricated by prearranged publicity on TV, newspapers, and other print media owned by the same firm, with commissioned flattering reports on staged news "events," press releases, photo opportunities, the paid-for "spontaneous" comments from celebrities, as well as the more mundane advertising repeated to the point of saturation. How can any product fail completely with the backing of such an integrated news, entertainment, and advertising effort? All this promotes the creation of a total cultural product that can serve all marketing purposes, and so presumably satisfy all human needs. When fully constituted it should be capable of fashioning a whole "style of life"—with the sole proviso that it must be one of short duration only, lasting no longer than when the next such product line comes on stream for the next run of the market. This business strategy has been most successfully realized where there is least resistance—in youth culture. This bodes extremely ill for future generations and raises some daunting questions about the fate of culture in the coming century.

In a global situation of concentration of ownership and product integration the question that touches on the cultural destiny of the whole of mankind can be put as bluntly and crudely as this: is it desirable or even acceptable that the major part of the cultural lives of all human beings should be in the hands of a dozen or so media moguls, the chief executives of the future cultural conglomerates? What kind of Orwellian dictatorship of the soul does this amount to? Is this kind of cultural oligopoly any the less threatening than the possibility of an ecological catastrophe to which it is linked as one of the twin evils and globalization?

Anyone who is at all struck by the force of these questions and who agrees even partially with the diagnosis that leads to them is bound to ask the further question: what can now be done about all this? Are all the people of the world likely to accept it helplessly, held spellbound by the media magic like a rabbit mesmerized by the stare of a snake? And when there is a revolt against it, as there is bound to be sooner or later, is it not likely to take some violent form of utter rejection such as we are already seeing in the rise of fundamentalism? It seems that the longer a sensible reaction is delayed, the more such an outcome is bound to occur. But any such countervailing action is now very difficult because global culture is a consequence of a general globalization that seems the inevitable trend of the future. Globalization in some form or other will be impossible to avoid, for though in its most developed form it is very recent, its roots go back deep into the past.

Historically considered, the present era of globalization is but the second of the great waves of capitalist expansion. The first occurred during the period between the French Revolution and the First World War and was largely confined to Europe. However, it also had profound consequences for the rest of the world, for it initiated the period of colonial conquest and imperialism that brought most of the world under direct European rule or hegemonic influence. This led not only to political domination and economic exploitation but also to the debasement and debilitation of all the subservient non-European cultures. The European form was meant to take their place for this was seen as the one true, rational, enlightened, and universal culture for all of mankind. This view, held by almost all Europeans, was enforced on others in the course of one or another *mission civilisatrice* launched by the colonial powers. Thus this first wave of capitalist proliferation did not directly threaten European culture itself, which maintained its privileged status and continued unimpeded. But all the other cultures of the world found themselves reduced to the degraded position of native lore or primitive customs. Only rarely did any of them succeed in retaining any self-respect, dignity, and cohesion.

This first period of global capitalism as imperialism came to a halt in Europe and America with the First World War, followed by the Great Depression. In Europe the war and its ruinous course, resulting in the establishment of totalitarian dictatorships in some of the major countries, brought about a slowdown of capitalist expansion that was further accentuated by the Great Depression. This produced a reaction of cutthroat protectionism and predatory military adventurism that almost inevitably led to the Second World War. The world capitalist economic system only recovered gradually after that calamity, pulled out of its trough by the mighty engine of the American economy. And fairly soon after, the other countries of the Western alliance also reached unprecedented levels of economic development. But in these countries capitalism was partially controlled and restricted by quasi-socialist welfare state or Keynesian policies; it could not develop its full potential for uninhibited economic production as well as cultural destruction such as it has since demonstrated.

That only happened in the present phase of global capitalist expansion called globalization, which started in the West in the early 1980s—in Britain under Margaret Thatcher, in the United States under Ronald Reagan, and also partially in Japan; it has since been followed at staggered intervals by all the other countries of the world. It was then that there began the great free market reforms and privatizations leading to the end of protectionism and the partial winding up of the welfare state in the West. The rest of the world soon followed suit with the collapse of the communist regimes in the East and the acceptance of market freedoms by all the Third World countries, including most importantly China and India. Thus an almost unfettered capitalist system has prevailed all over the world. This has generated a surge of investments of capital to the poorer countries and the shifting of production capacity to low-wage labor markets. Thus undoubtedly many, though by no means all, of these countries have profited from globalization.

However, even the narrowly considered economic balance sheet of the gains and losses of globalization has not yet been drawn: at first the credits were apparent, but of late some ominous debits have also started to appear. The main Western societies, with America in the lead, have enjoyed an unprecedented period of prosperity; or, better put, the leading strata in these societies have done so, those who through wealth or talent have been able to take advantage of the new opportunities. For the others there is employment, but often in poor-paying, dead-end jobs. This has created even greater social inequalities; a new class, that of the working poor, has arisen, and many now subsist below the poverty line. The situation in most of the non-Western countries is far worse. Some, such as Russia and others of the former Soviet empire, are now going backward; some who initially prospered, such as Indonesia and Argentina, are also declining catastrophically; Africa is on the point of collapse and currently facing famine that only international relief can avert; the Muslim world is in the doldrums. However, China and India, the most populous nations, are markedly improving. Thus the overall economic picture is extremely mixed. Nevertheless, the world seems to be coping with an unprecedented population level, one that only a short while ago was generally believed would lead to mass starvation almost everywhere in the Third World. Some of this must be due to globalization. It is to be hoped that in time its economic benefits will be more widely and evenly distributed.

The present stage of global capitalism is obviously not its final stage. How capitalism will develop in the future and whether this will or will not benefit the majority of mankind in the long run is not for us to know. But we might surmise that the symbiotic nexus between capitalism and global culture need not persist, and might not do so for all that much longer, if adequate corrective measures are taken that are necessary for the survival of local culture. Though currently it furthers and makes use of global culture, capitalism does not depend on it and might function just as well, perhaps in the long run even better, without it. Thus opposing global culture need not entail being against capitalism as such. Those who attack globalization in the name of anticapitalism are mindlessly repeating the revolutionary slogans of the past at a time when revolution is no longer a serious option. Our opposition to global culture must not be confused with any such sterile revolutionary impulses. We will return to this issue in the last chapter and set out at greater length just how and why our position differs from the many kinds of critics and defenders of either capitalism or global culture.

The relation between capitalism and culture has varied in each of its major stages. But it is now scarcely deniable that the overall effect of capitalism on European culture during the long period of its initial growth, at least from the Reformation till the First World War, was generally favorable. Up to this point the countries that were economically most developed were also culturally most advanced, and those that were economically backward lagged behind culturally as well. This was no mere coincidence. Capitalism did stimulate culture in Europe and later in North America. The situation was, of course, very different in the non-Western colonial world where during the first great global expansion of capitalism irreparable damage was done to all the old traditional cultures. Now in the second period of globalization the threat is as much to European culture as to every other.

In the first period of capitalist global expansion trade followed the flag; now trade has gone ahead and been followed by the flags, rags, and riches of global culture. Wherever globalization has penetrated economically it has brought in its wake a cultural invasion. The mainly American produced or licensed cultural products have flooded the world through the same channels as its trade and media. This was made possible by the fact that huge technological advances occurred in transportation and communication: the cost of moving bulk cargo by container and ship was much reduced; air travel and transport became cheap; and, most crucially, interconnectedness throughout the globe was established by the new satellite facilities now linked to computers. Television and telecommunication reception is omnipresent. There is almost none so poor as to be completely without radio, television, or telephone. And so by these means all have access to the cornucopia of global culture. The whole world can now simultaneously watch the same shows, and sometimes almost half of it does so, as with the great sporting fixtures or beauty contests. The Internet and the Web have extended this reach even further, also offering every kind of "information" and consumer product. Who can resist such offerings when they can be had with the least effort at the mere touch of a button and perhaps the incurring of an invisible electronic debt?

B. FLIGHT-CULTURE AS A PREMONITION OF THE FUTURE

So what is this global culture we have been talking about in such ominous terms? It hardly seems daunting at all—who is afraid of Mickey Mouse or the computer mouse or any of the other countless quotidian mice we unthinkingly make use of every minute of our waking lives? It is there all about us, we float in it like fish in water or birds in air. Like air it is intangible, it yields to every pressure and offers no resistance, so that it seems impossible to oppose it, and to struggle against it seems a futile waste of effort. Emblematically considered it is most apt to designate it as the culture of the air, for we are most in it when we are off the ground and no longer in touch with our earthy local roots; then, like Anteus, we are at our weakest.

This can be almost taken literally for one is most seductively tempted by and immersed in global culture when one is in the air, inside the pressurized cabin of any ordinary airliner taking off from anywhere and landing anywhere else—the names of the places hardly matter for they are all the same as far as air travel is concerned. The hours in the air are usually spent passively absorbing the cultural products that are made so freely available: one watches the latest films or hears the latest sounds, which almost invariably come from Los Angeles by the grace of the big studios and recording companies; or alternatively one watches and listens to the farrago of news, entertainment, sport, and advertising beamed by the major TV networks; or one reads the newspapers, magazines, and pulp literature best sellers from the publishing arms of the same firms; or one plays with the onboard computers, caught up in the new gambling hobby of share-market speculation, or indulges in computer games mainly produced by Japanese media companies. Every so often this media immersion is interrupted by the obligatory offering of plastic food in plastic containers with plastic utensils that tastes more or less the same no matter what its original ingredients. Soon after one is tempted with a wide range of consumer goods with renowned brand-name labels and all manner of alcoholic drink with equally well-known brands.

This, on average, is what time spent in the air is like, and those who spend more of their time in this way than others, busily globe-trotting from one airport to another, are considered the most important and celebrated people on our planet.

Life in the air has also its own temporal rhythms, liberties, constraints, and other sociocultural peculiarities. Strapped in their seats and nearly immobile, the passengers become passive recipients of a wide range of sights, sounds, tastes, and smells; some of these emanating from neighbors who are anonymous strangers with whom conversation is restricted to a few phrases, usually couched in the pidgin English that almost everyone in the air now understands. There is unlikely to be any real interchange or contact established, as was often the case in the older and slower modes of transport. The new ethos of air travel inhibits any personal encounters or any displays of personality. Anyone who acts beyond the narrow permissible limits of mobility is branded a troublemaker and disciplined by the cabin crew or, even worse, handed over to the airport police. This creates an ethos of complete docility and conformity that exceeds by many levels that usually enforced on the ground, though of late that difference is diminishing.

The recent terrorist outrages have vastly increased the levels of surveillance and policing at airports and, consequently, greatly magnified the required conformism. This will inevitably also have a major impact on ordinary life environments, which will also become more restricted. It is impossible now to say whether this will be merely a temporary or a permanent feature of travel in the future. Much depends on how long the terrorist threat continues, which is at present unpredictable.

There is not much difference between the consumerism and conformism of the air and that on the ground in the airports. These are vast bazaars, commercial emporiums, and duty-free shopping malls that are almost the same everywhere on earth and provide the same range of consumer goods, those tending to the luxury side of indulgence. In every place there are the same affiliates of the global chains of fast-food restaurants, department stores, haute-couture designer boutiques, amusement parlors, and media dispensers purveying everywhere the same records, videos, books, journals, and toys for children and adults. Everything can be had for a price provided one wants what everyone else wants. In the airports, too, a strict conformism rules and one dare not step out of line, for policing is thorough and omnipresent. The spick-and-span ambience of modern architecture, with its shiny, sterile cleanliness, prohibits any littering and inhibits any loitering or even lingering, for everyone is either on the move or sitting in a stupor waiting for the call to move.

For those who leave the airport to retire there are the many standard hotels in the vicinity, nearly the same ones throughout the world. The facilities they offer are also almost the same, calibrated only according to the various grades of luxury depending on the price. They all offer the same range of brand-name entertainments, media resources, foods, exercise facilities, licensed gambling, discos, massage parlors, and, usually in a more covert way, the same narcotics and prostitutes that so many travelers now require to properly relax. If these travelers are tourists, as so many are, then they will end up in the same kinds of hotels in more scenic places and be surrounded by the same appurtenances. Regional differences make little difference, as they are only there to provide local color: the for-tourists-only shows of native art and lore, the local adaptations of global merchandise and media, the guided tours to select sites for their sights, sounds, tastes, and smells, the latter carefully muted so as not to offend foreign sensibilities. If the tourists are headed for the old cities or metropolises of the world then their offerings will include specially prepared versions and editions of the old high-culture classic of the local civilization, such as theater, opera, and musical performances, adapted to the limited tastes and capacities of those reared on mass and global culture. In every such city hordes of tourists swarm like locusts: they come and consume and depart again and leave nothing behind except for the money they have expended to fructify the local economy. That money will circulate to be used eventually by the locals to import more global culture or for themselves to become tourists elsewhere. And so all the cities of the world almost seem to live by taking in one another's tourists.

Air travel and the flight-culture that surrounds it is such a perfect emblem of global culture in general because it exemplifies nearly all the key forces of globalization: the most developed form of capitalist enterprise; free and open markets; individual freedoms to move and consume; state-provided infrastructure and state-policed law and order; bureaucratic systems of management, administration, and crowd control; the most advanced scientific methods in every aspect of the technology of flying; and the most up-to-date machines and instruments, joined together into the one gigantic technological system. These technologies, at their most efficient, concentrated, and cumulative, function almost identically wherever they are located. They also carry with them the same cultural milieu that we have described as flight-culture. Everywhere it extends, the airport system and airline industry bring with them the same cultural forms and contents, those initially stamped on them in America where the system first arose in the context of an internal mass-transit service. The same flight-culture was extended to all other countries as these, too, became part of an international traffic network. The technology of flight did not mandate these particular cultural usages of its own accord. It is easily conceivable that air travel might have been launched on a quite other cultural basis; but that did not happen for many reasons mainly to do with the American dominance of this industry. However, once established on this cultural pattern, it has become almost impossible to change it.

Flight-culture has now become one of the main carriers of global culture, for wherever it proliferates it brings with it the same joint ethos of functional operation and consumer commodification. This is extremely appealing to masses of people all over the world whose sole common factor is that they are moderately affluent, socialized in modern styles of living at least to a degree that makes it possible for them to utilize the basic amenities, and sufficiently literate to be able to follow the signs and obey the regulations. But even such barely competent independent travelers, once they have experienced the gratifications of flight-culture, become avid consumers of such cultural commodities even when they are not flying. Flight thus acts as an enculturation experience par excellence that massively promotes global culture.

The aspirations of flight-culture work on both those who fly and those who remain grounded, being too poor to take to the air. Those among the poor who service the tourists themselves become imbued with the same needs and desires. Envy for those who have makes the have-nots want the same kind of things. Even if they cannot afford the more expensive versions of the commodities of global culture, they can occasionally indulge in the cheaper ones. And many of the products of global media are free of charge: television shows, pop music, advertising, and so on. It is a mistake, therefore, to suppose that global culture touches only the privileged elites who can take to the air and are not bound down to the one place, whereas all the others, being grounded, are thereby rendered local.

It is this kind of error that Zygmunt Bauman perpetrates in taking too literally the distinction of the global and the local as purely a matter of mobility and space. Thus in this vein he writes that "a particular cause for worry is the progressive breakdown in communication between the increasingly global and extraterritorial elites and the ever more 'localized' rest."[3] On this view the distinction between the "globals" and the "locals" becomes synonymous with that for the rich and the poor, who in fact have no trouble communicating because both sides watch the same shows, want the same goods, and share the same assumptions as to what is good; what separates them is only the disparity in the acquisition of these things.

The distinction between the global and the local, as we are developing it here, cuts across all these differences between rich and poor, masters and proletarians, mobile and immobile, exclusive enclave and ghetto, and increasingly so between First World and Third World. On both sides of these social divides there are those who are more given to the global and those who have stuck to the local. Bauman seems to have allowed his evident sympathies for the poor, immobile, and excluded to cloud his sociological judgment as to which are the "globals" and which the "locals." Nor does he seem to fully realize that all are subject to the same homogenizing pressures.

To a lesser degree all modern systems of technology have the same propensity to lead to cultural uniformity for rich and poor alike for very similar reasons as flight-culture. Car-culture has displayed the same tendencies, though on a lesser scale, for whenever the system of transportation by privately owned motor vehicles is introduced, and is affordable to all classes, it is conducive to similar conditions of living in major respects. It leads to commuting on highways and freeways, to service stations, overhead displays and advertising, to drive-in shopping and parking lots, to malls and motels, to suburban living, and to many such general social effects as the yearning of the poor and young to possess their own cars with their seductive promises of mobility and escape away from any supervision. Cars not only transform the outer landscape and cityscape, but also the inner mindscape of subjective being. The new information technologies will very likely have even more drastic social and cultural effects, and through these affect the mind to a commensurate degree, though what these will be is not yet fully apparent. However, it is a fair assumption to make that as they spread throughout the world they will make it even more culturally homogeneous. This is as inescapable as it was with every other large-scale technological change.

Propelled by the same technological and other uniform socioeconomic systems, life everywhere on earth is tending to the utopian aspirations of flight-culture—or, at least, this becomes a more or less realizable goal for the affluent classes in every society, for which the others also yearn and to some small degree struggle to achieve. When achieved, such a life, immersed fully in global culture, displays some very strange existential effects. It is a most peculiar utopia. Literally so, for it is situated nowhere because it could be anywhere, at no time because it could be at any time: it blurs temporal distinctions of day and night, yesterday and tomorrow, last year and next year, past and future, merging all times into a continuous present of increasingly shorter duration. This leads to an erasure of the historical past and the cultural traditions by which it is carried, as is evident in myriads of ways from such arrogant pronouncements as "history is bunk" to the deliberate confusion of historical realities with science fiction fantasies in the literature, films, and theme parks that cater to the barely literate young. As temporal distinctions—on which so much of our fundamental sense of reality is based—disappear, so people's awareness returns to the preliterate and even the prerational state of myths, superstitions, and collective cults, each with its own account of the scheme of things. These are now rife in all modern societies.

In such a distorted and shrunk world of time and reality the sense of self and personal identity is also diminished. People become alienated from others and incapable of relating; each one appears to others as an anonymous quasi-passenger or individual nomad among hordes of fellow travelers who share nothing but common amenities. All are subject to the same restraining rules and regulations that punish eccentricities and render choices down to the same few possibilities for everyone. These are like the supermarket choices of rival but near-identical products graded according to cost and selected according to affordability. From such a meager range of genuine differences it becomes increasingly more difficult to constitute an identity that is distinctive or a self that is one's own creation. A uniform set of possibilities for self-constitution is imposed that is like a single wardrobe of uniforms from which one must choose what to wear and what to be. It is in these ways that people are becoming more alike.

Such people also begin to lose their cognitive bearings: deprived of any independent orientation, all kinds of fundamental epistemological, moral, and aesthetic separations begin to become hazy. The strongly emphasized distinctions present in all civilized traditions between truth and lies, reality and illusion, right and wrong, beauty and mere attractiveness are slowly but surely becoming elided in global culture. The communications media offer a continuous and barely differentiated stream of news, entertainment, and advertising; unless one is extremely alert and critical, the one function merges into the other, so that fact, fiction, and fantasy fuse into a cognitive phantasmagoria that is a kind of virtual reality.

What is real and what is illusory are barely to be distinguished as media celebrities or so-called glitterati play out their public lives before the cameras and are themselves no longer separable from the roles they enact. To their adoring and addicted fans their own character and the characters they act out fuse and are held to be the same. In their lonely lives these fans identify with such composite personages, so much so that the sudden and often tragically pointless death of a star or celebrity is felt by masses of people as a personal loss and whole nations all over the world go into traumatic mourning at such an event. The mass outpouring of grief at the death of Princess Diana—a media creature if ever there was one—was a graphic case which no doubt will be repeated on other such occasions. The media executives and program producers work deliberately to break down the distinction between reality and illusion by eliding the difference between real life and fantasy games. Voyeuristic shows are concocted in which people have to live out play activities of survival or seduction under the constant stare of the camera that broadcasts the pictures around the world. Other kinds of shows are staged as mere vehicles for advertising, such as quizzes and beauty contests and all manner of sporting competition with their "larger than life" heroes and fabulous icons.

Even the basic and supposedly objective reporting of news is not free of such distortions, for the separation of fact and fiction or commentary is disappearing; and in any case, what is selected as having news value is often the same real-life stuff as figures in the shows. Scandals involving public personages are serialized like "soaps." Whole professions have arisen whose main job it is to provide staged news and to otherwise manipulate the media—that is, to massage the message so as to obfuscate the difference between truth and lies: such are the lobbyists, public-relations managers, marketing consultants, spin doctors, talk-show hosts, impresarios, publicity agents, and so on. In this way, too, any clear distinction between right and wrong is steadily eroded away. This is also done by fictional means when heroes in stories and films behave much in the same way as villains and cops as crims, merely being on the right side of the law. By such means goodness is mocked as weakness and beauty reduced to sex appeal. So one by one all the traditional separations are undermined and there begins to emerge a devalued world of phantom realities and real illusions—that is, until every now and then something happens and "real" reality from outside the media world intrudes, when some shock or other compels people to wake up from their artificial paradise dreams and face the stark choices they have to confront in their lives. Those who refuse to rouse themselves and remain fixated in their delusions invariably suffer whether they know it or not.

The flight-culture to which everyone aspires is, as yet, only fully enjoyed by a minority of the affluent, though increasingly larger numbers in the so-called developed societies and the emerging middle classes in the underdeveloped ones can already afford some vicarious taste of it for short periods. Even workers who are drudges for most of the year can save up for brief holidays as tourists in faraway places. In this respect, flight-culture, though expensive, is not exclusive, but of the masses; it gives the bulk of people what they want and what they are prepared to pay for; the range of goods and services it provides caters to the tastes of the great majority. It is a mass culture ruled by the free choices of countless anonymous buyers on an open market. Nobody is forced or in any way compelled to buy or pay for anything that is not wanted. Nevertheless, masses of people from utterly different societies have been so influenced and conditioned that they have come to want more or less the same kinds of things.

How such a uniformity in desires and tastes is achieved can only be explained by an extended analysis of the techniques of mass marketing, particularly of advertising, and an examination of the kind of society in which these are so successful, which we will postpone until the next chapter. Here we merely note that these are mass societies of individuals—an oxymoron that expresses the seemingly contradictory nature of societies in which everyone is an individual, free to choose what to prefer and how to live, but where such freedoms are, in practice, exercised alike to prefer and do what everyone else does and chooses, and so for these individuals to behave en masse. We can term this a conformist individualism of the masses, which is quite unlike any earlier type of individualism. It is the individualism of a democratic egalitarianism, one which is also, seemingly paradoxically, riven by enormous class and status differences. Everyone is in principle equal, yet in practice huge inequalities abound based on wealth, profession, educational qualification, family background, and so on for other advantages. Thus, for example, everyone can vote and all votes are counted as equal, yet only the wealthy, educated, and otherwise privileged can stand for office with any hope of success.

All these apparent contradictions reflect themselves in flight-culture and its more humdrum adjuncts in ordinary quotidian life. In both these contexts the types of things made available express the preferences and desires of the masses. There is no question but that the choices of the majorities rule the culture market. Both through direct sales and through other techniques for establishing majority preference, such as polls and ratings, every marketing effort is made to determine what the masses want. And, then, on the basis of all such soundings, these putative desires are satisfied within broad ranges of goods and services. But within these ranges of things, the not-so-openly expressed—but through buying-power demonstrable—desire for exclusivity, to reveal the inequalities of class and status, is also affirmed through careful qualitative calibrations. Thus within the one line of goods there appear enormous differences in grades of quality based on cost; as, for example, within any ordinary item of clothing, such as jeans worn uniformly by the young, there are many standards of quality marked by great price differentials that are usually indicated by designer labels. This satisfies the aspirations of the rich and privileged both to appear to be like everyone else and yet at the same time to subtly flaunt the marks of their status exclusivity. In this way they can have it both ways—subscribe to egalitarianism and affirm their superiority.

Flight-culture has made an art of this contradiction and has managed to combine equality with superior status in all kinds of ingenious ways. It is the mass merchandising culture with designer labels, par excellence. Everything in it is a standard item, but always graded into qualitative categories according to price. Thus the same thing can be had in numerous versions depending on what one can afford or is willing to outlay. This has become the standard procedure for establishing differences of quality in all of global culture.

For example, all cars are more or less alike and fulfill the same basic needs and requirements of reasonably comfortable transportation, yet the differences in cost between one make of car and another, or even between one range and another within the same make, can be enormous. Much rides on this difference as advertising has made us all acutely aware; what is at stake is a demonstration of income, status, power, even profession, age, sex, and other such differentials. It is the same with nearly all cultural goods and services.

Global culture can in general be referred to as mass-merchandising culture of branded goods. The only qualitative distinctions or grades it permits are those determined by price—money stands in for value. If the cynic, according to Oscar Wilde, is the person who knows the price of everything but the value of nothing, then global culture is that of mass cynicism. Unfortunately, in a commercial world in which such cynicism is an implicit assumption, those few who wish to object have nothing to appeal to, for no other standard or criterion of quality is given any credence. Ethical, aesthetic, cognitive, even practical utilitarian standards have been devalued and count for little. In a mass culture with designer labels it is what everyone can be made to want and how much they are willing to pay that matters. Any other value is of marginal consequence.

Hence, a defense of values is for us of crucial concern. Indeed, the very right to make value judgments can no longer be taken for granted, for it is questioned on all kinds of grounds by various parties. Judgmentalism, so called, is now often denounced as a new kind of sin of the intellect. We shall return to this most fundamental of all issues in the last chapter and seek to offer a rationale for explicit judgment as well as a critique of the implicit judgments usually made in the realm of culture.

C. AMERICANIZATION, OR THE ORIGINS OF GLOBAL CULTURE

Like flight-culture, most of the rest of global culture originated in America, but it has now spread throughout the whole world. It has been carried abroad by all the means we have previously examined: through trade and communication, flight and tourism, the media and the Internet, and many other more subtle ways. And wherever it goes it devastates all the existing local cultures; it distorts, displaces, and destroys every other culture that stands in its way, both those that have already existed for thousands of years as well as modern ones that only arose relatively recently. Just as the monoculture of single-crop agribusiness wipes out both the remaining virgin lands and wilderness as well as traditional agriculture, so, too, global culture eliminates all other cultures and spreads a kind of monocultural wasteland.

This holds not only for the exotic cultures of non-Western civilizations, or the ethnic cultures of still-tribal people, or the very few remaining primitive cultures; it also applies to European culture as well. The culture that only all-too recently thought itself superior to every other and invulnerable from any attack from outside barbarians is itself now succumbing to its own self-generated barbarisms. It is crumbling in the face of the onslaught of global culture. This process began even earlier with the gradual inroads of mass cultures, the different national precursors of the present global culture that is mainly American. The reasons that traditional and modern European cultures could not resist these internal and external invasions are many and varied, and we shall examine them in greater detail in the next chapter. We shall briefly mention some of them here in anticipation.

During the course of the twentieth century, Europe underwent numerous disruptions of wars and revolutions that exacted a heavy cultural toll. The despoliations wrought by the different kinds of totalitarianisms were particularly severe and gravely affected some of the leading countries directly, and all the others indirectly, through the ideological conflicts they fostered. Traditional European cultures were discredited and could not offer much resistance. At the same time there occurred a creeping process of cultural commodification under the pressure of the capitalist market, which gradually transformed cultural goods into mass-market products. In this way a mass culture was constituted in each major European country, a culture which was in some respects alike, due to the same prevailing conditions; yet, in many others it was distinctive, each major nation or cultural region fostering its own mass culture, one generally deriving from its own popular resources. Thus, for example, there arose characteristically different film industries in the major linguistic regions. All this was still very far from the uniformities of globalization we now have to endure.

Mass culture, however, began the process of transformation toward global culture, for it involved a change in the mode of cultural production: the earlier manner of creation, which utilized the hand-crafted labor of individual writers, painters, and composers, or at most the organized workshops and ateliers of sculptors, engravers, and printers, was displaced by a quasi-industrial factory-style method requiring a large workforce practicing a division of labor and utilizing advanced technological machinery. The latter had great advantages in providing a more technically finished product of uniform quality and generating a much greater output. All these differences are clearly apparent in the traditional operations of a theater company as compared to the advanced production methods of a film studio. Traditional culture, such as theater, could not compete with the new mass culture, such as film, for economic as well as other reasons: films can play to vastly greater audiences at a fraction of the cost per spectator to that which theaters have to charge; they call for less prior education or understanding and so can attract a much bigger public; they are captivating and create an oneiric world that is both mesmerizing and arousing; they promote shared pseudo-intimacies with the actors who very quickly emerge as stars with a mass following; in every way they seem more modern and fashionable; and so on. In this way, in most areas of cultural endeavor a commodified mass culture arose that took over in public appeal from earlier high and low cultures, from the previously widespread elite, folk, and popular cultures at once. Some of these have still survived, but now only in much attenuated forms.

This new mass culture, one that is solely a product of twentieth-century developments, must not be confused with earlier forms of popular culture—which have always existed, especially in cities, and which still exist to some extent—as is so often done in common parlance as well as in academic studies. Contemporary commercial pop art is not popular art in any meaningful sense except that of having wide appeal—in fact, it is far too widespread to be really popular. This confusion has been systemically and often cynically exploited, for it is part of the sales pitch of mass culture to disguise itself as popular culture and to appropriate features of real popular culture for this masquerade. The differences between the two are patently evident, though in some intermediate cases difficult to draw: popular culture arises out of the spontaneous practices and preferences of identifiable groups of people who constitute a public sharing a common cultural style; mass culture is produced as a saleable commodity for anonymous buyers on as wide a market as possible, utilizing all the sales techniques of modern advertising, publicity, and marketing. Popular culture is that in which the people who partake of it are themselves to some degree participants in it—they are actively involved in one or another way. Mass culture is that of passive consumers, who might be stimulated by or engrossed in the cultural product, but who themselves contribute next to nothing in its conception, reproduction, or reception. This difference, which is now often ignored, was until recently well understood both by conservatives who wished to defend traditional cultures as well as by radicals protesting against the inroads of mass culture into working-class popular culture and the pernicious effects this was having on working people and their families, a process of debasement that is now almost complete.

The difference between popular and mass culture is also apparent in the relation between the producers of either culture—the artists, creators, inventors, performers, exhibitors, showmen, etc.— and their respective publics— the people who listen, look, enact, react, and frequently pay for the privilege of doing so. A popular culture addresses a local public, where a relation of commonality exists between artists and their audience who feel that something of themselves is expressed in the message conveyed back to them and who, therefore, identify closely with the creators or performers. Mass culture, which tends instead to rely on stars or media-generated celebrities, addresses a nondescript public of standard categories of consumers and appeals to them with something that is usually foreign to themselves, something enticing or exotic or marvelous or technically miraculous or simply seductive. At its most developed, as global culture that is intended to appeal to everyone on earth, mass culture tends to the condition of Muzak: innocuous and bland background sound in public places played by nobody to be heard or not by anybody who happens to be there.

Such omnipresent sounds of mass culture drown out any spontaneous, unmarketed, and unmanipulated upsurge of popular culture, insofar as this is still capable of occurring. As against the now global pop music industry, with its backing from the major media companies and its ubiquitous reach, what chance have styles of popular music arising among usually poor itinerant musicians in out of the way places? If these musicians happen to be Americans, then there is a small possibility that their popular style will be spotted by talent scouts of the big recording studios and recorded and tried out on a mass public, but usually only after it has been polished and refined—that is, altered and adapted to make it fit for mass consumption.

Put in the simplest of terms, the difference amounts to this: popular culture arises from below, from the populace, and is always local and specific; mass culture is imposed from above, from the production sources, and if not completely constituted there, at least distributed from these. The latter is indifferent to local character, for it is designed to appeal in all places to as wide a range of people as can afford to buy it, irrespective of their character or identity. This contrast, which we have so sharply set out for heuristic purposes, is in reality often a matter of degree, as there are always many intermediate cases that are difficult to neatly categorize. The further one goes back to the earlier stages of mass culture the more this is so, for mass culture developed out of the preexisting popular cultures over a long period, extending at least from the last decades of the nineteenth century to the early ones of the twentieth century. It is a matter of some historical controversy just when the decisive split between them occurred, some historians placing this as late as the 1950s. However, as mass culture constituted and established itself over this period, it removed itself ever further from its sources, and so its relation to popular culture became more distant and tenuous, until eventually it separated itself completely from the latter. When mass culture became global, it had no longer much to do with popular culture, and so it became much easier to tell them apart.

The history of mass culture is a long story that has often been told, and need not be retold, in full here. In brief, it was simultaneously conceived in late-nineteenth-century Europe and America, but it was sooner incubated and hatched in America. There the vigorous and buoyant capitalism of the post–Civil War period was the goose that laid this golden egg—a fast-expanding economy that took full advantage of the new lands, resources, and people eventually gave rise to a new culture of mass appeal for a society where a stratified European class system with its established traditions did not obtain. The fast-growing cities that began to accommodate the melting pot of uprooted immigrants—who had mostly abandoned their traditional mores—were an extremely fertile ground for new commercial forms of mass culture. Cultural entrepreneurs, entertainers, and showmen quickly learned how to utilize the new technological marvels made available by inventors in

Europe and America for the creation of new media and the revolutionizing of the old. This was the start of whole culture industries based on new devices, such as photography, film, sound recording, radio, television, and in our time, video and computers. The process was already well under way in America before the First World War; for example, Hollywood and Tin Pan Alley were already established, but it had as yet little impact on Europe or anywhere else in the world.

Eventually, as America went so did the rest of the world. The steady growth of the American economy and its political power and influence during the course of the twentieth century ensured that a mainly American-produced mass culture would become predominant in all other places and that it would eventually supersede those generated elsewhere. In our time it has become a global culture that is sometimes loosely referred to as Western culture. But this is a particularly confusing designation, for this global culture has little resemblance to traditional Western cultures, either European or American. However, it bears some relation to popular American culture. This connection needs to be spelled out better so that the two can be distinguished.

Traditional American culture—in all its various modes (elite, folk, and popular)—was historically a local outgrowth and native adaptation of the European traditional styles that the settlers, mainly English, brought with them from the Old World. In all three modes it developed its own local forms that were as varied and rich as anything to be found in the same period in Europe. It was particularly profuse in regional folk forms, some of which still survive to this day, though now in a very vestigial state. Added to this basic WASP stock were later grafted stems from other immigrant groups: African American popular styles, particularly in music; elements derived from Irish, Low German, and French Creole cultural influences and, most recent of all, the input from such exotic ones as Yiddish. Thus there arose a composite American traditional culture that was the fertile soil out of which a mass culture grew; as it did so it took up themes, motifs, tunes, and steps, mainly from popular culture, but utilized in its own way. The materials it took from the preexisting store of cultures it invariably reduced to formulae and clichés. It was in this form that American culture as a mass culture was reexported back to Europe in the course of the twentieth century.

This happened in three well-demarcated stages. The first was the between-the-two-wars period when Europe was in turmoil and American mass culture influence started to make itself felt mainly through cinema, music, and dancing. Hollywood became the symbol of a wish-fulfillment, dream way of life, free from the poverty, squalor, and violence of Europe, to which so many aspired. However, the educated elites held themselves aloof and were contemptuous of such commercial pandering to the mob. The totalitarian regimes banned it completely, and as a result made it all the more tempting as forbidden fruit holding out the mirage of freedom and personal satisfaction. This became apparent after the Second World War when the fascist powers were defeated, and it has now repeated itself again with the dissolution of communism in Eastern Europe.

The second and more decisive period of American cultural influence was during the Cold War, when its mass culture became paramount throughout most liberal democratic societies, with the possible exception of a few, such as France. American cultural sway was particularly effective in transforming its two defeated enemy countries, Germany and Japan, both of which had previously resisted any Americanization by means of authoritarian fiat and censorship, but now had it imposed on them by the occupying power. In any case, American prestige was overwhelming and easily lent itself to the notion of culture superiority. Britain and the other English-speaking countries succumbed to Americanization even without any compulsion. However, to some degree in all these countries and to a greater degree in a few, there was still considerable cultural resistance from all classes. The elites, who were generally political allies of America on ideological and economic grounds, nevertheless held themselves snobbishly aloof from cheap and demeaning foreign cultural imports; the workers, who were frequently enemies of America on the same grounds, were inimical to the culture of a hated capitalism.

Such oppositions were only decisively overcome in the period of Americanization after the Cold War at the conclusion of these great ideological battles. In this period American mass culture took on global dimensions and now is paramount throughout the world. This is sometimes symbolically referred to as the McDonaldization of the world or as its Cocacolonization, to invoke but two of the most potent symbols of American culinary culture to which many others from the consumer market can be added as well. American brand names and the names of its stars and celebrities in every cultural activity from sport to song to satire are household names throughout the world, known in all metropolises as well as the most distant, out-of-way villages. The American media, which are omnipresent, have ensured that this be so. American cultural prestige and influence is at its apogee; it has become the hegemonic cultural form of the world and is likely to persist as such for a long time to come.

As can be seen from this account, the relation between American culture and global culture is a particularly close one, but that must not be taken to mean that they are identical. Globalization in cultures is not solely and simply a matter of Americanization. It is true that at present most of global culture, though far from all of it, is either made in the United States or licensed by American-based conglomerates for production elsewhere. It is also the case that global culture mostly derives from and continues a previous American mass culture. Hence global culture persists in utilizing mainly American cultural material in both its form and content. This material frequently goes back in its origins to traditional American elite, folk, and popular culture. Between P. T. Barnum in the nineteenth century and today's celebrity-producing publicity machines there is an unbroken historical continuum, as there is between the nineteenth-century folk and popular musical styles and present pop, and so on for many other such examples of continuity. Often, indeed, it is difficult to tell where the one ends and the other begins.

However, this must not lead to the mistaken conclusion that global culture is an authentic American culture. It is not any other kind of authentic culture either, but a surrogate for real culture or what the Germans would call an *Erzatz Kultur*, a derivative substitute culture that takes the place of real culture. Hence it could in principle derive its materials from anywhere and still utilize them in the same way for the same commercial ends. It so happens that for largely historical reasons it originated in America and derived its inspiration from there. It is conceivable that had historical circumstances been different this could have happened somewhere else, so that now a global culture would be circulating that had quite another basis, perhaps a wholly European one. Instead of American blacks sweeping the world with their jazz it might have been European Gypsies who developed and propagated their tzigane or flamenco musics or Jews with their klezmer music, to mention only those from the backward corners of Europe. Political repression and sheer extermination certainly disposed of any such

Gypsy or Jewish dreams. Hence it is not inconceivable that at some distant time in the future the American elements in global culture will be attenuated and displaced by others, but that would not change its basic character as an *Erzatz Kultur*.

To some limited extent this is already starting to happen now. Non-American and largely non-European elements are now steadily infusing themselves into the global cultural brew. Every major non-Western culture is contributing something to this cultural mix. The Japanese, who are the wealthiest and most technologically advanced of these, have been buying up media companies and through them propagating a few of their cultural clichés to the rest of the world: samurais and ninjas, judo and Zen, sushi and *tamagotchi*, a fascination with bonsais and dwarf electronic gadgets. The Chinese have not yet had such comparable success, but their culinary culture is prevalent wherever the Han people have immigrated, and a small following, mainly of youthful fans, for kung-fu flicks is starting to emerge. The Indians have succeeded in the Western world with the widespread practice of yoga and to a lesser extent with theosophy and gurus of various small cults; in the poorer countries they have been selling their cheap cinema products and now even Hollywood is showing an interest in Bollywood. Interestingly enough, the Arab people have not as yet managed to market anything of their Muslim culture for a global public, nor have the Africans done much better. The reasons have obviously to do with their economic, political, and technological backwardness and consequent lack of power and prestige on a world stage.

Success in global culture is mainly a matter of power, prestige, and pre-eminence in the other things that matter in a technological civilization. At present these have mainly to do with productive capacity, high standards of living, technological inventiveness, ideological influence based on military and political superiority, control of transport and communications (especially of the media), and the accumulated cultural prestige of previous influence and achievements. To some extent this has always been the case in cultural matters. The ancient Greeks and Romans spread their culture for some of these kinds of reasons. But these were not global cultures, only the specific cultures of a classical civilization that generally only appealed to ruling aristocratic elites. And they never extended their cultural sway much beyond the areas of their effective political control. In a global technological civilization such limiting conditions no longer apply.

America is now for all the above reasons in the preeminent position to exert cultural influence all over the world. Hence global culture is effectively in American hands. In fact, so much has America become the world's salesman of culture that exporting the goods, services, and images of the American Dream to starstruck foreigners is now a mainstay of the whole American economy. Protecting this lucrative trade has become a key plank of U.S. commercial and diplomatic policy, and its agencies of state do not hesitate to deploy their full panoply of power to make sure that such things as its intellectual property rights are everywhere upheld and that protectionist barriers to the free flow of its cultural commodities are broken.

This identification of America with global culture, promoted as much by itself as by others, is now so well established that any opposition to the latter comes to be taken as an attack on the former. This misunderstanding must be redressed for the sake of any meaningful discussion. To emphasize firmly once again: to be against global culture is not necessarily to be against America; to act against it is not to mindlessly attack what have come to be taken as the symbols of America. Nobody in their right frame of mind would advocate the cultural terrorism of bombing McDonald's restaurants; nor should any sensible person wish to uphold the taboos of the mullahs against rock music or disco dancing or scantily clad girlie-ads; it is one thing to denounce Coca-Cola culture and the hedonistic vision of life it purveys in its advertising, but it is quite another to ban the drinking of Coke. In any case, it would be tactically foolish to do any such thing for it would alienate the very people whose support is so crucial for any concerted action against worldwide cultural pollution. For just as the environmental movement began in America, where so much damage had already been done to nature, so one might hope that an analogous cultural reaction might also start there where so much cultural devastation has already occurred. Where the danger is at its highest, the battle is at its keenest.

D. IN DEFENSE OF LOCAL CULTURE

If this is the correct diagnosis of the world's cultural ills, the question that arises is whether anything can be done about their cure. It would be foolishly hopeful to believe in any kind of complete remedy: global culture will not somehow be overcome and vanish—it is here to stay for the indefinite future. However, this does not mean that everybody need completely succumb to it and allow it to become the world's sole culture. People can resist its claims to hegemonic exclusivity and its attempts to insinuate itself into every other culture so as to surreptitiously take it over. It can be reacted against and countered in all sorts of ways both public and private, whether through state legislation or through individual initiative, as well as by organized movements on the model of the environmentalist ones.

People wishing to act against cultural pollution might begin by taking a leaf out of the environmentalists' book: if their catchphrase is "think globally, act locally," the forthcoming culturalist credo might reverse that to "think locally, act globally." To defend the local one needs to act globally, for what is being opposed is itself global and can only be countered by a joint worldwide effort. But to do so one needs to think locally—that is, to think through, feel oneself into, and commit oneself to one's own local culture, one that is not shared with people from other places. The future cultural battles will be between the one global culture and the many local cultures. Somehow the oligopolistic monoculture will have to be broken to permit a variety of local cultures to bloom once more.

Local cultures come in many forms. Some are very narrow, though very varied, such as tribal cultures and those of small communities; others are very broad, though much more uniform, such as the cultures of civilizations and universal religions; in between these two extremes fall the intermediate cultures of nations, ethnic or linguistic groupings, regional societies, civic entities, and so on. Local cultures can be very old and traditional or modern and "progressive"; both of these forms can be found in European cultures, often in interaction with each other, as, for example, when a religion adopts an enlightened stance, thus melding age-old traditions with contemporary currents. Local cultures need not always be coherent and unified—they can be internally diverse and structured along numerous stratified divisions: those of town and country, upper and lower classes, elite and popular publics, adults and children, men and women, sacred and profane, oral and written, traditional and fashionable, and so on. There is almost no limit to such internal differentiations; each culture to some extent shapes its own patterns of segmentation and separation.

Thus local cultures maintain differences and promote diversity, whereas global culture breaks down differences and tends toward uniformity and homogeneity. Local cultures need not be exclusive of each other, for in any one locality—even within the same population—there will always be a great many diversified local cultures available to which people can choose to adhere or not. It is in terms of such alternative choices that individuals establish their unique identity and define themselves. To what extent these choices are free or conditioned or compelled will depend on historical circumstances and the balance of social forces at any one time. In general, the more modern a society the freer they tend to become, allowing, of course, for exceptional circumstances, such as the all too recent totalitarianisms. But there is always considerable scope for any person to define himself or herself by choosing to partake in certain local cultures and not in others, in such ways that are different from those of relations or near neighbors, adopting some roles and not others, cultivating specific status differences of group or personal exclusiveness, or deliberately choosing not to do so but to practice instead egalitarianism or the common touch, and so on for all the other almost unlimited possibilities of establishing and affirming identity differences.

Global culture, by contrast, works in almost the opposite way: it offers everyone the same limited choices, the choice of cultural products that are as nearly the same as Coke and Pepsi or *Time* and *Newsweek*, which only leaves open the difference between those who prefer to drink or those who prefer to read. By making people define themselves through consuming products within a few broad scales of income and buying-power differentials, global culture forces them to mold themselves in standard ways and to assume uniform identities within these few ranges as upmarket or down-market buyers. For consumption is a poor marker of identity differentiation, since it does not really establish character differences. Changing one's pattern of consumption and, indeed, even changing one's lifestyle need hardly make a crucial difference to who one is. One is what one eats (*man ist was man isst*) has some truth only in a highly impoverished or caste-ridden society. In an affluent society defining people according to what they consume, as advertisers are wont to do, is but a way of reducing them to a common denominator and so in effect rendering them the same. These and other homogenizing trends, if carried far enough, will eventually lead to a society of classes of clones such as Huxley envisaged—differentiated on genetic grounds, though really cultural in intent.

CHAPTER 1

Many academic exponents of culture studies prefer to ignore these sad facts. Those who take pride in discovering minutiae of difference, even in the appearance of identical twins, also find fine distinctions among the products of consumer culture. And if there are no such discernable differences among the products themselves, then they will hasten to find them in the ways they are consumed or received or, more loosely speaking, processed. The idea that the very same Coca-Cola advertisement is understood and appreciated differently in various localities and culture contexts, and that this matters to the effect it has, is the delusion of myopic theorists determined to see difference for its own sake. Advertising executives have obviously decided that such differences do not matter to the success of their trade. They do not significantly vary their pitch in different countries. No doubt there is some semantic variety in how the same "message" is received across different societies, as well as across different classes, groups, and individuals within the same society. But to use such divergences to argue that it reveals the persistence of cultural diversity even within the most homogenized milieu is dangerous wishful thinking that is oblivious to the evident effects of Cocacolonization, which show that the same barrage of Coca-Cola advertising will be received in the same way in the respects that matter across the whole world.

It will not be easy to repair the damage already wrought by Cocacolonization or other inroads of global culture, but it is possible to limit it. To this end local cultures must be maintained at least as a holding operation to prevent the unresisted flood of cultural trash sweeping everything away. For once lost local culture is irrecoverable. Local cultures, as we have seen, come in many forms—elite, folk, and popular—and there are numerous varieties of each still available in different parts of the world. All kinds of cultures, both traditional and modern, count as local. However, what do not qualify are the locally produced versions of global culture, or variants of it, more or less adjusted to local tastes and sensibilities. McDonald's in India has not changed the basic flavor of its offerings even though it does not serve beef burgers for obvious religious reasons, but some other meat filling; "spaghetti" Westerns to not belong to local Italian culture even though they are made in Italy largely for Italian audiences; Nigerian sitcoms are still the same slick comedy routines despite their local humor, which is attuned to the more earthy tastes of Africans. Such minor adaptations must not be allowed to confuse the basic distinction. All spurious theorizing to the contrary—arguing that there is diversity even in reproductions since they are never quite the same as the originals—is mere exception-mongering that panders to the powers that be of global culture. The Murdoch media executives like to believe they are going native because they add a dash of local color to their standard program lines.

Much more interesting than such mere adjustments of global culture to local conditions are the genuine hybrids between the global and the local that more rarely tend to arise at a popular level in different places, especially now in Third World countries. Such cultural cross-fertilizations occur whenever local forms are infused with global content or global forms with local content. This can occur at a simple level, as in African versions of African American music, or at a highly sophisticated level, as in postmodernist art, which is a cross between European modernism and American pop. There is no denying that such hybrid or "creole" cultures are very frequently colorful and daring; but, unfortunately, they are not hardy and tend not to last. Like mules, they can be strong but infertile, unable to reproduce themselves. They cannot consolidate themselves as stable cultural species, for they all too quickly revert to their global paternity and are absorbed back into it. Hence, most often these are merely transitional stages to full globalization. Even in the case of postmodernism—which is in many respects different, since it arose within an already established mass culture—there is an analogous tendency to be tamed and commercialized as merely a distinctive fashion style; what began as a gesture of mockery and defiance of the art market and consumer culture has now ended up as luxury-line styling catering to the tastes of the more sophisticated wealthy elites, especially their younger cohorts.

Postmodernism has been hailed by many cultural theorists, particularly in America, as a new cultural era. If it is, indeed, a transitional stage to global culture, then this puts paid to any such assumptions. Mistakenly thinking they were affirming a populist point of view, such theorists have battened on to it in order to discredit a modernism that was favored by the cultural establishment and, moreover, was European-derived, and so, supposedly, had elitist predilections; and in opposition they pushed for a pop-inspired, youthful art that they thought might appeal to a broader public. But in upholding an art that was already heavily infused with pop culture, they had in effect brought high culture halfway down to mass culture and so began the process of winding it up altogether. The modernist movement in art can in retrospect be criticized on many counts, but at least it did not give up on the perennial aspirations of serious art, which it still partly embodied and which are in no way against popular art. Brahms once paid tribute to the music of Johann Strauss, which he admired, by saying that he wished he were the composer of the "Blue Danube" waltz. But he never placed it on the same level as one of his own symphonies. Both are masterpieces of their kind, yet there is an enormous difference between these genres of musical form, for the one is obviously much more elaborate and sophisticated than the other in terms of thematic content, formal complexity, and numerous other criteria of musical discrimination.

Postmodernist cultural theorists have a biased tendency to deny all such fundamental distinctions as they try to bring everything down to the same level. To achieve this aim they play semantic games with terms such as high and low, elite and popular, popular and mass, local and global, and so on, in order to make it appear that there is no basic contrast between them, that they are purely arbitrary, and that they do not stand for any value differentials whatever. These moves are now the stock-in-trade of academic discourse in the new burgeoning specialties, such as cultural studies, media and communication studies, and what is now rapidly emerging as a kind of pop sociology and pop politics. Almost invariably these studies are accompanied by a persistent, though usually disguised, prejudice: a fervently invoked, seemingly high-minded, value-relativism that in practice amounts to a value-nihilism. Thus it is sanctimoniously insisted that one is not to make value judgments—presumably on the charitable principle of judge not so that ye may not be judged; or if perforce invidious comparisons have to be made, then one must not do so on moral, aesthetic, cognitive, or any other autonomous veridical grounds, but rather on those of "exploitation" or "oppression" or "repression"—that is to say, on grounds of class, race, gender, or ethnic allegiance. The very word "quality" has been denounced as a catchword of the oppressors and so in effect as a biased word. Classical music is not to be judged as superior to pop music or in general the works of traditional culture to those of mass culture; and if a choice has to be made between them it should be in favor of that which is enjoyed by the multitude rather than by a select discerning few. Thus the democratic principle of majority decision has come to be applied in aesthetics and ethics as well as in politics; by which criterion, the Beatles are as good as Schubert, as *Time* magazine once egregiously proclaimed—indeed, going by record sales they are very likely better. Analogous claims have been made by art celebrities, media intellectuals, and some famous professors. Such braggadocio must not be allowed to go unchallenged because it is couched in an intimidating pseudotheoretical jargon that hides the fatuity of what is being affirmed. It is value-vandalism masquerading as value-freedom, a wholesale effort to destroy quality distinctions and devalue everything down to the one debased level where anything goes. All this makes it now necessary to undertake a fundamental defense of value judgment, which we shall embark on in the last chapter.

The basic judgments are unavoidable. Hence it must be firmly stressed that global culture is by its very design a meretricious or qualitatively cheap culture whose products are invariably inferior to those of local culture as judged on any autonomous valorizing criteria, such as those to be found in aesthetics, ethics, or cognition of any other kind. This is inherently so, for to produce something of quality—anything worth remembering, keeping, and passing on, that is, to become part of a tradition—would defeat the very purpose of a quick turnover trade. Its commodities are to be instantly consumed or disposed of so as to make room for new stock and another cycle of production–destruction to turn around. This holds not only for consumer durables, such as music, clothes, or furniture, but also for normally long-enduring edifices, such as buildings and monuments, which are no sooner up than they are being demolished and rebuilt. These cycles of obsolescence are geared to move faster and faster so as to generate higher profits in the shortest timespan on the capital invested. What is not quickly sold or disposed of as remaindered wares, paintings as much as videos, books as much as records, are quickly destined to be pulped as is implicit in the term "pulp literature." Nothing is made to last or endure, and if by some quirk of fortune it did, it would become a collectors' item and taken out of circulation. All kinds of devaluation strategies for making cultural commodities obsolete have been devised by publicity and advertising experts. Changes of fashion and styling now come almost with the seasons; every few years a new generational "revolt" or "revolution" in taste is invented and another "counterculture" discovered; new stars and celebrities are constantly conceived and launched, only to disappear almost as soon as they are born—in short, every trick of the trade is used to make it necessary for anything "dated" to be disposed of so that something more "up-to-date" has to be bought in its place.

This production–destruction process has the opposite effect on quality to that of the conserving strategies of traditional local cultures, which are ever intent on preserving and retaining over long periods the things that have been tried and tested and found worthwhile. In such a context the aim is to make and introduce something that will live and persist, that will retain its value as long as possible, with the ultimate promise of undying fame or immortality to the few things of superior excellence. Hence, local cultures are by their very nature dedicated to endurance and quality, whereas to strive for any such thing in global culture would defeat the whole purpose of the enterprise.

This is the reason that in general qualitative differences between the things of real culture and those of a manufactured *Erzatz Kultur* are so great and fundamental as to defeat the very possibility of making any meaningful comparisons between them on this basis. They are essentially so dissimilar that often attempts at comparison result in a mismatch of incompatibilities. How can one compare even a simple sung folk tune—which has intelligible verses and a melody that can be listened to and remembered—with an electronically modified and amplified shouted rant against a noise background of a monotonous, mechanically generated beat that cannot be followed or even properly danced to? The former can be an aesthetic experience that is emotionally moving and that can be later recollected in tranquility; the latter works at a visceral level like a quasi intoxicant, one that very soon wears off leaving nothing behind—that is, provided the often vicious and hate-filled rantings of the "rapper" are disregarded or not heard in the first place, as is, mercifully, more likely. In a similar vein, how is one to compare a children's puppet show on a familiar story line with the senseless scamperings and knockabout antics of copyright cartoon figures on a screen or in comic books? What meaningful comparisons can be drawn between novels and "soaps," or between paintings and ads, or between film scenes that make dramatic sense and MTV videoclips? Such incompatibilities can be multiplied almost indefinitely. They illustrate the unbridgeable gulf separating genuine culture, which is invariably local, from the global surrogate. The former is a repository of the collective treasures of mankind; the latter is the temporary storage bin of disposable waste products born of a throw-away-after-use mentality, the rubbish that pollutes our cultural atmosphere just as industrial rubbish pollutes our air.

We know something of what polluted air does to the health of people, especially young children, but we are still largely ignorant of the psychological effects of prolonged exposure to cultural pollutants, especially if this persists over a number of generations. The results, as we can now already foresee, are likely to be all too startling in the future. The initial symptoms, especially as evident in young people, children, and others most susceptible to such problems, are even now starting to appear. Manifestations of serious damage are coming to hand all the time in ever-newer guises. That violence in films and television predisposes children to aggressive behavior is now officially acknowledged; it is even experimentally demonstrable: very likely it also reveals itself in the ever-growing statistics of delinquency and bullying in all schools, as well as the occasional massacre in a few. A cult of illicit drugs is now prevalent among the young, and it is linked to sex and rock music as promoted by the media and by revelations about famous stars, some of whom die or barely recover from well-publicized overdoses. Their example is not lost on their numerous fans. The large incidence of depression and the rising rates of suicide among the young, among whom such things were previously rarely heard of, is at least partly attributable to their cultural malnourishment; a steady diet of pop culture passively absorbed is bound to take its depressive toll since it mainly deals with negative emotions, such as rage, hate, lust and fear, as well as playing on vanity, envy, and insecurity, and extolling greed, instant gratification, and the cunning necessary to encompass these ends. It is noteworthy that those societies longest exposed to mass culture and its global successor display to the greatest extent the corrupting effects of such negative experiences.

This fact is particularly evident in Los Angeles, the very epicenter from which so much of this culture emanates, and the location of the headquarters where it is planned and produced. The breakdown of civic and communal life is there amply apparent and has been repeatedly demonstrated in numerous incidents that reveal the disturbing manifestations of delinquency, gang warfare, and riots by the poor, and a flight to safety in walled-off and heavily guarded enclaves, away from any responsibility, by the rich. Family breakdown, illegitimacy, drugs, and pornography are prevalent among all classes. A cheap streetwise cynicism rules the behavior of the young; the egoistic cynicism of what has been called the "me-first generation" dominates the mentality of their elders. In this society, civic standards are low; policing is poor, making up in brutality what it lacks in persuasiveness; justice cannot always be relied on; corruption is rampant. Altogether a not very desirable society, yet one where enormous private wealth and glamour hide the public squalor, where the American Dream turned nightmare still manages to entice streams of immigrants from all parts of the world. Obviously, not all of this cheapening of the quality of life that has come with rising standards of affluence can be ascribed to cultural factors, but some of it is undoubtedly due to what is produced there to such profit. Los Angeles lives by exuding the poisons that are slowly killing it.

Beyond such glaring and dramatic effects there are even more subtle, but no less insidious, consequences of global culture, such as the threat it poses to literacy. Literacy, broadly understood, is the basis of all the cultures of the book or its textual equivalents. The decline of literacy, which is so apparent among those most exposed to pop culture, is not due to the usual self-congratulatory reasons adduced by the exponents of such McLuhanacies as that the era of print is over, and that the book, as an obsolete print medium, must give way to the more technologically advanced electronic media of imagery and information storage. In fact, far from displacing books, the new era of electronic media has promoted a huge increase in printing and book production. The number of titles published rises year by year and now runs into well over a hundred thousand; not even the biggest libraries in the world can keep up with the constant flow, and electronic computer means are required to tabulate, catalogue, and make even marginally accessible this plethora of print; indeed, this might be one of the most useful functions of the computer and the associated Internet, as the handmaid of print.

The book as a technical manual or as a best-seller entertainment commodity is an inherent part of global culture. This means that the book as a mode of literacy has undergone a drastic change. Book reading is now a different kind of activity to what it was in former cultures. Nearly all people are now capable of reading—that is to say, they are literate in the purely technical sense of being able to decipher script. But this is only the lowest degree of literacy that schools inculcate at an elementary level. In itself it is far from adequate for being able to read and understand a text of any complexity of meaning in whatever subject. For such accomplishments the much higher literacy of interpretation and appropriate knowledge is required, which is usually acquired in high schools and universities or equivalent institutions to be found in all literate civilizations.

The culture of the book as literature or other such texts is at the heart of all such civilizations. It is in this sense that the book is now under threat from global culture. An addiction to a constant diet of pictures and music, such as are incessantly beamed by television screens and DVD players, or the easy reading of pulp fiction and such printed matter cannot but weaken (if not blunt) any capacity to study and absorb a text with any complexity of meaning that needs to be interpreted and explicated. The comprehension of concepts, theories, and complex ideas, all of which require definitions and arguments to back them up, is made very difficult for those who can only deal with blocks of "information" and data segmented into bits. The imaginative apprehension of a fictional world that is not pure fantasy, but casts a critical light on reality, is stunted by the constant absorption through pictures or texts in a make-believe world of unreality. These are just a few of the ways in which the high literacy of previous generations is giving way to a low literacy that is but one step removed from illiteracy.

Closely related to literacy are all kinds of other cultural competencies that involve "reading" and understanding in some sense or other, and these, too, are severely impaired by global culture. The capacity to "read" pictorial representations and comprehend their subtle conventions is undermined by comic book and cartoon codes of the crudest kind, and by optical camera imagery that reproduces mechanically the look of things. The ability to correctly hear and interpret tunes, to speak only of the simplest level of musical appreciation, is subverted by rap and rock that demand nothing from their listeners but rhythmic swaying. Such capacities, as most people used to acquire in childhood, are now being lost to the young. Youth culture—which is a key component of global culture, since so much of it is addressed to youthful audiences—functions on such a level of aesthetic incompetence that it might be considered an anesthetic, acting like a drug that dulls and blunts perception.

It will be readily appreciated that there are no simple solutions to problems of this magnitude. To advocate local as against global culture is merely one step in the voyage of recovery, but it is the necessary first step without which the journey could not begin. It might seem like a highly traditionalist or even reactionary move to take, and it can be that when it is taken in an antiquarian spirit intent on merely preserving the past for its own sake or with a religious fundamentalist mentality that refuses any adjustments to contemporary conditions of life. However, it need not be understood in this way, but rather as a flexible conservationist approach to the past by means of which traditions and their cultural forms can be maintained, yet kept vital, by being transformed to meet the changing needs of society. Traditions that are held to as fixed and unalterable standards become the taboos of a dead traditionalism; traditions whose spirits are alive are continuing to grow and to remold the shape they assume. Such a conception of conservation is consonant with the best conservatism of the past, in its most enlightened forms, which, in a sense, it also conserves and transforms. But it is purely cultural and in no way bound to political conservatism or any other of its ideological baggage.

Hence, criticisms that such a stand abandons the universal for the particular, the humanitarian for the xenophobic, the inclusive for the exclusive, the cosmopolitan for the parochial, and so on for all such charges likely to be brought by opponents, are based on misconceptions of what is meant by the local in opposition to the global. Such contraries do not work in favor of the global, for that is far from being universalist, humanist, inclusive, or even cosmopolitan or internationalist. It is global culture that is itself particularist for it is fashioned in a few localities, mainly in America, as the derivative of a narrow range of forms, also mainly American; the fact that it is then purveyed and accepted throughout the world does not make it universalist. It is also far from being humanist for it espouses none of the values of an ideal humanity, but rather those of hedonistic material affluence; it does not aim for excellence and promotes neither enlightenment nor liberation. Hence it is not inclusive for it acts as a status differential that permits the rich, who can afford more of it, to assert their superiority over the poor, and in general for rich societies to lord it over poor societies and feel culturally smug and self-satisfied in doing so. At the same time it induces resentment and envy by encouraging the flaunting of status goods and other costly symbols of wealth and affluence. And, finally, it is the opposite of cosmopolitan for it immures people within the constraints of a narrow monoculture and makes it seem unnecessary for them to have to communicate across cultural divides, as is so patently apparent in the behavior of tourists. Hence, it is not internationalist either, for it does not recognize the rights of other cultures.

Global culture is not universalist, humanist, inclusive, cosmopolitan, or internationalist; some local cultures can be so—to be specific, those of the European Enlightenment. The culture of the Enlightenment and its numerous successors is, of course, not only to be found in Europe, but throughout the world where European influence prevailed, most prominently so in America, which to begin with was simply an overseas extension of Europe. This was the political culture on which the U.S. Constitution was founded, one of its most impressive practical realizations. In the non-European countries of colonialism its legacy is not as impressive and not as lasting. The liberal–democratic socialism of India has not really taken root, and the Chinese version of Marxism, an extreme communist creed, produced the totalitarian horrors of Maoism. In Europe itself the culture of the Enlightenment in its various political expressions was productive of great achievements and enormous failures. The legacies of its liberal and democratic socialist movements are still there to humanize the quality of life and to harmonize social relations between classes. The grand utopian projects of its extremist movements are everywhere in ruins. Despite its checkered history, much of this culture still survives and manifests itself both locally in some higher educational institutions and their surrounding circles of intellectuals, such as those in Paris, as well as internationally in such things as UN-sponsored projects of cultural conservation and human rights—in these respects ably backed by American foreign policy.

Thus it is still possible to invoke something of the surviving spirit of a European universalist humanism against the inroads of global culture, or at least conjure up its ghost to haunt it. This, too, as we have shown, is a kind of localism against globalism. It is not to be imagined that this can defeat the overwhelming forces of globalization, but it will give some of its more sensitive exponents a bad conscience and so perhaps prevent it attaining intellectual credence and flaunting itself brazenly in triumph. The immediate aim is not to overcome global culture, merely not to completely succumb to it. But for even that limited goal to be achieved will require mustering the full resources of every local culture throughout the world in a common collective effort against a common danger. That means that people everywhere will have to learn to act globally even while they think locally.

Those people who consider themselves Europeans by origin, upbringing, or choice will naturally turn to their various native cultures, such as those of the separate regions and nations or those of the continent in general, so as to protect them against the ravages of globalism. Americans, too, those who are still alive to their own authentic traditions, will wish to prevent them being overwhelmed by the commercial trash sweeping their country. All kinds of protective measures will need to be taken both in private and in public, through organized social movements and by the legislative actions of the state, to limit and restrict the influx of global culture. Those who oppose this with the usual shibboleths of free trade need to be reminded that protectionism in defense of culture is no crime.

The defense of local culture can be misused in all sorts of xenophobic ways and these, of course, must be attacked whenever they occur, for they compromise and discredit all that is worthwhile in this endeavor. Currently in Europe some perverted versions of something like it are being invoked in narrowly chauvinistic and even neofascist campaigns, often leading to outrages against metics, auslander, and other immigrants, especially those of different race from the old colonial countries. In some of these newly independent countries of the Third World even worse forms of revenge racism, ethnic cleansing, and religious fundamentalism are being perpetrated under the banner of upholding native rights, indigenous lore, or the traditions of the faith. In such situations global culture appears by contrast as a liberating, enlightening, and tolerant alternative and is appealed to especially by the young under the mistaken impression that it represents Western culture. However, the fact that there are things in the world even worse than global culture must not distract us from its clear and present danger.

The defense of any one local culture is in no way directed against others; on the contrary, it acts in support of others, for no local culture can survive on its own, but only through the mutual cooperation of a collectivity of cultures that uphold each other while distinguishing themselves from each other. Neither is such a defense of one culture exclusive of others that are also present among the same people. Hence, it does not render a sensible form of multiculturalism impossible. In many ways it can even justify it and support it. Individuals and groups need not always be unicultural but can also practice various forms of biculturalism, adhering to distinct cultures in different contexts or situations. This is no more odd or difficult than being bilingual and using one or other language as the occasion warrants. In fact, in a global world people should be encouraged as much as possible to become bilingual and bicultural, to reach out to other local cultures even as they remain in firm possession of their own. The fact that English is becoming the other language that most people in the world are learning does not go against localism and need not in principle support global culture, even though in practice it often does so. For under contemporary conditions of globalization, the acquisition of English is often seen as the passport to the world enabling those who speak it to escape their own societies and acquire the trappings of global culture; in this way it becomes the conduit through which global culture enters and subverts the cultures of other societies. But this can easily be avoided by detaching the language from the cultural cargo it now carries, one that promotes cargo-cult beliefs that affluence will somehow arrive once this language is learned.

Policies of biculturalism are especially called for in old societies that have experienced an influx of recent immigration from regions distant from themselves. Assimilationism cannot be expected from such migrants, who rightly prefer not to relinquish their cultural heritage. What can and must be required from them is that they become to some degree bicultural and where necessary also bilingual. For to become citizens of their new country they must understand and share some form of the local culture of the society in question, at least in its civic guise. Every society, if it is to maintain any civic cohesion, must require from its members a cultural modicum of shared values and assumptions, at least such as are inherent in the laws and institutions, especially the educational ones, that constitute the civil core of the local culture. Without such a basic commonality mutual understanding and cooperation become very difficult. However, that need not prevent individuals and groups also maintaining their own specific cultural traditions in private life or collective religious life or even in the communal life of ethnic diasporas. This is the sensible multiculturalism that is not only consistent with but made mandatory by a defense of local culture.

A world in which a thousand cultural flowers bloomed and people were able to pick some to participate in and admire others for their fragrance and color would be a truly cosmopolitan and internationalist world. It would be the opposite of one in which a monoculture prevailed. The exponents of global culture are not cosmopolitans; they are like tourists who expect to have their home comforts abroad, where there is more sunshine or where quaint natives abound, but where their favorite TV shows in their

own language will be available. A true cosmopolitan, by contrast, is someone who is at home in two or more cultures and well versed in others. Such
people are always rare, for just as a talent for languages is not given to
everyone, so neither is a talent for cultures. But that does not mean that
some degree of cosmopolitanism cannot be attained by everyone.

If the world were heading for cosmopolitanism and internationalism then
the key Enlightenment values of universalist humanism could begin to be realized. It is quite understandable that not everyone will share these, and there
is no question of imposing them on others against their will. Even a universalist ethics cannot be assumed to be acceptable to everyone. However, some
universal norms and values will have to be accepted and adhered to by
everyone if humanity is to live in peace with itself and if global mobility and
intercourse is to be maintained. Hence, a common core of principles that are
capable of being sustained in international law will have to prevail, such as
those associated with basic human rights and the protection of the environment. But this degree of universalism should not interfere with all other cultural differences, even such as extend to ethical beliefs involving a rejection
of all other Enlightenment values. But as the world becomes more interde-
pendent, humanity more unified, and as predicaments and problems arise
that are common to all mankind, so the necessity for such universal principles will grow.

Principal among such common problems are those of the environment,
on which the fate of all of mankind depends. Only second to these are the
difficulties of global culture, which also touch on every society and nation.
Our ultimate aim must be to attend to both of these problems at once in unison with each other, to repair the damage to nature step by step with that to
culture. Both are part of the same predicament of globalization in general:
the too rapid and often destructive changes wrought on the environment and
society by the forces of our technological civilization. In both respects, in relation to both nature and culture, conservationist and restorative measures
are necessary in order to establish an eco–cultural balance. And just as in nature conservation entails preserving species diversity, so in culture it also
means conserving the full variety of local cultural forms.

2

WHY IS GLOBAL CULTURE SO SUCCESSFUL?

The present worldwide success of global culture, and the triumph of technics that it represents, is the most remarkable achievement of any culture in human history. No other culture has spread so far, so fast, and to so many people at once as global culture. The rapid expansion of the great classical cultures, such as those of Greece and China, or of the world religions—though some of these, above all Islam, spread very rapidly indeed—pale by comparison with global culture. In somewhat less than a century, the fatal twentieth century, global culture has emerged from almost nothing to world domination.

How was this achieved? What forces were instrumental in bringing it about? Will it only come to an end when, like a raging fire, everything of value is consumed by it? Or is it still possible to save something from the approaching conflagration? Such are but a few of the key questions that will concern us in this chapter. Answering them fully requires more than a chapter, more than a book, and perhaps more than a single author can encompass, for the dimensions of this issue are awesome. Nevertheless, some leading pointers toward putative answers to these questions can be provided even within the limited scope of a chapter.

The issue must be approached historically, for the current outstanding success of global culture is the culmination of a historical process involving a number of more or less demarcated stages. A somewhat different account will be called for to explain it at each stage, though the same or very similar forces will be found to be continuously at work to a cumulative effect. Just as

the force of gravity can accelerate a falling object from standstill to any imagined speed depending on time and space, so, too, the same historical force
can work continuously to alter the movement of culture to any imagined extent depending on the times and circumstances. The crucial forces we will
be considering continually in what follows are these: capitalism, the state,
technology, and mass society. These are the more or less operative factors
throughout the whole trajectory of the historical process. Any one of them
taken by itself does not explain what has happened to culture; it is the interaction of all of them that matters.

In this process there are two distinguishable stages: first, the rise of mass
cultures in America and the various countries of western Europe which took
place approximately in the first three quarters of the twentieth century; and
second, the proliferation of a global culture, out of a largely American mass
culture, that began in the last quarter and is still continuing, now at an ever
accelerating rate. In many ways both of these are the phases of the one continuous historical sweep, and the influence of America was paramount
throughout. But in other respects each of the stages presents different features, and different issues arise in explaining them. The extraordinary success of global culture builds on the previous, somewhat slower, achievements
of mass culture without which it could not have even started. However, mass
culture was not yet global and had a somewhat different character in every
major country.

Mass cultural phenomena began to make themselves felt toward the end
of the nineteenth century in every developed society. They were the cultural
responses to the rise of mass society brought about by the ongoing development of capitalism, the state, bureaucratic organization, and technology
throughout the course of the nineteenth century, ever since the industrial
and political revolutions of this period. Industrialization and standardiza-
tion of products and services, the constitution of an open market for goods
and labor, and the growth of cities connected by rapid modes of transport—
these were the economic aspects of the process. The growth of an administrative bureaucracy, of state regulation (above all in ordaining compulsory
military service and compulsory education), the rise of organized political
parties, of labor unions, of clerical and anticlerical associations, of nationalist sentiment and revolutionary ideologies—all these were the political aspects of the same process. Both of these general trends had their social ex-

pressions, which took a mass form as they became more entrenched. Mass-market merchandising and advertising, mass spectator sports, mass movements ranging from scouting for children to voluntary associations of all kinds, mass political parties, mass entertainment, mass tourism, and mass media were all beginning to appear toward the end of the nineteenth century. Eventually these mass social phenomena began to affect every aspect of life, in both work and leisure for all classes in society. Individual behavior in all its varied modes was influenced and shaped by these mass manifestations: whether it was the care of one's body or sartorial appearance, or the cultivation of aptitudes and tastes, or the rules of propriety or the roles that could be assumed, hardly anything remained unaffected by these mass currents of society. All this cumulatively and conjointly constituted the basis for the buildup of a mass culture.

Here we cannot possibly examine all the varied forms of this culture, so we shall largely concentrate on one of its most crucial components—the mass media. The media are the commanding heights of mass culture, overlooking and dominating all else, for they literally mediate and amplify the other aspects. Thus, for example, mass spectator sports are inconceivable without the media; without the sporting press, to begin with, and later without radio and television broadcasting, it would have been impossible to whip up a mass sporting following and create a reliable spectator public. Indeed, the media have even partly determined what kinds of sports will be played and how they will be played; basketball, for example, would not have attained its present eminence without television, and there are many other such cases. The benefits, of course, are mutual, for mass sport has in turn contributed to the rise of mass media. Newspapers grew in size and circulation as they devoted more space to the sporting pages and attracted a new readership of mainly working people by these means. This symbiotic relation between sport and media is well understood by the media magnates who have been buying up sporting clubs and acquiring exclusive rights for the broadcasting of matches. There are analogous links between the media and other mass cultural activities. Entertainment and the media are almost synonymous. Tourism and the media are also closely connected.

It is the mediating and amplifying role of the media that made them so crucial to all of mass culture right from the very start. Global culture is even more dependent on the media. The technological revolution that enabled global broadcasting and the easy and quick circulation of media products throughout the world is one of the key preconditions of global culture. Jetliners and the flight-culture they fostered had made a good start for global culture, though at first restricted to a wealthy elite, but it took the media to expand and enlarge on this to embrace almost everybody on earth, for nobody is now out of reach of the media.

Thus focusing primarily on the media is by no means as restrictive and partial as it might appear, for everything else in mass and global culture can be referred back to its mediation. This also has some methodological advantages, for media products are clearly identifiable and surveyable. In particular, the economic factors of media production can be calculated with great precision. Indeed, partly for this reason we shall begin our study of the media with this aspect in view, for it provides the first important considerations in explaining the success of mass and global culture. This must not be taken to mean that we are in any way bound to an economistic approach, Marxist or any other variety. Far from it, for there are other aspects to be considered that are even more important than the economic and these we shall discuss later in the chapter. However, the economic dimension reveals most clearly and obviously the enormous advantage that global culture has over every other. Hence, it is to it that we turn first.

A. THE ECONOMY OF THE MEDIA: SUPPLY AND DEMAND

The economic aspect of anything has two sides to it: supply and demand. The two are inseparable, for without demand there would be no supply, and without supply no demand could be formed. Hence, it is idle to wonder which is prior or more important, whether supply-side economics is more basic than demand-side or vice versa. Purely as a matter of heuristic convenience we shall begin with the production of media commodities first and then go on to consider how the demand for them is constituted.

Perhaps the single most remarkable economic fact about the supply of mass and later global media products is that they are incredibly cheap for consumers. They are perhaps the cheapest cultural products ever offered, being frequently given away at no cost at all or sold for purely nominal prices compared to the cost of production. At the same time the production of media goods is one of the most profitable and lucrative businesses ever devised, providing very high and safe returns on the sums invested. How is this economic miracle achieved?

The secret lies in a unique combination of funding and technology that is specific to the media. The funding, involving enormously large sums, comes from sources outside the media, usually from business firms and state agencies—though sometimes, and much more rarely, other outside interests such as unions and churches also contribute. All of these are buying media attention, measured precisely in terms of so much space or time, usually for hardheaded and self-interested motives, though very occasionally more high-minded and altruistic concerns also arise. The media operate on the ancient adage that "he who pays the piper calls the tune," and it is usually quite clear what ditties all these diverse patrons wish the media to play.

These large amounts of capital made available to the media permit them to invest in the latest technologies as soon as these become available, and also to hire the most expert and talented people to man them. As we shall show in the next section, this kind of utilization of technology, especially for reproduction and broadcasting, permits the almost unlimited delivery of the same media product to an ever-growing audience, one that ultimately can include the whole human population on earth. Hence, it is media technology that enables the constitution of a mass public, which business interests and the state are especially keen to address with their particular messages. For that privilege they are willing to outlay very large sums indeed.

This ability to deliver the same message to a very large public is the demographic basis, so to speak, of mass media culture. This culture is different from earlier forms of culture because of the very mass appeal it must make to so many people at once. The messages that can circulate in the mass media must have very special characteristics that distinguish them from other kinds of messages that were current earlier in folk, popular, or elite culture. For the more people a message has to appeal to the more unexceptional and innocuous it must become: it cannot afford to disturb, upset, baffle, or seriously displease any significant segment of its public; it must seek to interest, amuse, titillate, and captivate as many as possible as quickly as possible. These conditions are usually fulfilled by entertainments, amusements, harmless fun, games of chance, and games and sports in general, as well as anything that is of very broad interest, such as ordinary human foibles or specialized activities that arouse curiosity. As the size of the audiences addressed by the mass media has grown progressively, so step-by-step has the anodyne, trivial, and pointless nature of its typical offerings increased. Now, when the one television program can be watched by something approaching half the human population, it is sporting events, song and beauty contests, special ceremonial occasions such as coronations, and outrages, assassinations, or other acts of violence that alone can keep such a vast audience enthralled.

The sums expended on the propagation of global culture are truly staggering, and most of the money comes from the big corporations for purposes of publicity, especially for advertising. The world allocated around $435 billion (in U.S. dollars) to advertising in 1999; approximately half of that was spent by U.S. firms, of which sum about $120 billion was spent in America and the rest throughout the rest of the world; this amounts to well over 2 percent of U.S. GNP (these figures come from Robert McChesney).[1] Undoubtedly these sums rise by a few percentage points each year. This is the money that pays for the free or very cheap products of the mass and global media. It is the hidden subsidy of global culture that is the economic basis of its superiority over every other culture. For no other culture can be produced so as to be given away free of charge or at nominal cost. Of course, business concerns are usually not interested in subsidizing any other kind of culture. It is very profitable for them to invest in mass and global culture, especially in publicity.

Investment in advertising makes much more economic sense for producers, above all the large firms manufacturing consumer products, than almost any other kind of investment. It is far more profitable to pay for advertising of a product in order to create demand rather than to lower the cost of the product. This is the reason that producers usually do not compete on price, but mainly through advertising. Of course, it is consumers or the general public who pay for the advertising in the long run, but that is not a calculation that they are willing or able to make at the time of purchase. Hence, in effect by paying for advertising through the higher costs of products, consumers are also paying for the media products that this advertising funds, and which they believe they are getting for nothing or for very little. At the same time they are supporting a commercial media industry that has now assumed global proportions and a commensurate advertising industry. Both of these are in collusion in promoting and propagating global culture.

Media productions that do not directly depend for finance on advertising, such as films or recorded music, nevertheless still rely on it indirectly for their publicity. The radio and television stations that plug hit records and blockbuster movies are usually part of the same commercial chains as those that produce them. It is only such companies that have the requisite large sums of capital to invest in such expensive media products utilizing the latest technologies and the most expert production teams. Without such built-in advantages in production and prepublicity necessary to bring such a media product to the attention of a large public, no film or musical record can now succeed. The small, independent producers have now been pushed to the margins. Hence, in mass cultural fields, too, no autonomous and unaffiliated culture can now compete with global culture.

The need for ever-larger investment of capital in order to succeed also explains the extraordinary concentration of ownership in the era of global culture, with all the consequent homogenizing effects this has had on media products. Those with great capital resources are continually buying out those with less, and so eliminating the once small, independent, and sometimes more courageous producers. Production is then managed by functionaries of bureaucratic marketing departments. At this point the accountants usually take over and begin dictating to the so-called "creative" people what will or will not make for bigger profits. This has usually a culturally disastrous effect on the product. Thus, for example, as the small publishing firms, previously run by family concerns or small boards of directors, were taken over by the media moguls, the whole nature of book publishing and the very quality and meaning of a book changed irrevocably. Writing, commissioning, editing, marketing, and reviewing of books is no longer what it used to be even a few decades ago. Now it is the blockbuster book published to prearranged and orchestrated fanfares that alone succeeds. Such a book is usually commissioned from prospective authors who have already attained fame or notoriety through the media for other reasons; they are frequently paid large advances which they use to hire "ghost" writers and other helpers; and eventually the finished product is released in huge marketing campaigns that have now assumed international scope. What kind of a book results from all such inducements and pressures? This question more or less answers itself.

Apart from business firms it is the state that directly or indirectly pays for the media; which also means that in the long run it is citizens, as taxpayers, who foot the bill. The state subsidizes directly by paying for media products that are of service to it, or when it funds whole media channels, as with public broadcasting in many countries. The state subsidizes indirectly by giving away publicly owned radio and television bandwidth frequencies either to privately owned media enterprises almost exclusively, as is the case in the United States, or to private firms as well as its own domestic or foreign broadcasting corporations, as happens in many other countries. This is in principle no different to giving away other scarce resources, such as land or water. The effect of this is to create oligopolistic controls of all broadcasting media and to reduce competition to negligible proportions, so much so that, as Lord Thomson, the Canadian media magnate, once put it, to be granted a bandwidth allocation is tantamount to being given a license to print money. The state also supports other forms of media in even more subtle ways; thus, for example, a reduced rate of postage for papers, magazines, and other commercial print materials is an indirect subsidy for advertising and permits the wider distribution of such goods at public expense.

Business firms and the state have two major motives for lavishly funding the media and thereby subsidizing mass and global culture: promotion and propaganda. Promotion means advertising and other forms of publicity, such as brand-name and lifestyle constitution, that are part of the whole marketing effort so necessary to the arousal of a demand for all the products of factories, farms, and other enterprises; all those products that were at first sold on national markets, but which now have extended to global distribution. Without the creation of a demand for what is produced, the whole system of mass production could not function. But to create such a need for mass-produced products, a special kind of consumer has to be constituted—the mass-market consumer. This is the function of advertising and commercial publicity in general. Now with globalization the market embraces the whole earth, and so promotion has for the very first time in history to address an audience of global consumers. Hence promotion, too, must become global. This is the economic basis for global culture.

Propaganda is not all that different from promotion and it works in much the same way, though for different ends. Its aim is also to persuade, convince, sway, habituate, and eventually to indoctrinate; but instead of commercial products and, in general, a consumer style of life being promoted. it is the dictates, doctrines, and legitimating beliefs of the state or the ruling party that is propagated. Both advertising and propaganda utilize psychological techniques that were developed on a quasi-scientific basis during the course of the twentieth century, which have proved to be very effective in the political and commercial fields.[2] Like advertising, propaganda also works with slogans, catch-calls, images, and enticing scenarios to arouse desires and emotions, to inculcate beliefs and attitudes, and to affirm credos and causes. The arts of the advertiser and propagandist are so much the same that people skilled in the one craft can easily switch over to the other, as was soon discovered in the democracies during the previous wars when advertising people were enlisted in the propaganda departments. This is still the case even now, for such people are usually hired to run the election campaigns of politicians; they claim that packaging a product and a politician is just about the same. Both activities involve the formation of an image, a process that we shall examine in the next section. Frequently, too, the one entails the other, for there is implicit propaganda in advertising (for a lifestyle, the free enterprise society in general) and there is advertising in propaganda (to buy bonds, perform patriotic deeds).

Apart from promotion and propaganda there are also other motives at work in state and business support of the media. Such alternative purposes are likely to be more evident in the media involvements of other groups and organizations, such as churches, labor unions, universities, and some cultural and civic organizations. They can be roughly grouped under two headings: public policy and special interests. Public policy considerations are all these that are intended to contribute to the well-being of society, such as policies for promoting citizenship, democracy, education, and providing the necessary knowledge and vital information on matters of general concern. Special interests are all those purposes that work in favor of specific interest groups and organizations such as the ones previously mentioned, those that are partisan and partial rather than common to all members of a society. Obviously religious beliefs, political ideologies, group values, and exclusive cultural ideals are of this kind. Public policy and special interest ends are still being pursued by the media to some limited extent, but funds for such purposes are now restricted. Neither the state nor business is keen for such involvements and other social groups lack the necessary means.

At the start of the twentieth century the opposite situation obtained, for down to the First World War the then-available mass media, mainly print with just the beginnings of film and recording, were frequently in the hands of special interest groups, above all political parties, labor unions, churches, universities, and cultural organizations. After the war, all-out control of the media by special interest groups declined very rapidly, until by now there is almost nothing of it left. During the war nearly all media in the combatant countries were mobilized for propaganda purposes. It was at this time that the state became concerned with media production in a big way. In the nascent totalitarian countries, such as Russia, Italy, and eventually Germany, the state took over the media completely and used them almost exclusively for propaganda. In democratic European societies—above all, in Britain and France—the state established special quasi-autonomous broadcasting agencies, such as the BBC, ostensibly for public policy reasons. In America this never took place, for all the media were left completely in private, mainly business, hands, with the exception of propaganda broadcasting usually beamed to other lands. Public broadcasting only took off in a very limited and marginal way in the 1960s. The media in America have overwhelmingly been devoted to advertising and commercial interests; for short periods, mainly during wartime, they were also engaging in propaganda at the state's behest; and right throughout, to a very minor extent, also serving public policy and special interest goals.

Thus since the First World War three distinct patterns of media control and funding have emerged, giving rise to three kinds of media systems. There is the wholly commercial or capitalist system, as preeminent in America; at the opposite extreme there is the wholly state-run or totalitarian system, as used to be prevalent in the communist countries and to a large degree still exists under dictatorial regimes such as that of China; and between these two extremes, there is the mixed or liberal system, with some proportional sharing of the media between commercial and state-funded public service agencies, such as is still partly current in Britain and continental Europe. However, this mixed system is now under concerted attack by the forces of globalization and might not survive much longer. Once this happens then the whole world's media might become integrated as the one commercial system, closely modeled on that of America and mainly controlled by American conglomerates such as the ones mentioned at the very start.

On the back of this American system of media ownership and control rides the full panoply of global culture. Hence, it is crucial to understand its nature and functioning if anything is to be done to limit it to acceptable proportions. As it functions at present, it is a system of private ownership by business corporations, run for profit and fully integrated with the capitalist market system. The state took a hand in it only during periods of war or national emergencies such as the Cold War, and then mainly indirectly by exerting pressure and influence rather than assuming control, which was still left in private hands. But the state's need for the requisite propaganda effort was still served even without any explicit directives to this effect. Film—which showed itself to be such a wonderful propaganda medium ever since D. W. Griffith's *Birth of a Nation*—was easily co-opted through the Hollywood studio system to the war effort. And even after hostilities ceased, what the state required, by way of anticommunist propaganda, for example, could also easily be enlisted either by crude tactics, such as McCarthyism, or in more subtle ways. Similar measures also worked for privately owned radio stations and newspapers. Their owners were only too willing to cooperate for they reaped the joint rewards of profits and patriotic kudos if they complied with what was expected of them.

Even though it hasn't established any proprietorship itself, the state in America has been closely involved with the media, especially the electronic ones, through all kinds of licensing and supervisory bodies that have a semi-autonomous role. It was such a state agency, the Federal Communications Commission, that allocated the radio spectrum during the late 1920s to at first but two commercial networks, NBC and CBC (out of which a little later a third, the ABC, emerged). These three, plus the much later established FOX network, owned by the Murdoch companies, is about the sum total of broadcasting media ownership in the United States. For a while it seemed as if the new technologies of cable and satellite transmissions might break the near oligopolistic stranglehold of these conglomerates, but this has shown itself to be an illusory hope, for the mergers that ensued established new media concentrations that have succeeded in absorbing all the new forms of production and emission. The state has in no way interfered with this process, being loath to act against such centers of power and influence.

Since the key concerns of all commercial media are profits and growth, it follows that their main preoccupation is with advertising, which provides the bulk of their revenue. Their whole mode of production and programming is focused on attracting high-paying advertisers. Everything else becomes secondary to that dominant goal. As a result, the advertisements are frequently the costliest items in the whole production schedule, the ones on which the most care and concern is lavished, requiring the most advanced technical means and equipment and employing the best specialist talent in the field. Frequently the ads are of greater interest and have more quality than the programs between which they are sandwiched.

The main purpose of these programs is to attract and hold an audience for the advertisements. The quality or character of the program is ancillary to this aim—anything that will muster a large public will do. Hence, the supreme importance of ratings for the commercial media. Ratings measure pure exposure to advertising, irrespective of people's interest, focus, or concentration on the program that is being listened to or viewed. However, there is also invariably a commonality of point of view and attitude between the advertisements and programs; both promote a consumerist lifestyle and the values that reinforce and encourage it.

Advertising in its latest manifestations is no longer simply concerned with advocating single commodities on their own; it has transmogrified into the superior form of promotion known as branding, or the establishment of general brand names. The difference is that the older style of advertising, characteristic of the earlier stage of mass culture, promotes a specific product, such as toothpaste or soap; the new form of branding develops a whole product "concept"—that is, a range of goods embedded in a particular style of life. The brand name and its associated logo are portrayed through continuous and consistent advertising campaigns in such a way as to stand for a way of bearing and comporting oneself, associating with others, living out one's fantasy aspirations, and assuming a role in society. Thus, for example, Nike does not merely advertise running shoes, which are what it primarily sells, but a whole youthful, sporty style of life. It celebrates sporting superheroes—such as the basketballer Michael Jordan—as admirable role models, and presents gala sporting events of all kinds as spectator entertainments. Naomi Klein has explored the process of the creation of a brand that can then be applied to a whole range of related products, or eventually, to any product whatsoever that the company chooses to market.[3] Thus the brand names Calvin Klein or Virgin have very wide currency across all kinds of products. To achieve this branding effect companies such as these have to associate their products with all kinds of desirable activities, hence their endless sponsorship of sporting, youth, musical, and all kinds of other events and festivals.

Because of such practices, the older distinction between the advertisements and the media materials that carry them is being elided as the brand promotions and programs fuse into each other. Articles in papers or magazines that promote tourism or clothes or the pop scene or gastronomy are at once news and ads in inseparable combination; the celebrities who feature in music or films become brand-name icons by association with certain types of products; the development of MTV, a combinations of music and videos, has meant that though apart from the records themselves, no single line of goods is advertised, yet a whole way of life directed at young viewers in their teens is promoted, combining everything from attitudes to aspirations, to activities and their accessories. These examples show that the main aim of branding practices is to inculcate values associated with consumerism. The transformation of culture to pure consumption is the consummation devoutly wished for by the whole advertising effort.

Branding is a very costly affair; it far exceeds the old styles of advertising that could be done with modest means. Only the biggest companies can engage in it. Often those that do have become purely marketing entities that do not themselves manufacture the goods they sell or that are sold by others in their name. The manufacturing process is then relegated to subcontracting suppliers who might be scattered all over the world, and are frequently located in Third World countries where labor costs are the cheapest. The selling might also be licensed to smaller semi-independent enterprises and individual proprietors. What the main central enterprise does primarily is to produce the brand identity—which is really a cultural product and no longer a purely economic entity. It is a cultural value as much as a utility in the economic sense. Thus many of the global companies have in effect become culture merchants. The cultural wares they produce constitute a large part of global culture.

This is the economic rationale for the expenditure of such vast sums on the production of global culture, and it also explains the purely economic advantage that this culture has over every other. No other culture can compete with a commercial culture in which so much money is invested that its products can be given away free of charge or at a fraction of their cost of production. Thus the branded culture of commercial promotion can very quickly displace every other that stands in its way. The incredible success of the Disney Corporation throughout the world illustrates this argument. As it advances and its sales increase, it is more or less eliminating all the traditional children's cultures of fairy tales, festivals, fairs, and ceremonies, with their costumes, characters, and semi-ritual games. All that children in different countries used to enjoy in their own different ways over ages past is now giving way all over the world to the same few Disney-branded products that are available everywhere at any one time. Disney is, in effect, manufacturing and selling childhood. The new generation is being brought up almost exclusively on its products.

It is because of such facts that cultural production has, in significant respects, become the apex of the whole present capitalist global system. America is the leading world economy in considerable part because it is the leading cultural producer—it produces the great bulk of global culture. This is the prosaic reality behind the high-minded theories of a so-called postindustrial society. It is not so much science and technology as sheer forms of knowledge or inventiveness that make for a postindustrial society, but only the products of science and technology transformed into cultural icons through the power of promotion. Industrial production is meanwhile delegated to less developed societies where labor is cheap and controls nonexistent.

A clear case in point is the so-called information revolution of recent times, which is to a considerable extent also a cultural revolution, American-style. Certainly, the invention of computers and their interconnection is a scientific-technological accomplishment of a very high order; but the fact that the ownership of a personal computer by almost every single individual, and that using it for all kinds of private activities has become almost de rigueur socially—that is a cultural phenomenon. It was achieved by a coordinated promotional campaign of an intensity never before experienced in history. The hype was unrelenting and it came from all quarters. Vast sums were invested directly and indirectly in touting computers for all purposes for everyone. This strategy, pursued assiduously over the last decade, clearly worked all over the world. Governments were won over and persuaded to completely restructure their education systems in order to make every child "computer literate." Enormous amount of capital were invested on the stock exchange in firms in any way connected with the Web and Internet. A whole commercial revolution was anticipated. The vast losses incurred of late have some-what dampened the ardor of investors for dot-com companies and burst the computer bubble. But as yet there has not been any rethinking among the general public about the utility and role of computers in their lives and in the education of their children. The influence of promotion is so powerful that it inhibits ordinary common sense.

The media industry played a key role in promoting the information revolution at the behest of business and will do so again when another such occasion arises. The whole process of advertising and branding depends on the media, so it is crucial for business that these persuasive means be predominantly in private hands and so available for deployment by commercial interests. This requires that publicly owned public service media be eliminated, reduced, or brought into the commercial ambit. In fact, it is the process now taking place in many societies where previously the public service broadcasting media used to predominate, such as Britain and other European countries. Many strategies are being employed for the purpose of "privatizing" the broadcasting media. Governments so disposed are cutting funds to the public broadcasting bodies and forcing them to make up the shortfall by resorting to the commercial means of selling their products or accepting advertising. Commercial media with far greater resources of finance are allowed to import whatever media products they need to achieve the high ratings that advertisers require. Not being burdened with any public policy goals or inhibitions means that they can unrestrictedly compete for audience approval. Thus, for example, if pornography is found to work, it will be used. And the general public is proving itself responsive to their appeal and abandoning the public media for reasons that we will presently examine. Thus the public media are being squeezed both from the top and the bottom, from governments and audiences.

However, it is not yet inevitable that the public media should be completely displaced by the commercial ones. If adequately supported they can still hold their own, as they have done since their inception. In Britain, for example, a proper balance of public and private media was maintained from the introduction of commercial radio and television in the mid-1950s until the onset of the Thatcher government's policies of privatization in the early 1980s. Until then the BBC, as a state-endowed autonomous public institution, was the dominant media organization setting standards of public policy programming that even its commercial rivals had to try to match to some extent. It committed itself to the goals of objective news reporting and fairness in presentation, to the cultural and educational values suitable to its various audiences, and to the pursuit of public issues of concern to the nation. Internationally the BBC became a byword for probity and impartial objectivity.

Now all this is being lost as Britain is becoming engulfed in global culture and the BBC is forced to subscribe to market values and act more and more like a commercial enterprise. It is not above importing American "soaps" to try to boost its waning popularity. A similar process is at work in all the state-endowed public media throughout continental Europe. In Italy the Berlusconi media empire is taking over from RAI, the public media network; a process that will surely accelerate now that he has settled in for a lengthy period as prime minister. In France the Vivendi-Universal conglomerate—now the third largest in the world (behind Time-Warner and CBS-Viacom, but ahead of Newscorp)—is having a similar effect on the state-owned media. Outside Europe the situation of public media devoted to public policy goals is, if anything, even bleaker. In America the PBS network only subsists on charity from its viewers and few high-minded businesses. In Australia the ABC is suffering from government-induced interference (its appointed director is gradually dismantling it), and SBS—a unique Australian-devised, multilingual, international channel that has received worldwide plaudits—can only sustain itself by taking in advertising. A similar story doubtlessly repeats itself elsewhere in the world as well.

The destruction of public service media represents an important facet in the victory of global culture. The reasons for it we have already adverted to: misguided government policies of "privatization" and the shibboleths of market competition, coupled with a flight from public policy values by an audience that is increasingly becoming more habituated to global culture, especially the younger age groups. Thus a version of Gresham's monetary law operates: bad media drives out good media. It follows from this that a defense of public service media is tantamount to a resistance to global culture. If more people understood this crucial point, they might begin doing more to save public media.

It is indubitable that mass media is necessary in a mass society. The issue is merely one of what kind of mass media this will be: who will own or control it, and to what purposes will it be put? People in mass societies need television to have something to focus their leisure hours around, to inform themselves on general issues, to have things in common to communicate with each other, and to be instructed and entertained. A form of mass culture is, therefore, unavoidable, but it need not be global culture, nor need it solely serve commercial ends and be dominated by advertising and branding. A good balance of public service and commercial media would best satisfy the requirements of mass culture. Public service media dedicated to public policy goals can best provide for all the diverse interests of various groups in society and for the needs of the social whole. Commercial media, working under publicly specified conditions of programming, can cater to more general tastes in entertainment, sports, drama, and investigative journalism.

What must be avoided—by law or other restrictive means, if necessary— is the wholesale importation of global culture. The purveyors of global culture, mainly American media companies, practice a commercial strategy that is often little short of cultural dumping. In order to create markets for their commodities they will give away for nothing or next to nothing shows that have already recouped their cost of production and reaped a handsome profit on the wide and wealthy American market. Such shows, once amortized, can then be exported around the world with the main purpose of building audiences, and so creating a demand for such cultural products as will eventually have to be paid for, vastly increasing the profits already gained. It is by such give-away methods that American television production companies have created a worldwide market for pop music, "soaps," and sporting events. Basketball has built itself up from almost nothing to one of the world's major spectator sports through the initially free distribution of its telecasts. This kind of one-sided competition is another major reason why global culture has been so successful against its mass media rivals in other countries. It would be perfectly legitimate, and not necessarily infringe on free trade practices, to legislate against cultural dumping, as it has been done against every other kind of products-dumping.

As we have so far shown, there are very good economic reasons why global culture has been so successful on the supply side of cultural competition. But this by itself does not account for why it has also succeeded so well on the demand side. Why do masses of people all over the world prefer global cultural products to any others? Answering this question is not a mere matter of economics, but rather of all the other constitutive factors that determine the choices, tastes, and aspirations of masses of people. Such are the predominantly psychological, sociological, political, and general cultural or ideological conditions that we will discuss in what follows. However, there are also economically relevant issues—that is, ones closely bound up with the economic function—that we can raise even in this context.

Demand for media productions does not occur spontaneously nor out of any inner need or necessity. It is a created or constituted demand, just like that for many other kinds of products. And just as the media stimulate a need for all kinds of manufactured products through advertising and branding, so they also arouse a demand for their own products through publicity. Publicity is the self-advertising of the media. One part of the media is constantly boosting another part through all kinds of publicity devices. The commercial media, in particular, have perfected such methods whereby they constantly advocate their own productions. The media products that emerge from the one conglomerate are in all kinds of ways tied by cross-referencing to each other. The news programs, entertainments, sporting events, talk shows, and straight-out advertising of the one television company are constantly backing each other up and molding the viewer's preferences in all these fields. The newspapers, magazines, books, and other publications of the same company will also be incorporated to enlarge the publicity effort. At the same time all the companies working together, or the commercial media system as a whole, is self-reinforcing and self-perpetuating through mutual plugging and boosting. In this way, through the operation of the interlocking wheels of publicity, the media create a demand for themselves.

This can be neatly illustrated by considering the publicity process involved in the creation of celebrities or stars and then the use of these constituted icons to boost all kinds of other media products. A cinema star, for example, does not appear out of nowhere, but is an assiduously nurtured and groomed studio "property" whose stellar luster is polished out of the raw human material in well-honed and carefully crafted publicity campaigns and calibrated screen exposures. The star's daily life and private affairs are promoted through all the relevant news media, to be observed and studied as closely as the appearance of a new comet. Popularity is generated through fan clubs, tours, and other newsworthy events. Good opinion is secured through paid agents, impresarios, columnists, and other such tastemakers. All this is very expensive, but if successful, it can recoup tenfold in profits:

for the star, once shining in the media firmament, can then be used to illuminate all kinds of other products, beginning with the films and advertisements in which the said star stars. Some stars even have a political usefulness and can be employed to sway election results by backing a preferred party or candidate. This in turn provides even more publicity for the star and the other products thereby boosted. It all constitutes a circular process of mutual causation that creates demand for all kinds of media productions and other things as well.

In the competition for audiences, global media have all kinds of inbuilt advantages over local mass media. Thus, for example, the publicity, and so consequently the glamour, surrounding global stars are of many dimensions greater than those of mere local stars. The stars of Hollywood outshine those of any other film-producing country. Indeed, local stars tend to gravitate to this great global galaxy of stardom with its inordinate star-making facilities. Being so prominent throughout the world makes a global star all that much more newsworthy in every locality. Such people are names to be conjured with; they are famous for being famous, if for no other reason at all.

However, publicity by itself would not create a demand unless there was some need, no matter how spurious, that was being met. So we must consider what satisfactions media products offer to people, for that is a sure indication that a need is being served. The media mostly offer distraction, relaxation, and mild stimulation—all that is necessary to while away the hours. Given the nervous exhaustion of pressured work and the stressfulness of most people's city lives, their need to have the radio or television on all the time, while at work, at play, or resting at home, is very understandable. Film-going, though requiring slightly more planning and effort, is also an escape route from the daily round of chores, mostly to lose oneself in a fantasy dreamworld. The press and the other print media provide other satisfactions, which differ according to age, cohort, occupation, education, and even gender. Yet generally they cater to no more complex needs but such as satisfying curiosity, awakening mock horror or outrage, providing titillation and tittle-tattle, and all the other small pleasures that most people get from the reading of papers, magazines, and increasingly so even from books as well.

Media products, whether they be shows, films, or articles, compete with each other in providing such sought-after satisfactions. Other things being equal, it is generally those demanding least exertion that win out. There is a kind of law of efficiency operating, that those products of the media are most sought after that satisfy needs with least expenditure of effort. Global media are extremely efficient in this sense. They specialize in the quick thrill, the easy sentimentality, the tantalizing search for information that is absorbed without fatigue, the simple exercise of basic intelligence, and so on. Whole cadres of specialists are enlisted to test and make sure that nothing is too difficult or demanding for as large a public as possible. Everything is aimed at the lowest common denominator. As the old cynical saying has it, nobody has ever lost money by underestimating the intelligence of the public. Hence, continuous exposure to global media results in a process of dumbing down; people are fixated on a much lower level than they might in other circumstances achieve. The law of psychic economy that aims for media efficiency condemns them to a kind of stupor.

The exponents of global culture and its more theoretical defenders argue that people are only being given what they want, so it is their own choices that are responsible for what they become. After all, if people are even prepared to pay sometimes considerable sums to get what they want, then this surely indicates that it is really their own preferences and desires that are at work. The same argument is utilized by drug pushers who also maintain that they do not force anyone to buy narcotics and that they are only meeting a perceived demand. But just as the demand for drugs is created, so, too, is the demand for the products of global culture. The process of demand creation is different—though there are some surprising analogies, as we shall see—yet in both cases people are being given or sold what they can be made to want.

Demand creation for media products is, of course, nothing as crude or simple as drug addiction. It is a long and subtle process of inculcation and habituation that starts in childhood. Its outcome is partly unpredictable, for there is no way of determining precisely the molding of taste, what given people will actually like or need later in life. But it can generally be ascertained that long exposure to the media results in a dependency on media products of some kind. Which media product will gain a following and which will fail is also unpredictable. Even though the marketing gurus can avail themselves of numerous quasi-scientific techniques for anticipating audience demand, they still have to rely on hit-and-miss methods in gauging the likely outcome. What succeeds and what fails frequently takes even the experts by surprise. There is no sure-fire formula for best sellers or blockbuster movies or hit records. However, nothing can possibly succeed unless it has the backing of a whole concerted marketing effort involving a complex sales and publicity organization. That is the precondition that enables a product just to compete, for otherwise it is not even in the running. The quality of the product in itself is not particularly relevant; it succeeds not because it is good, but because it has something that catches people's momentary attention or interest, which the publicity apparatus can latch onto and boost.

Over time the general tendency in mass media products has been to decline in quality. This can easily be ascertained by comparing the most successful products of present global culture with those from other decades of the twentieth century, particularly from the period before the First World War, at the start of the mass media. In comparing newspapers from the beginning of the century with those at the end of the century, it becomes amply apparent that the quality of "news," both in terms of what is considered newsworthy and how it is presented, has markedly declined; trivialization and sensationalism have taken hold; even the sheer level of literacy shows a drastic drop despite the great increase in the years of schooling that contemporary readers have experienced as compared to their grandparents or great-grandparents. Hollywood in its early years produced much better films than it does now, and Broadway had much better musicals. The infantile rap and hip-hop music that black "musicians" play now cannot be compared to the ragtime, jazz, boogie-woogie, and other musical styles that their predecessors created much earlier.

It is almost as if to compensate for this loss of quality that the global media have to rely much more on publicity and sheer advertising to create a demand for their products. The sums expended on these efforts have continually increased and have now grown vast, frequently exceeding the cost of the product itself. It is a concerted effort that, as we have already seen in discussing branding or the creation of brand names, focuses not just on single items, in the way the old styles of advertising did, but on a whole style of life and the values associated with it. Thus the branding of consumer commodities translates into the inculcation of lifestyle values that in turn promote all kinds of other media products. The advertisements for cars that extol the glamour, prestige, and status afforded by certain makes merge with the films in which such cars feature with handsome heroes at the wheel. In an earlier period, this strategy was used with cigarettes with such good effect on whole generations of smokers that the sales generated still continue to exact their toll in lung cancer victims. The cars or cigarettes and the film heroes and actors who play them, both on and off screen, all fuse together into the one lifestyle image. It is this image that is then held up to masses of people for emulation. In this way the whole of global culture acts as the one integrated system of products and publicity.

Advertising plays a crucial role in this cultural system and is the key component in it for the creation of demand. As Stivers observes: "[A]dvertising is so pervasive that it is the background to everything we do. Taking into account billboards, logos and labels, as well as television, radio and Internet advertisements, some studies estimate that we are exposed to 16,000 ads each day."[4] It is not only a demand for the specific commodities advertised that results from this barrage, but also a general demand for the values and style of life that the advertisements show the commodities as representing. Thus the commodity, a car or a brand of cigarettes, acts not merely as an object of utility, but also as a symbol of cultural values. Indeed, the main aim of advertising is to add cultural value to every economic utility. Thus a hamburger is not merely represented as a certain quantity of bread and meat, but has a value-added content as a promise of togetherness, as a kind of communion. For lonely, isolated people in mass society, this is a potent appeal. In advertising nothing is what it really is objectively, but through the media magic it is transubstantiated into something else, something rich and strange. This enchantment that advertising weaves around quotidian articles is a fetishism of commodities that Karl Marx could not have imagined. It is a fairy godmother that waves its magic wand to turn every frog into a prince and every pumpkin into a coach. People who normally have no need for frogs or pumpkins suddenly develop a great yen for them. If cultural value can thus be added to frogs and pumpkins their price rises commensurably and the profits from selling them soar. Adding value to every conceivable mundane article is the key to marketing and economic success.

This media magic works even better for media products themselves. It can turn the girl next-door into a fairy princess—that is, a star who illuminates all the other girls next-door who in turn shine by reflected glow. It turns the sportsman into a hero who can be admired for everything else that he chooses to grace. But, of course, none of this would be possible outside the context of global culture. People en masse must already be imbued with the values of this culture and bereft of any other countervailing ones, whether those of tradition or modern education, for the media publicity to be effective and cast its spells on them. For people who have never been exposed to this culture, it can take a generation or more to make them susceptible to it. In America, where the process first began, it took a number of generations. But now in Eastern Europe and east Asia it is proceeding with incredible rapidity, and just the one generation might be sufficient.

The efficacy of media magic is enormously boosted by the extra magic of technology. This is particularly evident in the new electronic media, where for most people on earth voices coming out of boxes or pictures appearing on glass screens initially seem like supernatural occurrences. And even when this stage passes, the belief in technology remains and the fascination with it increases. People look at it as the panacea for all the ills of life, and they become obsessed with acquiring the little gadgets that save them toil and trouble. Media gadgets in particular are eagerly grasped as soon as they appear. The romance with the computer is still sweeping the world, though there are early signs of disillusionment starting to creep in. But it is still the case that any cultural product that is presented by means of a high-technology medium always attracts more attention than one presented by means of a low-technology medium, regardless of the nature or quality of the thing itself. The medium is more important than the message.

This triumph of technics has an economic dimension that is of great advantage to the firms that purvey media culture. These commercial interests have the financial resources to invest in the latest and most expensive technologies. Almost from the start of the mass media new technologies have nearly always been first taken up and exploited by capitalist entrepreneurs. This was inevitably so, as most of these developments took place in America. The technical improvements that occurred in film making in Hollywood were ahead of those of any other film industry. Radio and television first developed into mass broadcasting networks in America. This process of technological innovation at the behest of commercial interests has continued on a global level. It is another part of the explanation of the success of global culture. Hence, it is to technology that we must turn next to take our account beyond economics.

B. TECHNOLOGY AND THE MEDIA

The triumph of technics that is represented by the success of global culture is much more than a matter of technology, for there are all kinds of other modes of human technics that have little to do with instruments, and these we leave for consideration later in the next chapter. But to begin with we shall focus on the technologies of the media alone. These are those technologies without which most of the modern media are inconceivable. This does not mean that technologies by themselves give rise to media that dispense global culture, for obviously the whole historical context of the twentieth century during which they arose must be taken into account. All these other aspects, apart from the economic and technological, we shall go on to discuss in the next section. Here we shall focus on technology, while being fully cognizant that technology is neither autonomous nor imperative; on its own it determines nothing in cultural life, but in a specific sociocultural context it can be decisive in pushing developments in a certain direction. In the present globalizing context technology is extremely conducive to global culture. All these are contentious theoretical issues that we will not attempt to fully justify in this text, so here they must be taken as mere presuppositions.

Right from the very start of modern developments, the technologies of the media provided the basis of mass media culture. In fact, its main periods and stages correlate closely with the invention and deployment of new technologies. In approximate historical sequence these came as follows: first, the technologies of mechanical reproduction, such as the printing and graphics media (for which photography, invented earlier, was a precondition); second, the electronic reproduction technologies, such as film, recording, and others; third, the broadcasting technologies, such as radio and television; and finally, the information technologies of computers and satellites. These stages are not discontinuous, but overlap with each other—each technology undergoes a continuous technical evolution parallel to and in conjunction with the others. The most revolutionary changes do not necessarily come from new inventions, but from new interconnections among the technologies that already exist singly by themselves, as, for example, when sound recording and film were synchronized to produce the talking movies. Now nearly all of these technologies are interconnected to constitute a whole network of media systems. A still higher level of connectivity will be attained when digitalization of all information takes place, such that it will be possible to transfer automatically from any one medium into any other and also to manipulate and alter any message at will as required. As these linkages grow and expand, so the more complex the technological system becomes and the greater the resources necessary to own and control some part of it. This is the technological rationale for the formation of ever-bigger media conglomerates, such as the present multinational companies.

Printing is the oldest of the mechanical reproductive media, going back to Gutenberg in the mid-fifteenth century, but it is also the first of the mass media, which appeared in the form of the popular press and mass publishing in general. The technical changes that made mass publishing possible toward the end of the nineteenth century were the many small incremental improvements during that whole century in printing presses, paper, ink, and machinery for folding and cutting. A key new development that culminated all these improvements was the invention of graphic reproduction, including that of photographs, and eventually this could be done even in color. This linkage between printing and photography gave rise to the new medium of the illustrated press and had a great impact on the printed press in general. Thus the press became at once more topical and more visual, with less attention given to literary journalism or serious articles. Headlines and pictures become more prominent. Drawn pictures in the form of syndicated comic strips and cartoons were also introduced to appeal to a younger and less literate readership who previously did not look at newspapers. Dramatic incidents stemming from acts of violence, disasters, and wars, usually accompanied by photo-illustrations, became the staple news fare. The decline of the written word that then began has continued, until now most papers are no better than the television news coverage in content.

The dominance of the image over the printed word began with photography and graphics, but it was really consolidated with film and television. Recorded music acting as background accompaniment contributed to the same outcome. These technologies were able to generate and address simultaneous audiences across whole continents, and now, throughout the globe. As we have already indicated, this afforded enormous economies of scale that no other media could rival. Once the initial costs of the media product had been met, the further expansion of the audience cost either nothing, as with radio and television, or very little, as with cinema and other forms of recording. The product could either be given away for free, through the subsidy of advertising, or sold initially very cheaply and eventually, when amortized, also given away, as was the case with old films. All these economic benefits could only be achieved thanks to technology.

As audiences for the new media grew ever larger, this made them more and more appealing as vehicles for promotion and propaganda. Advertising flourished as never before because by the grace of technology it could almost simultaneously reach everyone in the one society. Thus its impact was concentrated and not dissipated over time, and it could be continuously maintained in this form through strategically planned campaigns. Propaganda gained the same advantages. Statesmen and politicians in all countries, democratic as well as dictatorial, realized that in these new media they possessed an unequalled tool for arousing, swaying, and influencing the people of a mass political society. First radio and later television have played an ever increasingly important role in the political life of all societies. The electoral contest in democracies is now almost inconceivable without them; it has become a media process. As we shall eventually see, this fact has affected all kinds of changes in the very nature of democracy and what it means for voters to take part in the voting procedures to choose their representatives. As is well known, those who command the media exert a preponderant influence on the outcomes of such choices. This places media proprietors and those who can afford to pay for their services in a very advantageous political position. He who pays the piper calls the tune even at advanced levels of technology.

The electronic media have technological features that render them particularly suitable for purposes of promotion and propaganda and make them, in these respects, exceed all other media, which find it very difficult to compete with them. Primarily this is so because technologies that mechanically reproduce an aspect of reality have the effect of authenticating what is represented by these means. Mechanical mimesis convinces by its sheer factual authenticity. Thus what appears on the television screen looks as if it were a slice of unmediated reality itself. The fact that this can be manipulated to any desired result is momentarily lost on the viewers. It is overlooked for the instant, sufficiently long enough to have an emotional impact and leave a lasting imprint of sheer affect that can even escape the censoring guard of the conscious thinking processes. It sways the viewers even without their being fully aware of it. And the more technologically advanced the medium, the more vivid the image and the more realistic the simulation, the more avidly and uncritically it is received. The ultimate culmination of this technological drive for perfect simulation is virtual reality, where the very distinction between appearance and reality is temporarily elided, since for the duration of the "show" the two merge. This should have enormous potential both for promotion and for propaganda once it becomes widely used.

The paradoxical irony of this striving for technical perfection is that the better and more faithful the image, the easier it becomes to betray the viewers by its means. High fidelity in engineering results in low fidelity in trust and meaning. Or putting this in pseudo-scientific jargon, the more engineering information the message contains, the less cultural information it carries. On the whole, other things being equal, the older media are invariably more culturally significant than the newer media. This inverse relation between engineering and cultural information expresses the sad historical fact of our time that as technology progresses, culture declines.

The second, and perhaps even more important, reason that the electronic media are technologically so well adapted for promotion and propaganda is that they make it possible to achieve a level of habituation, dependency, and even sheer addiction that could not possibly be attained by the older media. It has been empirically established that promotion and propaganda work best through constant and incessant repetition of the same message, only slightly varied to fend off boredom. The electronic media, working through mass media broadcasting, are so technically engineered that the one message can be repeated to a mass population over and over again, twenty-four hours a day, and made available everywhere, in both private and public places. The message thus becomes inescapable, and every person becomes subject to its influence and suasive power, whether this is desired or not by the given individual. Most people, in fact, surround themselves by these media messages almost for every minute of their waking lives; some must have the radio or television on to do their work. Those who wish to escape this ubiquitous reach of the media have to take extraordinary steps to do so. For this kind of total media immersion, the electronic media are particularly apt.

People in contemporary mass societies all over the globe become habituated to living constantly inside a media environment, which is a cultural atmosphere that surrounds them like a kind of bubble of air. They breathe in the media messages of promotion and propaganda even without being fully away of it. Those who control the output of the media rely on this fact. They know that the same propaganda lie, repeated often enough, will sooner or later be accepted as the truth; that the same advertisement featuring in an extended sales campaign will prove efficacious. Hence they do everything in their power to bring about a habit-forming attitude to the media—and the electronic media make it easiest for them to achieve this.

Thus the main aim of commercial television programs is to create a loyal audience that will become conditioned to come back to the same show time and time again, sometimes extending over years, for this alone makes it possible to subject them to the same advertisements over and over again. People must be made to want more of the same, only slightly varied to make it seem different. As the history of commercial television has demonstrated, this effect can be best achieved by a number of tried and true methods: telling an endless tale around the same characters, as in "soaps"; establishing audience rapport with the one "personality," such as a host, compere, or newsperson; establishing a format or formula that can be repeated with variations, as in the sitcom, detective, and murder-mystery genres; relying on the same ceremonial rituals, as in game shows and sporting events; and a few others of the same ilk. Repetition and more repetition, repetition varied just enough so as not to provoke a sense of déjà vu works best. The reason for this is that people who lead routine and predictable lives prefer predictable and routine media. This has now become a global condition and so the same formats and formulae are repeated everywhere in every language; they are so fixed and settled that hardly any further innovation is possible within their limits. What is it now possible to change in the news-reader routine that audiences will accept? In a striving for novelty, the attempt has been made to have nubile female news-readers do striptease while they read from the teleprompter, but this is only likely to be tolerated by a small minority.

This media law of the eternal recurrence of nearly the same has made it possible to institute new and highly rationalized methods of production. Once a winning formula has been found—frequently relying on old-fashioned hit-and-miss procedures—then whole production teams can be assembled to exploit the discovery and mine the material for all it is worth. Such teams embody a very high level of the division of labor, with each segment of the task allotted to its own specialists. The extensive credits at the end of any typical Hollywood film give one but a fleeting glimpse of the specializations involved. Once such a team is on the job it can go on endlessly, which in practical terms means for as long as ratings and audience-appeal hold.

Technology once again plays a large role in such production methods. There are special machines and technical devices for every step of the production process. All kinds of special effects can now be routinely utilized, such as recording actors in one place and the natural scenery against which they are shown in another. The utilization of computer simulation has opened up a veritable cornucopia of special effects, including all kinds of "morphing" and other reality enhancing or altering techniques. This, too, is part of the technological miracle of the media that appeals to so many, especially among the young.

Technology also permits not only the production of new material, but the constant revival in slightly varied forms of the old as well. Since everything recorded is stored away, it can always be reutilized later at any desired time. This makes possible a strategy of revivals of the old with seemingly new materials. Thus the "stars" of the past can be heard or seen again at any time in the future with "lost" takes and film footage being brought out of storage for this purpose. Thus Elvis, the Beatles, or Marilyn need never die—they can sing, dance, prance, and mime from beyond the grave. The libraries of old stock are among the most valuable properties that the studios possess.

However, this must not be taken to mean that technology serves unequivocally for the preservation of the old. It can also work to the contrary, for, like the Hindu gods, as technology preserves it also destroys. The whole nature of the library, which is still supposedly dedicated to the preservation of books and other printed matter, is now undergoing a dangerous transformation under the impact of the new technologies of recording and information. On the pretext that such things can better be preserved on microfilm, the most prestigious libraries in the world have destroyed a considerable part of their holdings of old newspapers. Nicholas Baker has documented the further destruction of printed texts in libraries, including books that are taken apart to be photographed.[5] At the same time the digitalization of texts has made their preservation insecure. It has transformed the very process of researching a topic and restricted it to accessing databases using computer search engines. Books need no longer be consulted. Collecting preformed and predigested information has taken the place of reading books not only among students, but among their teachers as well. Digitalized information has also a very short life span as the equipment necessary to "read" it goes out of use. Hence, it is possible that everything now stored in digital form will be lost and that a "digital dark age" will ensue.

As technology makes possible freer access and bigger audiences for media products, it at the same time transforms the nature of these products. For the bigger the audience to be addressed the simpler and cruder the message must become. Audiences of billions all over the globe can only be mustered and held by the most trivial of shows, such as sporting events, beauty contests, song competitions, or special ceremonial occasions that everyone knows about. This is not, of course, inherent in the technology itself, but in the use to which it is put in the sociocultural context of global civilization. In the hands of multinational media conglomerates, most often American-owned, the new technologies are invariably used to beam global culture around the earth. Commercial interests ensure that hardly anything else can be presented. Undoubtedly, the very same means could also be made to work in other ways for other ends, but the willingness to do so is absent among those who control these technologies. To redirect the present uses of media technology will call not only for changes in programming, but also for sheer inventive genius that will only flourish in a quite different cultural environment.

Under present conditions technology serves to create a demand for global culture and almost no other. This, together with the economic advantages this culture has, which we previously expounded, explains to some extent its extraordinary success. But not completely, for all kinds of other factors must also be at work. All of these must come together as the partial aspects of the full historical process whereby global culture came to predominate. This process had two major temporal phases: firstly, the transition from a period of a largely popular culture to mass culture; and secondly, the move from the many national mass cultures to the one global culture. In both these phases the question to be answered is not merely why mass or global culture succeeded, but also why the other cultures they came to displace failed. We must study these failures, for without them the triumph of global culture could not have been as overwhelming. It was not only its own strength that gave it victory, it was also the weakness of the opposition.

C. FROM POPULAR TO MASS TO GLOBAL CULTURE

The success of global culture is inexplicable without taking account of the wholesale collapse of all the traditional cultures that occurred largely in the period from the mid-nineteenth to the mid-twentieth centuries. Apart from the earlier conquest of the Americas, it was during this time that an intensification of colonialism took place all over the world, from central Asia to North Africa, from India to Indonesia, from China to Indochina, and by the close of the nineteenth century Africa had been absorbed and a little later the whole of the Arab world. This is the historical background to the present phase of cultural globalization that is succeeding so easily despite the abrogation of colonialism during the last half century and the independence of all countries on earth. And the reason for this is that there are no viable local cultures left to provide any kind of concerted opposition.

China is at the moment a prime example of this fact. From the Taiping Rebellion until the Cultural Revolution, China had been subject to wave after wave of cultural devastation, until eventually there was little remaining of traditional culture. The cultural vacuum thus created is sucking in global culture at an accelerating rate now that the communist regime has opened itself up to economic globalization. Only politically induced censorship is keeping the full flood at bay. But the global media conglomerates, with the Murdoch-owned News Corporation in the lead and Disney not far behind, are only too willing to make the necessary political compromises in order to capture the Chinese media market. The upholding of basic freedoms and civil rights has never been high on the agenda of the media proprietors. The communist government in its turn has no problem in collaborating with them in importing what appear to it to be politically unthreatening aspects of global culture. Shanghai has been officially designated as the conduit of global culture and is competing with Hong Kong in this respect.

This process is proceeding somewhat slower in India, for under paternalistic British rule it did not experience the same degree of cultural destruction as China. But already there are all the telltale signs of global incursion into the heartland of Indian cultural life. Television antennas are sprouting everywhere and the Murdoch interests are once again well placed to beam their programs into every village hut and city dwelling. The growing middle class, numbering as many as a few hundred million, is rapidly developing a taste for affluent Western lifestyles. McDonald's franchises are starting to proliferate, which, like the early swallow in spring, is the harbinger of a cultural change in the season. Hindu fundamentalist mob violence against hamburger outlets for supposedly dispensing beef products—probably a slander—is not likely to provoke another Indian Mutiny and is bound to subside in the long run. A much more self-aware opposition to global culture is required, which traditional Indian society cannot muster at present.

The cultural situation in other parts of the non-European world offers even less prospect for any significant opposition. Sub-Saharan Africa is now a region of utter devastation both of the natural and cultural environment. Global commercial interests do not even consider it worth exploiting, and if there is anything worse than being exploited by the global capitalists it is not being exploited by them. Much the same is true of much of the Muslim world, especially in those countries where Islamic fundamentalism has made inroads—for this kind of puritanical xenophobic faith does preserve some indigenous traditions, but only at the cost of cultural sterility and isolation. Already the younger generation in these societies is yearning for the flesh-pots of globalization and it will not be possible to deprive them for much longer. The current war against terrorism is likely to increase the impact of global culture throughout the Islamic regions, an ironic outcome in view of the aims of the terrorists.

Apart from the Americas, this only leaves Europe for consideration. There the cultural situation is somewhat more complex because the historical process that took place during the last two centuries was more convoluted, with many more twists and turns. Europe suffered various kinds of cultural devastations, mainly in the course of its twentieth-century history of two world wars, numerous revolutions, and subsequent totalitarian regimes. This despoliation of traditional culture in Europe is also the background to the current success of global culture. Once again, it is as much a matter of local weakness as of global strength.

In what follows we shall concentrate on describing and explaining the two distinctive phases in the transition from traditional to global culture in Europe: first, the shift from popular to mass culture; and second, that from the various diverse mass cultures to the one homogeneous global culture. This second process is still taking place now, having begun not much sooner than about twenty years ago. But this would have been inconceivable without the first process, the rise of mass culture, beginning at the turn of the twentieth century. This was perhaps the more decisive change, for once a mass culture was firmly in place in every European society it proved not too difficult later to replace it with a uniform global culture. If traditional culture had remained more intact this second phase could not have occurred, or, at least, not so easily against so little resistance.

However, an added factor that explains the ease of the transition in Europe was the influence of America, which acted as a catalyst to speed up the process. So before dealing exclusively with Europe, some accounting is first called for of America's role. America exerted decisive sway in affecting the recent transition to global culture, but even much earlier it was also active in the first phase, the move from popular to mass culture. American mass cultural forms began to make themselves felt in Europe from the end of the nineteenth century onward, and from that point on they became ever more insistent. The two world wars markedly increased the cultural influence of America, but especially the Second World War, when America emerged as the savior of western Europe and its military presence in Europe became permanent. Eventually, with the onset of globalization, Americanization also took a leap forward.

As we noted previously, American and European mass cultures were more or less coeval, but almost from the start the American form was the leading one—the earliest to come to fruition, the more powerful in terms of prestige and wealth, and in many respects the more inventive and original. And so from the start it had steadily been infiltrating and influencing the formation of the European mass cultures. Wild West adventures, ragtime music, the silent cinema, musical recordings, and much more were already entrancing the youth of Europe before the First World War. After it, American themes, mores, and games became ever more popular and prevalent. Hollywood became the world-capital of film; American music, from jazz to rock, became the music of young people; fashion styles in almost everything—except for haute couture and a few other such exclusive things—almost invariably came from America. Thus, for example, the wearing of jeans became the hallmark of youth all over Europe. After the Second World War most things to do with the media were also derived from America. Americanization became ubiquitous in every respect.

However, though it is easy to understand why the forces of American-driven cultural globalization were so powerful and so influential in Europe, that in itself does not explain why the resistance to them proved so weak. To account for that we need to step back historically to the earlier phase, when mass culture took over from popular culture, and traditional culture in general declined. For this was the decisive step, since once mass culture was fully in place and traditional culture destroyed, there was little to prevent the national mass cultures giving way to a global form. Thus the lack of resistance to mass culture is even more surprising than the later usurpation by global culture. Why did the traditional European cultures fall prey so easily to the onset of mass culture?

In answering this question we shall consider it in relation to all of the three basic forms of traditional culture: folk, popular, and elite (that is, both low and high cultures). However, our main emphasis will be on popular culture, for that was the culture of the people that immediately preceded mass culture and out of which it developed. As we have already shown, popular culture must not be confused with mass culture, even though the latter is continuous with the former. But before we turn to popular culture we must first consider the fate of folk culture, the immemorial lore of rural people and those influenced by them.

Throughout western Europe folk cultures were already being eradicated during the nineteenth century as the traditionally minded peasant communities were transplanted to the growing industrial cities to become a deracinated urban proletariat. There they tended to abandon the religiously based rural rounds of festivities, celebrations, and ceremonies and instead took to urbanized popular culture and later the early forms of mass culture, such as sport, racing, and cinema. In brief, they generally preferred to watch football matches rather than attend church services; instead of missal or Bible, they now read the dailies of the mass press; they turned out for May Day parades and union fetes rather than saint's day processions and religious holidays; instead of dancing on the village green, they now danced in the burgeoning ballrooms. Their whole tenor of life had changed and the old folk culture had no place in the new environment. This happened in America as much as in Europe, and is continuing in a process spreading throughout the world. Now it is taking place in all the so-called Third World countries.

However, both in Europe and in America the forgetting of folkways led to an extraordinary flourishing of popular culture—the demotic culture of city people throughout the ages. The period from approximately the mid-nineteenth century until perhaps as late as the Great Depression proved to be the golden age of popular culture. In every European country a specifically indigenous popular culture was developed, but with considerable mutual cross-influence. Vaudevilles and music halls flourished; circuses, amusement arcades, and luna parks proliferated; cabarets and dance venues sprang up; and every kind of live theater was thriving. This was the great period of the operetta in all its various national forms, such as those of Offenbach, Strauss, Gilbert and Sullivan, Moniuszko, and many others, not forgetting the many composers of the Spanish zarzuela. Performed music was everywhere in abundance from brass bands to street ensembles; people entertained themselves singing a vast repertoire of popular songs around the piano in the parlor or the pub. Well-drawn posters were everywhere on display in public places. Demotic styles of architecture for both public buildings and domestic dwellings mushroomed in all the new suburbs of cities. Railways made travel possible to historical sites and so stimulated the popular historical imagination and led to a reconstruction of the past. Libraries and mechanics institutes arose to cater to the thirst for knowledge among working people. This was the heyday of the popular print media—newspapers for a diversity of publics arose, and every major city had a dozen or more of these; and they featured every conceivable kind of literary material from feuilletons to serialized novels (most of the great writers of this period first appeared in this way). The graphic illustrations that accompanied these publications were sometimes of an equal order of excellence—one need only think of Daumier to grant this. Book publication was also prolific, and not only of authors in the local language but also the rapid translation of popular books from all the other European languages. The popular culture of Europe and America was both richly diverse and coherently unified. It is for this reason, if no other, that the period before the First World War can rightly be considered the belle époque of popular culture.

This spouting fount of popular culture was gradually reduced to a trickle as it was diverted and dried up by the ever-greater flow of mass culture. The two were continuous with each other as mass culture rose out of popular culture, and only began to separate themselves by barely distinguishable stages during the early decades of the twentieth century. Mass culture began by simply imitating popular culture in terms of the new media. But what it copied it soon displaced. Popular culture, couched in the old media, could not compete for attention or mass appeal with versions of itself presented in a superior technological guise. Thus the popular theater and all other kinds of live performances found themselves outbid by the cinema. The film industry began simply as filmed versions of stage plays, music hall acts, circus, operetta, and other performing arts, featuring the best artists as star attractions. As the masses of people flocked to the cinemas to view the well-publicized simultaneous releases of the same films, they lost interest in live performances, and the many artists who earned their living in this way, apart from the few stars, soon found themselves out of work. Eventually the film industry and television completely destroyed the popular culture of performance, except for the spectacularly engineered and star-studded musicals, which are still current.

There are many reasons why mass-marketed films triumphed over popular theater and other shows. Films could be watched at a fraction of the price of stage performances because of the low cost of mechanical reproduction. They also required less effort and attention as they offered simplified and clichéd versions of popular forms, which were at once more absorbing and relaxing. At the same time, in the early decades of the cinema it was still possible for great writers, directors, and artists to make their mark and create the masterpieces that held the potential of a new art form. Among the huge volume of consumer trash that Hollywood churned out annually there were usually one or two distinctive films per year until sometime into the late 1950s. The European film industries continued their creative run until well into the 1970s, featuring a number of great auteur directors.

By now, unfortunately, the cinema as a creative art form has also almost disappeared; it has been destroyed by television, just as it had formerly eliminated theater, and for analogous reasons. Television viewing requires even less effort and attention than films, and can be had for no cost at all in the convenience of one's living room. It is a superior technological medium that can achieve far higher degrees of habituation and dependence that at times amount to a quasi addiction. It is backed by almost unlimited financial resources derived from advertising that can buy the most talented and, what is even more important, the most prestigious people on the culture market. It satisfies needs of socialization in mass consumer societies where its daily diet of news, entertainment, sports, and other consumer items is about the only thing that people have in common to talk about and interact around. It is swathed in the aura of publicity and glamour. What is now left of the cinema caters largely to the young and their need to escape from home and adults and to seek companionship immersed in their own youth culture.

A similar story repeats itself in all the other media of popular culture. Each one lost its popular form and gave way to a mass form. The popular press of a highly diversified range of newspapers, journals, and books is no more. Now the mass press, reduced to a few papers with gigantic circulations—usually featuring sensationalized trivia and often no more informative than television news—has almost completely captured the whole reading market. Journals specializing in pornography abound, also with high circulation figures. Do-it-yourself or cure-yourself manuals and blockbuster novels dominate the best-seller lists in all countries. The pop music industry has achieved similar results to the publishing and film industries; it mainly caters to the young with an extremely limited range of musical genres. How and why this ensued need not be spelled out in any detail here. It is all part of a process of transition from popular to mass culture, which is now culminating in global culture. In odd corners of the world it is still going on, and will continue until every last vestige of popular, spontaneous, unregulated, and unmarketed culture is absorbed into a technologically mediated, publicity-driven mass-market enterprise of one or another media industry.

Part of the explanation for the demise of popular culture in Europe must also be sought in political developments. The social disruptions of wars and revolutions and their associated ideological battles weakened the people's own freely preferred cultural activities and made them prey to state-regulated and prescribed mass culture. The totalitarian and dictatorial regimes that came to power in most of Europe in the decades between the two world wars were particularly intent on promoting various versions of ideological propaganda using the mass media to that effect. Popular culture that was uncontrolled and difficult to censor could not be allowed and was suppressed as a potential source of criticism or expression of dissatisfaction with the regime. Mass culture serving up propaganda was developed to take its place. Both the Communist and Fascist regimes of every variety were intent on promoting mass cultural forms to capture and hold the minds of their subject people. The print, broadcasting, and film media were preeminently harnessed to this indoctrination purpose. Once these regimes collapsed, people whose minds had been so debauched and bereft of popular resources became easy victims of a commercialized mass consumer culture. With some variations the same process repeated itself at different times in Italy, Germany, Spain, Russia, and throughout Eastern Europe.

In the liberal democratic countries of Europe, above all Britain and France, a somewhat different process ensued, but to similar effect. There popular culture gave way to mass culture without resort to state interference, but by gradual stages of attrition that went on longer. Many kinds of popular culture were still current within living memory. English theater was still flourishing in the 1960s and in amateur modes it still exists even now, but the professional popular theater has almost completely succumbed to Broadway-style musicals, mostly composed by Andrew Lloyd Webber. The French chanson was also keeping well until the 1960s, as the names of its foremost interpreters, Piaf, Aznavour, Trenet, and Montand testify, and it is only now coming to an end. Before and after the Second World War both the British and French film industries made remarkable films until roughly the late 1960s; now it is only the French that has survived, though in a losing battle with Hollywood. The public service broadcasting media in both countries, especially the BBC, were the best of their kind. But by now even these vestiges of popular resistance to global culture have been so weakened as to be no longer relied on to hold it back.

What happened in Britain after the Second World War can largely be ascribed to ever-growing Americanization, which, paradoxically, only increased after it entered the European Community. Common language, ease of travel and study, close political alliance, business investments—all this and more made the influence of America predominant in Britain and that brought with it American mass culture. All the American mass cultural forms were either directly imported or adapted in imitated local versions. Thus, for example, British youth eagerly took up rock music almost as soon as it had been mass-marketed in America. But they were not content to listen to the American versions alone—they began to improvise and improve on them. Almost in no time they produced the Beatles, punk rock, and other variants, which they could even export back to America. This is perhaps one of the earliest instances of mass culture becoming global culture, for rock music then spread to youth all over the world.

Mass culture also came to Britain through the commercialization of the broadcasting media, which began in the 1950s and provided a beachhead for the invasion of American media products. However, the BBC held its own until the Thatcher years in the 1980s, when government policies of privatization forced it to take to the commercial road. The British press, too, succumbed at about the same time. The entry of such media-magnates as Maxwell and Murdoch was the death-knell for the formerly independent British papers. By the grace of Thatcher, Murdoch was allowed to achieve a stranglehold over a segment of the press, with a whole range of papers from the *Sun* to the *Times*. He then used this base in Britain as a stepping-stone to acquire an American media empire, which has now become global. Thus by such insidious steps Britain was integrated into global culture.

France has offered much more resistance to Americanization, openly so during the Gaullist period, but now it is also succumbing. Soon there will be little left that is uniquely French. Disneyland outside Paris is a hit with the French public, easily outselling its feeble Gallic rivals. American fast foods are starting to cut into the traditional French cuisine trade. French children now celebrate Halloween with the same "spooky" masks and hollowed out pumpkins as elsewhere, encouraged by the showing of specially produced Hollywood films. Their slightly older siblings are plugged into the Internet and busily learning English to be able to follow the media fare on offer. The music they listen to pulsates with the same hip-hop beat as elsewhere. The commercial television stations show the same kind of "reality television" shows as are appearing throughout the world, and also thereby attaining the highest ratings. If France cannot hold out against global culture, which other country will do so?

The situation of elite culture is somewhat different to the one we have sketched out for popular culture. Elite culture survives, of course, for it is the culture of the establishments, the museums, concert halls, opera houses, art galleries, universities and university presses, and so on for all the other high-culture pursuits that are still being kept up, frequently only by virtue of public funding, within official institutions. In this form it might survive for some time, but it can hardly be called alive and thriving; rather, it is subsisting in a state of artificial preservation. Its hold is extremely tenuous anywhere outside these refuges.

High culture, just like folk and popular culture, is also succumbing to the blandishments of mass or global culture. It can neither insulate itself completely from its insidious influence nor come to terms with it through some kind of merger. As the art historian Christopher Allen puts it: "For high culture, no matter how much it tried to rise above or even to appropriate the manufactured trash of commercial culture, could see that it was drowned out by the cacophony of television, popular music, pornography of various sorts—soft, hard, sentimental or violent—and all of it linked by the manipulative technology of advertising."[6] Once even high culture disappears, then the triumph of global culture will be complete.

Until relatively recently this elite culture was still flourishing. Even though it catered mainly to the aristocracy and the educated bourgeoisie, nevertheless, it was not completely remote from the people and popular tastes. Down to the First World War there was no rigid separation between high and popular culture—they seamlessly merged into each other and sustained each other. Thus, for example, opera was at once an elite and popular art form, with composers such as Verdi, Bizet, and Puccini who appealed to both refined musical connoisseurs as well as ordinary people from all walks of life. The novel in the hands of numerous authors, including the very best, such as Balzac, Dickens, Tolstoy, and Zola, was read by almost everyone who could read. The posters of Toulouse-Lautrec and many other lesser talented artists were also enjoyed by everyone on the streets.

The separation between elite and popular culture involved a number of distinct developments working seemingly in opposition to each other, but ultimately tending to the same result. In the first place, there arose within the conservative elite an entrenched traditionalism that permitted little innovation; it was centered on the establishment institutions and academies. It prescribed an unvaried quasi-ceremonial repetition of the classics and only those contemporary creations that resembled them. This kind of academic conservatism had the support of the ruling strata, especially those gathered round the courts of Europe.

In opposition to it there emerged an avant-garde culture of rebellion. The continuing battles between the official Salon and the Salon des Refusées of the impressionist painters in France and a little later the various secessionist movements in other countries were manifestations of this ongoing conflict. So, too, were the various literary scandals trials, such as those of Flaubert,

Baudelaire, and even that of Oscar Wilde. The fiasco of Wagner's *Tannhäuser* at the Paris opera was another instance. Such scandals proliferated as the oppositional culture became more modernist and ever more aesthetically extreme; at first aestheticist (symbolism, imagism), the avant-garde eventually became abstractionist (cubism, futurism, atonality) and abandoned every link to traditional culture. Meanwhile, the official institutions—the repositories of tradition—became ever more moribund.

Because of all these turmoils in high culture, the link with popular culture was lost. Hence, elite culture could play no role in upholding popular culture against the rising tide of mass culture. In time it, too, began to lose support from the very elite groups that had formerly sustained it for countless generations. In particular, the young of each generation following the First World War lost interest in maintaining the cultural heritage of their ancestors. The novelties of mass culture became more appealing to them than the predictable ceremonials of high culture. They went to the cinema rather than the opera or theater; they wanted to hear jazz and later rock music rather than classical music; they danced to a syncopated beat rather than the staid measures of the ballroom.

Mass culture had an appealing egalitarian quality, especially for the young. It was the common ground on which people from all classes could meet and mingle. Dancing to the same music, listening to the same radio programs, watching the same television shows, attending the same sporting fixtures, and so on (though not as yet reading the same papers)—all this made people feel that they belonged together. In democratic societies, where an aristocratic or high bourgeois sense of superiority could no longer be openly flaunted, mass culture had the advantage over elite culture. The affirmation of class and status through aesthetic snobbery and the cultivation of refined tastes was replaced by the much cruder markers of designer labels, brand names, and other indicators of sheer money values. It was also much easier and required much less time and effort to buy one's marks of distinction rather than have to acquire them through arduous education. It was the obvious solution for the nouveaux riches. Thus were the last barriers to mass culture broken.

Once mass culture was accepted and dominant, and the folk, popular, and elite cultures completely in abeyance, the next stage of transition from mass to global culture was not such a large step. It ensued with almost no resistance as a consequence of all the other trends in globalization. People who are already habituated to mass culture consider it a matter of no great consequence whether it is produced nationally or imported from a variety of international sources. In a globalized world where all products circulate freely, where international staged events proliferate, where national boundaries and identities start to count for less, it becomes a positive advantage to assume a culture that is shared by all others. All over the globe there develop common interests and the same stock of ideas, the same symbols and signs are omnipresent, tastes and attitudes become homogeneous; the one lingua franca, English, is beginning to be everywhere understood among the educated classes; so it is only an obvious extension for the one culture to prevail.

But this does not simply happen of its own accord; there are forces at work that are propelling such developments and furthering the spread of global culture. These are of various types, driven by all kinds of motives, as many and varied as the ones we have been so far considering. We have already had much to say on this and need only to recapitulate briefly; we shall once more begin with the economic factors, but these are by no means the only ones—politics, organization, prestige, and symbolic issues also play a significant part, which we shall advert to in passing. The role of America in all these respects is at present crucial, but this must not be taken to mean that globalization is simply Americanization. Many other nations are also involved, though as yet to a lesser degree.

Considered purely from the economic aspect, the spread of global culture follows the general logic of contemporary global capitalism. And just as the multinational corporations have surpassed the purely nationally based ones, so, too, the global cultural interests have won out as against the national ones. Global culture has triumphed over the national mass cultures for sound economic reasons, as well as many others. As the multinational corporations develop global markets for their products and as they invest around the globe, they strive to further the development and spread of global culture. They seek to ensure that consumers everywhere buy the same things, and for this purpose it is necessary that they have the same needs and aspirations.

We can understand this nexus between global products and global culture better if we once more focus on advertising and branding, the subject with which we began this chapter. These are, in fact, the leading cultural products. The general rule of advertising is that where the same products are sold, the same advertisements are used to sell them. Hence, if a product is sold globally, the advertising will also be global. Once advertisements are made to be global, other cultural products that carry the advertisements will also be global. Thus piece by piece a global culture falls into place.

Advertisers have found that they can best sell global products, such as Coca-Cola, McDonald's food, Ford cars, or GE washing machines, by advertising them in the same way in every country regardless of the local cultural differences. Usually only minor adjustments need to be made to meet local susceptibilities or not offend local mores. This is so because they rely on the global cachet of such products to sell them locally. Thus, for example, people in various countries are not so much intent on quenching thirst by drinking Coke or slaking hunger by eating hamburgers, but in consuming a global product and participating in a shared rite of people all over the world. This brings them together in a kind of global communion, almost as if this were the global bread and wine. And if they come from a developmentally backward part of the world, this act of consumption holds out the promise of salvation through association with progress. If they cannot themselves attain the standards of America, they can at least afford to ingest something of America. Hence, to advertise such global products in local terms would defeat the appeal of these goods and be counterproductive. To keep such aspirations and hopes alive the advertisements must be couched in universal terms as the one panacea for all of mankind. In fact, the less the people are reminded of their usually backward local conditions, the better the advertising works.

Advertising is in turn linked by association to all other kinds of cultural products. For example, close links have been forged between McDonald's and Disney so that hamburger advertisements carry the whole menagerie of Disney comic characters, the latest films for children, giveaway toys, and even theme parks where these exist. Such synergies extend across whole complexes of consumer and cultural products. Pop stars, film stars, and sporting stars are often used as foci for many diverse kinds of commodities. All of these have to be global and can make no allowances for local particularities. The image of the star must be everywhere the same and be promoted as a global figure who transcends any local differences.

As globalization also proceeds in every other dimension of social life beyond the economic, in transportation, tourism, communication, sport, political integration, and so on, so there is every motive and incentive to promote the one global culture everywhere. As we already explained in chapter 1, people traveling from airport to airport expect the same products, facilities, and conditions everywhere. The multinational companies operating in numerous countries also expect uniform laws of investment, production, export and import, labor hire, and so on. International organizations prescribe the same standards and regulations in many global activities. The same games are played everywhere, and sporting associations stage international competitions that in some cases embrace most countries on earth. These and many other globalizing trends have their cultural consequences in bringing about uniform needs and expectations.

There is, however, an added specific factor in creating demand for a global culture product that must be given its due attention—the unique role that America plays in all this. America is not just like any other country in this respect. It is the cynosure of global culture to which every other country looks for a lead. People demand American cultural products before any others. In almost every respect they model themselves on American prototypes. Even those things that are not by origin American have to pass through America to be accepted by the rest of the world. Thus America acts as the essential incubator for all trends on their way to becoming global.

The primary explanation for this cultural dominance of America lies in the extraordinary prestige it has accrued. America stands preeminent in most of those things on which prestige depends in the modern world: wealth, power, technology, science, individual freedom, and the benefits of the affluent way of life. American propaganda has worked assiduously, especially during the long period of the Cold War, to extol its achievements throughout the world. Its failures have been given far less attention and tend even now to be overlooked. This propaganda effort—paid for by the agencies of the U.S. government, such as USIS and the CIA—was itself one of the precursors of global culture. There was, of course, considerable truth behind the propaganda, which is what made it so convincing. In this period America was a haven of liberalism and democracy with an economy, scientific establishment, and university system that was second to none. However, the promotion of acquisitive individualism and the free market system of corporate capitalism also served to create the consumerist preconditions of global culture. At present the U.S. government is still exercising its considerable sway—especially its economic power exerted through international agencies such as the World Bank and the IMF—to promote free market and privatization policies that are designed to facilitate the export of its cultural products.

These are predominantly products directed at the young of the world. The youth of every generation has always been particularly attracted to American mass culture, so that stage by stage each generation has become more and more Americanized. This started even before the First World War. it became more pronounced with the jazz generation after it. and it culminated with the rock generation after the Second World War. Thus. seemingly paradoxically, the radical and rebellious youth of the 1960s. who were most opposed to U.S. foreign policy, especially on Vietnam. were at the same time more habituated to American tastes and mores than their usually politically more conservative parents. The reasons for this are fairly obvious.

American mass culture has always been a culture of youth. Nearly all its values are those of youthfulness. Young. healthy, vigorous bodies and smiling, good-looking faces feature prominently, and sex appeal, if not actual sex, is seen as the gateway to pleasure and achievement, to having fun and a good time. The obverse to this is that age, feebleness, impotency, failure, and ultimately death are not to be mentioned and perhaps do not even exist. A play attitude to life is extolled, one that requires a liking for the new and shiny, especially if it is a brand-name product, for every new release that comes on the market, and for new gadgets for every purpose. A paliness that entails freedom from parental controls or those of any other authority figures is the preeminent social quality. This, too, has its obverse in the refusal to abide by traditions or superior standards or anything that smacks of authority; consequently the "arty" and "egg-head" are shunned. In its culminating 1960s expression this attitude enjoined a youthful "tribalism" of the gang and the experiments with promiscuous sex, drugs, and rock music of the Woodstock countercultural jamboree. Since that time things have quieted down considerably due to AIDS, puritanical feminism. and the career pressures of getting a job.

However, the media still extol a sense of fake rebelliousness. Mostly affluent and privileged young people with money to spend are urged to identify with the denizens of the ghettos and encouraged to view themselves as "revolutionaries" burking the authority of their elders, above all parents, pastors, and teachers, and to shun what are most frequently the values of their own local culture. Every new advertising campaign is billed as a "revolution" in something or other, overthrowing the staid old ways. Thus anything that the adult world demands of youth can be derided as old and "phony." The only things new and true are the "authentic" expressions of youth itself as conveyed through the media, of course. Only that which features in the media is to be admired and accepted, everything else is to be distrusted. Hence, every kind of offhand dismissal and the petty cynicism that it breeds is sanctioned—except that against the media itself. "Do what you like as long as you don't switch off" is the implicit imperative. The values of the media assume priority as media conformism takes the place of respect for tradition.

What is not so openly spelled out is that these media imperatives are in keeping with a ruthless striving for success, to becoming a winner rather than a loser—a fate to be avoided by every possible means. For this is preeminently a culture of success through competitive struggle for money and status. The main aim is to outdo every rival, to outdistance and outperform all others and rise to the top; for this end it is necessary to please more, to be more attractive and seductive, to win more friends and influence more people, and, what is most important, to make more money. The secret, almost subliminal, message of youth culture is that ultimately nothing succeeds like success.

This is the culture that has become prevalent all over the world among young people who have learned its terms from all the American cultural products they imbibe, from advertising, pop music, films, sporting competitions, and so on. They are charmed, flattered, and seduced by it. They come to believe that they, too, are entitled to its bonanzas as almost a natural right. If they cannot attain its rewards in their own societies, they at least strive to share in these vicariously by acquiring the few cultural products that they can afford. The familiar consumer items of youth gear, such as jeans, records, hamburgers, Coke, and so on, act as surrogates for that which most young people in the world cannot hope to reach.

This generational process of enculturation takes a different form in each of the major societies, depending largely on the period of exposure to youth culture and its intensity in a given society. In Western societies, which have been longest exposed to it, the process is almost complete. There is little to distinguish British from American youth in these respects. At least since the end of the Second World War both have been through the same generational phases, from the bobby-soxers and crooners, through the baby boom rockers to the despondent generation X. In other countries, especially in the Third World and newly liberated communist ones, the generational stages have been different. But everywhere they are converging to the same end point of cultural entropy or the heat-death of culture.

Youth is getting younger and younger with each generation. Small children are now being exposed to their version of youth culture, and soon one can foresee an assault on babies, for advertisers believe that consumers start in the womb. Those in their teens are the most addicted exponents of youth culture. They are the ones at whom the main barrage of pop music, films, television shows, and advertised fashions are directed. The best sellers in books, such as the *Harry Potter* fantasies, are pitched no higher than their mentality; and these are now being read in nearly all major languages throughout the world by young and old alike. The whole culture market, geared to their tastes and predilections, is becoming childish.

These youthful teens are neither children nor adults, but rather grown-up children and childish adults. Michael Jackson is their cynosure. Under the impact of media culture childhood and adulthood are disappearing as distinct stages in life—they are merging into the one indefinite state of youthfulness; children strive to make themselves as knowing as possible so as to seem grown-up and elderly adults try to keep themselves as youthful as possible so as never to seem old. The portly middle-aged man in jeans and matron in mini-skirt are familiar sights everywhere. People brought up on this culture become averse to maturity or ripening of experience. They grow older in years but remain fixated as adult children who knew no real childhood or adulthood: "thou hast nor youth nor age, but as it were an after-dinner's sleep, dreaming on both."[7]

How to wake up and arouse this dreamy, somnambulant youth is the problem of our age. The dream factories of the culture industry have habituated them to a star-struck gaze that must be broken so that they can look on their surroundings with more sober senses. They must be brought to understand what has happened to their cultural environment, just as they already know what has been done to the natural one. This is the great pedagogic task of the future—educating youth to an awareness of what has been done to them. The Moloch that is consuming the young in its cultural holocausts will continue to do so for as long as they themselves do not rise up against it and smash it together with all the other idols of the market-place.

Some of them have already shown that they are capable of symbolic resistance against the economic powers that be. They have organized protest movements against forests and jungles being cleared and animals hunted to extinction. They have launched charitable endeavors to succor the starving masses of poor during famines in distant parts of the world. They have agitated against children being put to work and workers being excessively exploited. They have lashed out, though in a much less clearly focused way, against world banking institutions that have brought about a debt crisis for impoverished nations and against trade agreements that are causing unemployment. Some are even beginning to get a hazy idea of cultural pollution and its effects. They do not always know what to protest against or how best to do it; frequently they are quite mistaken in their targets and hit out at the wrong things. But sometimes they are the only ones who are bringing such problems to the attention of the world. Sad to say this is only because the media cannot ignore demonstrations and street violence. The causes themselves would otherwise receive scant attention.

To educate these youth to the great task ahead and turn them against the global culture that has molded them will be a self-critical undertaking of enormous difficulty, but one with great potential for dramatic change in the condition of cultural life in general. It will require them to act against themselves, never an easy matter for anyone. It will involve them entering into strange alliances between groups that have never acted together before. The struggle will go on for a long time and have unprecedented outcomes that we cannot now foresee. But all that should not deter us from making a start.

For this purpose we have undertaken the defense of local culture as against the inroads of global culture. But we do not as yet know what this very general policy formulation amounts to in the specificity of concrete action. We shall postpone this consideration until the last chapter where it will be spelled out in some more detail and supported with further arguments.

However, before we arrive at that point, there is still one general matter to be settled first. As we have already shown, global culture is unlike any other that has ever existed. Its very success has been greater than that of any culture in history, for reasons we have just demonstrated. Its prevalence is such that it threatens to wipe out every previous culture. It is so different from these cultures of tradition that we have designated it as an *Erzatz Kultur*, a surrogate culture taking the place of every authentic one. But what this difference amounts to has not as yet been properly explained. This will be our primary endeavor in the next chapter, before returning in the final one to a discussion of how we are to defend our local cultures from being taken over by it.

3

HOW DOES GLOBAL CULTURE DIFFER FROM ALL OTHER CULTURES?

In this chapter we shall embark on a short theoretical detour which, however, does not take us very far away from our main theme, the concern with global culture. It is designed to answer the question why this culture is so very different from the cultures of the past or the still-surviving present local ones. To address this question we need to establish a theoretical basis for comparing cultures. Once we have such a general theory of culture in hand it can be referred to global culture in order to ascertain its peculiarities and idiosyncrasies.

We have established that global culture is the dominant culture of the present stage of predatory global capitalism in a technological civilization embracing the entire world. It is the leading cultural expression of all the globalizing trends that this world is presently undergoing. It reflects the changing conditions of life brought about by the growing integration, in so many diverse respects, of all the societies of the world. It has emerged as the very first common culture for the whole of humanity.

Some of the previous cultures of the past might have had ambitions to attain universality, but none could actually achieve it, each being limited by its origins and conditions of existence to a circumscribed local region of the world. Even the Enlightenment culture of modern Europe, which considered itself to be the acme of civilization, did not reach out far beyond its sources, extending at most to the privileged and educated few in colonial societies—those who had been brought up as honorary Europeans. Like all other previous cultures it, too, lacked the means to communicate itself to masses of people all over the globe and reach a large proportion of mankind.

The reason for this is that it, like all such previous cultures, operated on much lower technological levels within a restricted geographic sphere. It did not possess the advanced means of communication, transportation, and production in general that are now at the disposal of global culture.

It stands to reason that in a technological civilization culture will avail itself of technical means and itself becomes technified. What specifically this amounts to in each cultural dimension we shall see in what follows. It may be thought that to speak in this way of a technical culture is almost a contradiction in terms since, as usually conceived, culture and technology are opposed to each other. Some authors see technology as inexorably displacing culture. Conversely, other authors speak of two cultures, a scientific-technical in contrast to a literary-humanistic. In a similar vein many cultural studies theorists oppose computer literacy to old stylebook literacy. All these conceptions suffer from an inadequate understanding of the relation between culture and technique, which by no means constitute a direct and simple opposition to each other. As we shall show, the relation between them is much more complex than that idea allows.

Technology in itself is not culture, for the very same technology can lend itself to varied cultural uses, but the two are not in absolute opposition either. Every cultural form requires techniques that most often involve material means and media that are frequently technologies or allied instrumentalities. Culture must have a material basis, one that is usually technically conditioned. Even literary cultures, which seem most remote from anything instrumental, have a technical aspect in the techniques of writing and preserving literary texts.

Techniques are indispensable to culture, but obviously they do not constitute the whole of it. What other aspects of culture must there be apart from techniques? To answer this question we need to undertake a general theoretical analysis of culture. We have in fact already done so in other works.[1] Hence, what we are presenting here are but the briefest summaries of more extensive studies carried out elsewhere. But for present purposes that should suffice.

A. A GENERAL THEORY OF CULTURE

Any culture whatever can be analyzed in terms of three basic aspects: representation, ethos, and technics. We must take each of these words in its widest possible signification in order to arrive at an adequate theoretical concept. Thus representation means every possible mode of symbolic substitution of one thing by another, such as where one object stands for another or one person acts for another. Ethos means the whole social dimension of norms and values—that is, the form of life as it is governed and guided by all the stipulations and dispensations that control and direct action, feeling, and thought—such as laws, customs, manners, and morals. Technics means the whole ensemble of both instrumental and noninstrumental techniques necessary to achieve any given goal, such as is inherent in a cultural activity or such as is the means for other cultural ends. These three aspects of any cultural form or object are not separable components but merely analytically distinguishable features that will be found instantiated to various degrees and proportions.

Representation, ethos, and technics can also be distinguished by the differences in the standards or values, in the most general sense, which govern them. Representations are judged by reference to truth, objectivity, authenticity, authority, and other such criteria of reality and validity; modes of ethos are judged by reference to values bearing on goodness, duty, propriety, fittingness, beauty, and so on for all the other ethical or aesthetic standards; the various kinds of techniques are judged on the basis of utility, efficiency, functionality, virtuosity, skillfulness, and other such pragmatic considerations. Depending on the kind of thing it is, anything pertaining to culture will have some or other of these standards applied to it. Thus, for example, a work of art can be judged predominantly by one or another of these sets of standards. If it is primarily a representational work then it will be assessed on its truth or fidelity to reality; if it is more imaginative or expressive then the criteria of fantasy, feeling, or wit will be referred to it; and if it is mainly useful or skill-based then the more utilitarian terms of functionality, appropriateness to its ends, or technical achievement will be invoked. Most works of art are judged in all these three ways at once, but with varying emphases depending on the kind of medium it is and on genre and other stylistic considerations.

We shall not enter into the philosophical debate here as to which of these standards or values is the most important. But it is necessary to stress that none of them is to be taken as absolute or completely universal. Each distinctive culture develops its own versions of such general valuations and ranks them accordingly. But this does not mean that values are relative and that, therefore, cultures are completely sui generis and incommensurable. On the contrary, the various kinds of instantiations and realization of general values in different cultures can be compared to each other without having to be judged against overarching absolutes. Thus it is our prime purpose in this work to compare global culture to other locally based cultures on the basis of the three kinds of standards here outlined. Such comparisons do not necessarily have to tell for or against global culture in any one respect.

Cultures differ preeminently in the ways that they utilize forms of representation, ethos, and technics in relation to each other. This can be illustrated in the most obvious way by the extreme contrast between so-called primitive or tribal cultures and those of modern societies. The former rely on orally transmitted mythical and magical representations, on an ethos based on taboo and mana or some other notion of the forbidden and sacred, and on a repertoire of techniques that only use the simplest of handheld tools; the latter are the opposite in all these respects—they utilize scientific and other rational representations, their ethos is governed by a codified law and a secular ethics, and they employ a vast array of technologically based techniques. Between these two opposed poles of historical development fall all the other traditional cultures, both living and extinct, some of which are in many respects closer to primitive origins and others closer to the terminus of contemporary modernity. But these gradations must not be interpreted as falling on a unilinear scale of evolutionary progress in the way that so many nineteenth-century thinkers assumed. It makes some sense to speak of progress in relation to technics but far less so in reference to representation and ethos. This whole issue of progress and historical development cannot be dealt with fully here, but it has been considered in other works.[2]

What needs to be stressed here is that every culture is a complex of systems of representation, forms of ethos, and ensembles of techniques more or less integrated with each other depending on the consistency of the culture in question. Now we no longer possess cultures of any integrity. Parts or even fragments are all that have survived from the traditional cultures, for none is any longer fully intact. And even these are in danger of disappearing as coherent units and dissolving into the melting pot of global culture. In such a situation of dissolution it is all the more necessary theoretically to elaborate a basic understanding of the nature of culture. For this purpose we need to explain in greater detail each of our major terms.

Representation is a vast topic in itself, one that has been scarcely covered in a large book, *A New Science of Representation* (see note 1 for this chapter). In that work it is considered extensively and comprehensively from the simplest and most basic semiotic aspects to the most complex developmental issues of how systems of representation developed from culture to culture over the long span of history. Only a few key points from that treatment will be selected and elaborated here.

Representation in its simplest of aspects is the starting point for semiotic theory as first developed by C. S. Peirce and continued by his numerous successors. Peirce defined representation as follows: "To represent: to stand for, that is, to be in such a relation to another that for certain purposes it is treated as if it were that other. Thus a spokesman, deputy, attorney, agent, vicar, diagram, symptom, counter, description, concept, premise, testimony, all represent something else, in their several ways, to minds who consider them in that way."[3]

This definition lists some of the numerous modes of representation, each of which is a large topic in its own right. On first sight, they seem to have little in common with each other, for obviously the way a vicar represents is very different from the way a counter does so. Clearly different senses of representation are involved, and some might contend that the term is inherently ambiguous. However, as we have shown in our previously mentioned work, these senses (many of which are really nuances) of the term are not inherently distinct—they are all closely linked together by subtle gradations of meaning. Between any two seemingly disparate modes of representing there are always intermediate cases that span the gap of meaning. Hence, representing follows a semantic continuum going in all kinds of directions without any initial point of departure or center. There is no common essential core to the concept, but endless variation.

"Standing for" and "standing in for" are two distinct general notions involved in representation, but as they themselves assume numerous modes, they cannot be considered the essence of the concept. A description, a painting, a plan, a diagram, and a model all *stand for* something else, but do so in very different ways. Analogously so, an agent, a deputy, a spokesman or messenger all *stand in for* someone else, but also do so very diversely. Between these two types of functions of representation there are various others that share something with both. Thus role enactment or theatrical playing is like a modeling or reproduction of characters, but also like a standing in for fictitious or real people. Both these aspects are also to be found in other instances of representing, as, for example, when a barrister is both an agent for his client speaking on his behalf and a rhetorical performer making a plea before a judge and jury. A politician as an elected representative also fulfills something like this dual function. Even such widely divergent forms of representation as mathematical models of physical phenomena and mannequin models of types of physique—to make a comparison that borders on the ridiculous—are not without some similarity and connection as there are many intermediate forms linking these two extremes.

In any given culture there can be all kinds of representations: literary, pictorial, musical, mathematical, scientific, theatrical, legal, commercial, political, and religious. Those that are in fact present within the culture, in the particular form they take, will usually, though not always, be closely related and bound up with each other, thereby constituting a more or less coherent symbolic system. Each culture is a different system in this sense. The pattern representations that a culture constitutes mark its historical character and identity. As a culture changes and moves from one historical stage to another, so its whole system of representations undergoes a commensurate transformation. Some older forms of representation recede and newer ones emerge to take their place. In our previously referred to work we have examined such transformations as they occurred at three critical historical junctures: when primitive societies acquired civilization, when civilizations developed universal religions and philosophies, and finally when some of them entered the phase of modernity.

Even within the one cultural sphere, such as religion, there are many different ways of representing the sacred utilized by societies at different stages of historical development. In some tribal societies divine powers, spiritual forces, and mythic events were enacted by shamans in dances performed in a state of trance. In ancient Greek culture such enactments of sacred happenings were staged by means of the newly developed art of drama. In the Christian religion special highly symbolic rituals, such as that of the Mass, were devised for the purpose of conveying the central mystery of the faith. Christianity is particularly rich in its range of representational forms, both of the stand-for and the stand-in-for types. In the latter category fall the legitimating doctrines whereby popes, and later kings as well, saw themselves as vicars of Christ.

In direct contrast to such religious cultures, secular ones are much more restricted in their range of symbolic representational types. They are more given to realistic form of representation, such as those of science, democracy, and naturalistic art. Varieties of what might in a general sense be called rational representations predominate. Where this rationalization of representation takes the extreme form of technification, as has now happened in our global technological civilization, then representation is still further narrowed and its very character is drastically altered. As we shall show in what follows, in global culture representations are being displaced by images. In the most extreme cases of instrumental rationalization, representations are abandoned altogether in favor of computer models or some other information technology.

The transition from sacred to secular forms of representation reflects what Max Weber called "the disenchantment of the world." This process, whereby myth and magic give way to science and engineering, has its exact reflection in the changes in the forms of representation set out earlier. It is not, of course, in any sense a simple advance in progress. Nor does it mean that all forms of myth and magic disappear. On the contrary, as we have witnessed in the course of the twentieth century, new forms of myth have reemerged, such as those of the totalitarian ideologies, and a new recourse to quasi-magical means is also now in vogue, such as the resurgence of astrology and alternative health panaceas, not to speak of the magical potencies with which technology itself is invested in popular imagination. But these are no longer the myths and magic of earlier societies. They play a quite different role in our present global culture, for they cater to the sense of powerlessness and helplessness that ordinary people feel in the face of the technological juggernaut and the impersonality of the social forces that determine their lives.

The sense that people have of a loss of control in the course of their lives is also due to another decisive change in the character of representation. Whereas in past societies relations were usually personal, direct, and involved face-to-face encounters between people, even where these were separated by huge differences in status and power, today relations of most kinds are mediated by representatives and there is little that people can do directly for themselves. Representative institutions and agencies proliferate in our societies. Transacting any piece of ordinary business in life must usually be mediated by intermediaries, such as lawyers, officials, or professionals of one kind or another. Hence ordinary people experience a sense of a loss of self in being unable to do anything for themselves, but always having to rely on experts.

The diminution of a sense of self is closely linked to a reduction of a sense of human reality consequent on the previously described technification of representation. Between the information technologies of computer models and the virtual realities of the media images there is little room for the kinds of representations that give ordinary people a realistic sense of things. Global culture does not allow for very much reality. Hence the importance of maintaining a wide variety of representational forms, not just for the sake of cultural diversity, but also for the purpose of conveying realities other than those that can be captured by "information" or the "image." It is for this reason, perhaps more than any other, that it is necessary to preserve all the alternative representational forms still embedded in local cultures. These are like alternative windows on the world.

The same kinds of considerations also apply to the ethos, for in that respect, too, global culture works to narrow and limit the quality of life and reduce the options of living to a few standard types for all people on earth. The ethos determines the nature of ordinary quotidian life and experience just as much as representation for it governs the basic forms of behavior, the kinds of relations, the types of character, and the social forms available in any given society. As we have seen in the preceding chapters, global culture is particularly effective in determining the ethos of societies all over the globe because of its influence on ordinary practices and habits through the styles of life it promotes.

It is not possible to develop theoretically the conception of an ethos as fully as might be desired in this context, but we have done so elsewhere in another work, *Ethical Life,* and will continue this investigation further in a forthcoming work, *Aesthetic Life* (see note 1, this chapter). Here all we can offer are a few illustrative examples of fundamental differences in ethos in various kinds of societies, hoping that this will be sufficient to convey the scope of the conception. Historically considered, the three most differentiated ethos are those of primitive societies, the great classical civilizations, and modern societies. We shall try to indicate what these broad differences amount to.

The ethos of a primitive society is all of a piece. It coheres completely in its simplicity and there are few fundamental differentiations within it. People who are fully immersed in such an ethos have few hesitations as to how to lead their lives; they know what is right or wrong, obligatory or arbitrary, valuable or worthless, and so on for all the contrasting norm and value aspects of the ethos. Almost all imperatives in such an ethos are equally categorical. Reasons why something is right or wrong almost never enter into consideration and the motives with which something is done also do not matter. Every action is a kind of ritual performance—all that counts is that it be done in the right way. Anthropologists who have studied native people in different parts of the world invariably remark on how much the style of acting, rather than the ends to be achieved, is important. The correct procedures have to be carried out in the right formal way regardless of the reasons for or consequences of the action.

Such considerations only began to matter when types of actions were differentiated, which only began to happen with the rise of the classical cultures during the so-called axial age (roughly 700–300 BC) in the civilizations of Greece, Israel, China, India, and Persia. The major categories of the ethos—the good, the beautiful, and the useful—were distinguished and separated from each other and different norms were applied to each of these. Within these broad categories further distinctions were established, such as that between ethics or morals and mores or customs. What was of crucial importance for the ethos was that each of these civilizations developed a system of ethics, one which eventually came to be accepted as canonical for the duration of that civilization or its successors. Thus Judeo-Christian morality, as well as the ethics of Confucianism, Buddhism, and Hinduism, have maintained their position as determining influences on the ethos in their respective cultures, and classical Greek philosophical ethics has had a continuous impact throughout the history of the West.

The distinctions between the good, beautiful, and useful—that is to say between ethics, aesthetics, and utility or economics—were variously elaborated and treated within each of the great classical cultures. In the Judeo-Christian tradition it was morality—that is, God's commandments—that was given supreme importance for on it depended the salvation of the soul. Aesthetics had a subsidiary role, though in ancillary functions an important one. In the Greek classical tradition there was never any such discrepancy between them, nor was the value-weighting distributed in this unbalanced, one-sided way. The beautiful and the good were not seen as completely distinct and the one unified ideal of *kalon k'agathon* was expounded by the major writers and philosophers, above all by Plato. In Plato's philosophy love of beauty serves as the initiating impulse to virtue and the love of wisdom that lead to truth and goodness, the supreme ideals. This view had a persistent influence throughout the classical tradition in the West, and it is echoed in Keats's famous lines:

Beauty is truth and truth beauty—that is all
Ye know on earth, and all ye need to know.

All the traditional cultures treated utility as a lesser consideration not on par with the primary ones of goodness or beauty. Not even the practically minded Romans questioned this assumption. It only began to be challenged with the rise of modern secular societies and the consolidation of capitalism, which came together with the inauguration of modern science and technology. Incipiently implied in the new natural philosophy of Francis Bacon and his successors of the Royal Society, and spelled out clearly for the first time during the Age of Enlightenment in Mandeville's fable of the bees as well as in the *Encyclopédie* of Diderot and the Physiocrats, utility was gradually developed into the major category governing the new ethos of modernity. That which is useful is good because it is conducive to the happiness of society, that is, of the greatest number. The utilitarians of the nineteenth century made this judgment philosophically explicit and they were tacitly followed by the positivists in France and the pragmatists in America, as well as by most economists from Adam Smith to David Ricardo and onward. This had a profound impact upon the whole ethos of modernity for it led to a dissociation of value spheres such that the utilitarian assumed a dominant value in its own right quite irrespective of its effect on the ethical or the aesthetic. Thus technical progress for the betterment of society and social reform policies were pursued in a pragmatic utilitarian spirit without regard to their consequences for ethical or aesthetic life. Nevertheless, the traditional ethical and aesthetic ideals were not as yet given up, but only segregated and restricted to their own separate spheres of life—ethics mainly to private life and aesthetics to the special sanctuary of art, which was accorded a protected status.

With the onset of a global technological civilization the ethos has been transformed further in that direction and carried vastly beyond that current in the previous nineteenth-century era of European modernity. The utilitarian attitude has been extended to embrace almost everything. Values have given way to utilities almost in every sphere of cultural life. And furthermore, a narrowed conception of utility has expressed itself in the pervasive commodification of culture according to which cultural goods are solely judged by reference to market value or price. Global culture is a through and through commodified culture. We shall examine the consequences of this debased utilitarian attitude to culture in the next chapter and show how it is linked to the present stage of a predatory global capitalism.

The ethos purveyed by global culture is unlike any that had previously been current in any civilized society. It is largely based on the inexorable duality of work and leisure according to which everyone's life is split. The ethos of work follows that of a technically prescribed and regulated routine: the ethos of leisure that of the freely chosen lifestyle. The concept of a lifestyle, which is now current all over the globe, seemingly recapitulates on the level of advanced technical civilization the primitive unity of a cultural form in which the fundamental differentiations of ethics, aesthetics, and economics or utilitarian considerations are dissolved. The lifestyle is a pattern of consumption geared to outside appearances, cultivating an overall look and bearing based on designer-label goods and the comportment and attitudes that go with all this. To adopt the right style, together with all the accoutrements that are ancillary to it, is the prerequisite for being accepted in the affluent social circles to which top people aspire. To change one's lifestyle to fit in with one's changing fortunes and circumstances becomes socially de rigueur. Lifestyles are thus more akin to fashions than to forms of life within a traditional ethos with which they have little in common.

The lifestyle ethos of global culture is distinct from any traditional ethos not only because it is labile and ephemeral, but also because it is not embodied in people in the same way. A traditional ethos creates character, a set of traits that are firmly impressed on those who have been encultured in its forms and norms. By contrast, adopting a lifestyle calls for no character building, for it is more like role-playing or presenting an appearance. People present themselves as what they want other people to take them for or what they would like to become. This has more to do with self-projection, or really self-advertising, than with becoming a certain kind of person. In another sense it is also an instance of cultivating an "image."

The creation of images of whatever kind depends on techniques. There are technical ways of doing this and people who are proficient in these respects. Such techniques are skills that might be, but do not necessarily have to be, reliant on instruments or technologies. Technique is an all-embracing concept that covers all human activities. There are techniques of religious worship and meditation just as there are techniques of sex and all other aspects of lovemaking, including seduction. There is almost nothing that cannot be better practiced by learning a technique for this purpose.

Technics is the sum total of techniques current at any one time within any one culture. Ellul defines it as "the totality of methods rationally arrived at and having absolute efficiency (for a given stage of development) in every field of human activity."[4] The repertoire of technics of contemporary technological civilization is vastly more extensive than that of any previous civilization, and perhaps even larger than that of all previous civilizations taken together. The reason for this, according to Ellul, is that in the modern era technique has become an end in itself. Everything is now being technified in the name of progress or scientific advance or social reform or simply following the technological imperative that if something can be technified it ought to be. And, as Ellul makes clear, all these techniques do not simply function singly in isolation from each other; rather, they are linked together to constitute systems, which expand and eventually connect up with each other. This systematicity of techniques produces the total, all-embracing technics of contemporary technological civilization.[5]

This is the triumph of technics with which we are currently preoccupied. It is a triumph of technics over representation and ethos in every sphere of culture. Which does not mean that representation and ethos are completely excluded and eliminated—in itself a cultural impossibility—but only that they are themselves becoming pervaded by technics and so corrupted, degraded, and relegated to a secondary status. This means, as we shall examine in greater detail in what follows, that the representational system and ethos of global culture are becoming more and more enmeshed in technics. There is no escape from technics for even the most intimate of personal relations are often mediated by technological means. Pace Ellul, we shall maintain that not everything can be technified, but the general tendency of our technological civilization is to do so as much as possible. The ultimate extension of this is the resort to complete automation or pure technique where human intervention is no longer required. Even culture can be automated to a considerable degree, though never completely, and so rendered literally inhuman. This in turn leads to the partial dehumanization of people themselves.

In itself technique is not something to be avoided or opposed, it is one of the anthropological universals of all human culture. Every culture has its panoply of techniques that is more or less peculiar to itself. As we shall show, even the very same end result can be achieved by quite different technical means depending on the culture. However, in all cultures prior to our own techniques were subordinate to other nontechnical ends, usually those deriving from representation and ethos. Only in our technological civilization have techniques assumed priority so that the technically effective or efficient way of doing something is adopted irrespective of the actual ends achieved. It is this that we have designated as the triumph of technics and to explain it we shall examine technics in itself first before going on to also consider its effect on representation and ethos.

B. TECHNICS

As we have already intimated, global culture tends to the triumph of technics over representation and ethos, and that is to say, the meaning and value-endowing aspects of culture have been relegated to an inferior role. Techniques in themselves do not concern meaning or value but are pragmatic matters of practicality and efficacy. Hence the more techniques predominate the less scope is there for meaning and value creation. In a technological civilization where everything is subject to technification, there is an ineluctable loss in these respects. This is the cultural crisis of our time.

In global culture the tendency is for every cultural activity to be transformed into a technique and for every technique to become a surrogate for a cultural activity. Technique is what people all over the globe learn from each other because it is the easiest thing there is to learn. Hence techniques deriving from every kind of culture are taken up and transported everywhere else and allowed to circulate freely all over the globe. This circulation is a large part of what we mean by the term global culture.

The technical aspects of any culture are the easiest to understand, appreciate, reproduce, and acquire. By contrast, representations are only learned with great difficulty and the values constitutive of an ethos can only be mastered after a lifetime of effort. Techniques can be easily recorded and repeated for they are the most objective aspects of any human activity. They are also easily judged for obvious criteria of success and failure apply to them — does it work or does it not work, has one learned it or not, and so on. Thus technical competence can be used for competitive purposes to determine whether a thing or a person is better or worse than another. As we shall see, this is the main way of judging practiced today.

These factors explain why it is that techniques transfer relatively easily from one culture to another, whereas representation and ethos or meaning and value translate only with great difficulty. When two strange cultures encountered each other historically, it was always techniques that were first exchanged. This can be illustrated with innumerable examples; perhaps one of the most dramatic occurred when Japan was forcibly opened up to the Western world. The Japanese were, of course, most impressed by Western technical competence. Westerners, too, first appreciated certain technical features of Japanese culture. Western artists were struck by Japanese wood-block prints because of their unusual artistic techniques of close-cropping and bird's-eye-view perspective mode of representation. The representational content itself of the ukiyo-e or floating-world genre and its conventions only began to be appreciated much later, for it was so much more difficult to learn to "see" these pictures in a Japanese way. The Japanese aesthetic sensibility and the rest of its ethos, the "sword and chrysanthemum" thematic, was even more elusive; it was acquired by very few Westerners by the time of the Second World War and not too many even now.

The exchange of techniques is itself a cultural matter. Traditional societies generally had all kinds of inhibitions and restrictions on the importation and utilization of "foreign" techniques. In his study of the history of techniques and technologies, Ellul lists a number of such restraining conditions ranging from an indifference to improved efficiency to the emphasis on art or personal skill rather than on improvement in tools.[6] The guild restrictions on the tools of craftsmen held sway in European society until late into the eighteenth century. The loosening of such restraints and the consequent free adaptability of techniques in the pursuit of pure efficiency was itself a kind of cultural revolution in the West, one which the whole world is now forced to undergo. It is one of the main reasons why it is now so difficult to block the techniques of global culture because any attempt to do so is castigated as the work of Luddites and enemies of progress.

Techniques are also culture-specific in that they usually originate in a given cultural context. Each culture invents the techniques necessary for its own needs, and rarely are the techniques of two foreign cultures the same. Even the one purpose or end-goal is achieved in different cultures by quite different technical means. The work of Joseph Needham on Chinese science and technology shows repeatedly how the same end was accomplished by very different technical devices and practices in China as compared to the West. In his magnum opus he gives numerous examples ranging from ways of conveying food to the mouth or cutting timber to ways of bridging rivers or building boats.[7]

However, despite the fact that techniques arise within specific cultures, they can quickly transfer to others for they are the most detachable and free-floating aspects of a culture. The chains of transmission of a technique from one culture to others can be extremely long in space and time, frequently spanning the whole Eurasian continent over thousands of years. Mostly, until modern times, the movement has tended to be from east to west, as, for example from Mesopotamia and Egypt to Greece, and even further east, as far afield as from China to Europe across the intervening civilizations. The three crucial inventions that Francis Bacon had noted—gunpowder, the compass, and printing—had come to Europe in this way. But sometimes the movement of technical diffusion was the other way, especially during the Hellenistic and Roman periods. Later, of course, with the start of the colonial era Western inventions were exported to all other countries to facilitate trade or simply to impress the natives. It was in this way that Japanese artists learned the Western techniques of perspective—almost certainly from Dutch prints imported through the trading depot of Nagasaki. But they adopted and utilized this technique in their own way to serve their own aesthetic needs and altered it accordingly. It was this Japanese version that much later caught the eye of Western artists such as Manet, Degas, Toulouse-Lautrec, and van Gogh.

The exchange of techniques and technologies throughout history is an extremely complex process that has many interesting lessons to teach. The movement flows not only down the gradient from more civilized to less civilized cultures, but frequently also in the reverse direction. There are many fascinating examples of this contrary current, especially in the techniques of warfare. Everything to do with the use of horses from the earliest charioteers and bareback riding to all subsequent types of horsemanship, such as light and heavily armored cavalry, derived from the steppe-people of central Asia. And as with all warfare, these military techniques also brought with them allied techniques of human management, especially disciplinary techniques. The methods developed by Genghis Khan for his Mongol hordes in staff organization, intelligence, propaganda, the exemplary use of terror, and sheer disciplinary regimentation had not been equaled by Western armies until the nineteenth and twentieth centuries.

As this last example reveals, methods of human organization working as disciplinary techniques have always played a prominent part in all previous societies, both within and outside civilizations. These are the kinds of techniques of surveillance and control that Michel Foucault has highlighted in his work on contemporary societies, especially those utilized in the major institutions, such as hospitals, schools, and prisons. But he does not seem to have realized just how far back in history such techniques extend. All kinds of previous societies, especially the slave-holding ones, have practiced them at one time or other. What does distinguish the contemporary period is the concentration and systematic integration of these techniques and, furthermore, their amplification through technologies into the one comprehensive technics, as Ellul makes clear.

The introduction of novel techniques into contemporary culture proceeds without let or hindrance. Old techniques deriving from all kinds of cultures of the past as well as new specially invented ones are being continuously and routinely introduced into global culture. Such an onrush of techniques could not be fully absorbed into any local culture. It would destroy the fabric and integrity of any such culture. Local culture is in this respect invariably less flexible, and so comes to be considered inferior to global culture, which gives the latter a permanent air of superiority. Local culture cannot compete on a technical basis with global culture.

Whole swathes of global culture are almost completely dominated by technique with only the barest minimum of representational meaning or the values of ethos. Two such of particular importance are sporting and culinary activities, for these provide paradigmatic models that extend beyond themselves and influence most other practices of global culture. We shall explore each of these in turn.

Sporting and game activities in general are matters of almost pure technique; as a result they are very easily transferable from any one culture to any other. This makes them ideal vehicles for global culture. At present almost the same sports and games are played and—what is even more crucial—watched all over the world. Almost all people, especially males, now engage in one or another kind of football, most frequently as spectators. For some the time, effort, and attention devoted to this exceeds any other single activity apart from work.

In every other culture of the past sports and games figured only incidentally as folk customs, unless, as in a few key cases, they were given religious ritual significance, as among the pre-Colombian peoples of America and the ancient Greeks. Exhibition activities, or what we would now call spectator sports, were even more rare. The only significant instance was the gladiatorial games and chariot races in the circuses of ancient Rome and other cities throughout the empire, and these were closely bound up with political life. Today spectator sports bereft of any religious meaning or ritual or politics figure as autonomous practices without any symbolic import, and these have become the staple of weekend entertainment and weekday conversation.

If contemporary spectator sports have any significance whatever it is related to the technical cult of the body as a kind of quasi machine that is tested almost to breaking point in a continual process of record surpassing. Apart from this, sports are related indirectly to the competitive ethos of contemporary society, where winning or losing is all that matters. Either singly or in teams people engage in sporting contests that match the competitive pursuits they enter into in the course of ordinary life at work or at leisure. Thus the emphasis on sport in schools is meant to prepare children not so much to become players or athletes themselves, as to acquire the right competitive spirit for excelling in exams and for the team cohesion necessary to cooperate with others in group-work relations in offices, businesses, and laboratories. The playing of sport is usually abandoned in adulthood and substituted with spectatorism, mostly via television.

Sports and games exemplify a huge range of technical skills and prowess. Some are almost wholly bodily capabilities, such as athletics and gymnastics; others are almost wholly mental accomplishments, such as chess and bridge. Most sports and games involve a mixture of physical and mental aptitudes. The surprising thing is that nearly all of these skills—which most people spend an inordinate time cultivating in youth—are of almost no use in later life. They seem purposeless accomplishments without a goal, almost as if technique was practiced for its own sake alone, as it were an end in itself. This is indeed the hallmark of a cultural activity and it reveals thereby to what extent sports and games act as a surrogate culture, an *Erzatz Kultur*, which, as we have already noted, is a feature of global culture in general.

The same holds true of culinary culture, which also acts as an aspect of *Erzatz Kultur* in the context of global culture. It, too, is largely a matter of technique, a huge ensemble of practices in the preparation, cooking, presentation, and tasting of food and drink. The skills required at each of these stages can be of an extremely high order, as any gourmand who patronizes top restaurants is well aware. The gastronomic arts are highly cultivated in some local cultures—the French and Chinese varieties spring readily to mind, and there are some others as well. Culinary techniques of a much cruder kind, though employing higher technologies, also play an inordinately important role in global culture. One of its marks of universality is that anyone anywhere can now enjoy the same foods and drinks. Hamburgers or pizza, whiskey or brandy, coffee or tea, Coke or Pepsi, and many more such rival pairs are the culinary choices of the daily diet of people all over the globe. However, how this figures in global culture is very different to its traditional role in local cultures. In a traditional culture each stage in the preparing, cooking, presenting, and tasting of food and drink has usually a symbolic ceremonial role as part of a rite of conviviality or hospitality. The kinds of dishes presented, the order in which they are served, the vessels and utensils in which they are kept and with which they are eaten, the table used and its covering—all this and more is of great symbolic significance. In many societies all over the world such traditions of culinary culture are still maintained. But now they are everywhere under increasing challenge from the forces of global culture.

The preprepared and fast food industries are subjecting all local culinary practices to a process that George Ritzer has called McDonaldization, after the well-known chain of restaurants where it was first perfected. As Ritzer explains, this involves the rationalization and routinization of all aspects of culinary practice.[8] It is in nearly all respects the opposite of traditional culinary culture. As far as possible everything is mechanized and subject to technological controls that dispense with and eliminate nearly all human intervention or discretion. The food is preplanned and preprepared with scientific precision on an assembly-line basis, and delivered from a central dispensary to all the outlets where it is cooked in a standard way. This is done by unskilled and poorly paid young people who simply follow set procedures, timed to the second. What results from this is a uniform product without variation that is almost homogeneous throughout the world. Hence the customer is given little choice in ordering a meal. Techniques of human management and crowd control process each customer down a sequential route that is also unvarying. Yet, surprisingly, this suits masses of people who prefer to eat up and fill up rather than linger over a traditional meal.

In various degrees of McDonaldization, all the major culinary specialties of the world are now circulating in all major cities. One can eat French cuisine in Peking and Chinese in Paris, Japanese in New York and American in Tokyo, and so on. Every major city features all the world's culinary cultures. This has now become an indispensable feature of global culture. It attests to its apparent multiculturalism and the broadmindedness of all who share in it. And it is so easy to do so for it involves nothing but pure consumption. By consuming all manner of foods, it seems that one can become all manner of things. *Man ist was man isst* (one is what one eats) has become the implicit motto of the consumers of global culinary culture.

The two sets of examples of techniques so far discussed, sporting and culinary, by no means exhaust all of global culture, but they are paradigmatic instances of it. Many other cultural activities model themselves on these two types and mimic their features. These might be called processes of the sportification and culinarization of culture, which occur in many other cultural fields. The two can occur separately or in conjunction with each other, for they are not mutually exclusive. Any cultural activity whatever can be transformed to some degree in either or both of these directions at once.

A cultural activity is sportified when it is redesigned so as to be conducted in the form of a competitive contest that will result in winners and losers. This usually calls for precise rules as to what kind of thing or person is eligible to enter the competition, what is to count as an achievement or qualitative mark, and how this is to be assessed. Such competitive rules have been established in many cultural fields, so that there is hardly a cultural activity that is now not staged as a race or contest. There are pop song contests, classical music performance competitions, prizes for the so-called best in every genre of fiction, and all kinds of awards for films. The most popular are those that are televised, and among these beauty contests top the ratings charts. There are a number of different ways of determining winners, either through audience choices or voting (which is the democratic process), or through the authoritative verdict of a selected jury or a few judges who might or might not be publicly identified.

It is not only the "pop" arts with a mass following that have undergone a sportification process; this has been happening in the elite arts as well. Classical music has already gone a long way in this direction. Concerts are now regularly staged in the same way as sporting fixtures. Perhaps the most blatant recent example of this is the highly popular three tenors series of concerts held in stadiums all over the world before football-size crowds and telecast to hundreds of millions more. Opera performances before even larger crowds are now quite common, made possible by the new technologies of sound amplification. The musical stars of these show business galas promote their careers in much the same way as sporting stars. In fact, many of them are managed by the same agencies as the sports-people. The largest of these is the International Management Group run by the sporting entrepreneur Marc McCormack who, as Lebrecht puts it ironically, "had rightly identified an affinity between classical music and championship sport."[9] For budding beginners on their way to musical stardom there is the *gradus-ad-parnassum* of the graded steeplechase race through an array of musical competitions held in various parts of the world. Those who compete have had to train since early childhood, much like swimmers and tennis prodigies. For those who come first often enough, the rewards are prodigious. For those who don't make it there is no second chance; the great majority are lost.

As we have already previously indicated, there is a clear commercial purpose in this competitive system, especially for the arts. It is a technique for predetermining the market response. Once a winner in a given competition is declared, usually as the recipient of the so-and-so prize or award, maximum publicity in all the media is orchestrated to make this fact as widely known and celebrated as possible; then the public is solicited and cajoled to buy the particular things or to support the persons or groups who have come out on top. In this way a good start is made in initiating a self-boosting process that will lead to best sellers, hit records, sell-out programs, or future stars. The competition outcome serves to forestall people having to exercise their own judgment and make their own selections. They are told definitively which is the best and all they have to do is to go along with it and patronize or buy the things recommended.

As might be expected, there are very serious shortcomings in this system. Since so much hangs on the results of such competitions, it follows inevitably that every effort will be made by the contestants and other interested parties to bend the outcome in their own favor. Invariably, therefore, many such verdicts become suborned and corrupted in all kinds of ways. Some artistic competitions are rigged from the start, much like wrestling matches. And even if the process of picking winners is fair and above board, it still has unfortunate consequences. For, as in sporting contests, it is the winner and a few place getters who get all the rewards; all the other numerous contenders receive nothing and are declared losers. Inevitably they are consigned to oblivion. As in sport and business, a winners-take-all mentality begins to predominate in the arts. Those who cannot become winners soon enough—who mature more slowly and steadily or who have something original to offer that cannot be immediately appreciated—all such fall by the wayside and cannot survive. Everything goes to the very few who are impressive and showy or uncaring and unscrupulous enough to get in quickly and make an early hit. These become the future stars who eventually outshine everybody else and put all others in the shade.

Next to sportification, culinary culture is the other paradigmatic instance of all cultural consumption. On this model all cultural activities and goods become matters of taste that call for no moral or aesthetic judgment or for the connoisseurship, sensitivities, and education necessary to exercise such judgment. The good is what anyone likes—which sounds like a prescription for eccentric individualism ("I know what I like and let nobody tell me otherwise"), but in actual practice becomes a recipe for gross conformism ("I like what everybody else likes"). There are, of course, tried and tested ways of making sure that people go along with what they are supposed to like. Advertising and other modes of publicity are among the foremost of these methods, which are really techniques for the molding of taste and behavior.

Taste expresses itself not only in eating and drinking but also in seeing and hearing. Thus people develop a taste for certain kind of shows or spectacles—feasts for the eyes. The more sumptuous the show the more it approximates to the model of culinary culture. Musicals are among the few live stage shows left because they are the most spectacular. And many other kinds of cultural activities have also survived because they have been reduced to spectacles. Television has played a major role in this. Thus, for example, televised performances of symphony orchestras are less heard as musical concerts than watched as spectacles of group discipline—serried ranks of musicians playing under the strict baton and stern gaze of a conductor, whose expressive antics on the podium have become more interesting to see than to hear the music produced. In any case, a public long accustomed to hearing music merely as background accompaniment to films has habituated itself to switching off from the sound so that they can concentrate on the action.

The use of music in a purely culinary way to create a pleasant atmosphere or lend aural spice to an occasion is also now commonplace. The sounds so used are not really heard as music but as sound effects of an extended kind. Musak is, of course, the epitome of such interior soundscapes. But other kinds of music can also be used in the same way. Some of the works of the baroque masters, not excluding Bach and Vivaldi, lend themselves well to this purpose. There is contemporary school of "minimalist" composers who have even developed a style that is the sound equivalent of pleasing wallpaper—repetitive patterns that are always changing but always the same.

Both these models, the sporting and the culinary, reflect a culture that is centered on the body and its senses. But this is not really a sybaritic culture addicted to pleasure, but rather an achievement-oriented one intent on performance. The body is one's main tool and chief asset in a competitive marketplace struggle, so it must be kept in as fit and healthy a state as possible to withstand the rigors of work and leisure. For this purpose the ideal of sport and exercise is maintained, though practiced to a much lesser extent.

For purposes of conspicuous relaxation the ideal of taste refinement is indulged in and exercised on activities of consumption, mainly of expensive food and drink. For those who can afford it, wine tasting is a favorite sensual pastime. Other types of consumption are directed to enhancing the appearance of the body. It must be made to look as youthful and attractive as possible, regardless of its real age, so as to advertise oneself to those one wishes to impress or seduce. At the same time the body must be controlled through the senses so as to be in the required tone and mood for the activities one wishes to undertake. It is to be treated as the well-pampered *Klavier* on whose sensory keyboard all of life's melodies must be sounded.

To bring the body to its optimal sensory state a host of techniques have been devised and deployed. A considerable part of global culture is devoted to this purpose alone. The mass publishing industry devotes a large proportion of its production to bodily care of all kind. These are the "how to" manuals: how to gain weight or lose it, how to keep fit, how to be healthy and vigorous, how to have satisfactory sex, how to stop smoking, how to improve one's looks or anything else in one's physical appearance, and so on. Many of these are self-help books that teach self-applied techniques. Such books are usually on top of the best-seller lists in nonfiction. Specialized lines on sexual or bodybuilding techniques cater to the needs of people involved in pornographic or gymnastic activities that extend beyond reading into private rituals or organized practices of a semi-cultic kind. There are whole subcultures to which such activities constitute a raison d'être. These, too, have now assumed a global dimension.

The technification of the body has now gone a long way and extends way beyond ordinary gratification or exercise. It now involves a whole panoply of bodily controls, among which therapeutic means are in the forefront. Diet regimens, food fads, drugs, and other supplements—taken both under medical supervision and self-prescribed—are now routinely employed to put oneself into the right bodily state. There are specific means for every such purpose, such as assuaging pain or calming nerves or focusing attention or attaining euphoria. Drug culture, both the licit and illicit, is the overt manifestation of a general preoccupation with the body that in many cases turns into an obsession. The narcissistic aspect of all this has, of course, not escaped psychoanalytically minded commentators such as Philip Rieff and Christopher Lasch.

Therapeutic techniques for bodily control merge on a continuum into those for mind control. The medical pharmacopoeia hardly distinguishes between them, especially since the arrival of the new generation of mood changing drugs, such as Prozac and its successors. But there are also numerous mind bending and mind altering techniques that do not rely on drugs but on various types of behavioral therapies and talking cures deriving from all kinds of psychiatries and psychologies. Resort to these quasi-scientific therapeutic methods has taken on a mass dimension and become part of ordinary life activities for a significant proportion of the population, including children. Thus in line with the previously referred to authors, we can now speak of a therapeutic culture which is a key aspect of global culture at least in the more affluent societies, for the poorer ones cannot as yet afford such privileged special treatments.

However, in all societies there are also available cheaper techniques for self-help of a more contemplative kind, various types of spiritual exercises that people can practice mostly without professional assistance. These usually have a religious provenance but are now mostly utilized outside their original context and deprived of any transcendent meaning. Many of them rely on autosuggestion, which in extreme cases can amount to self-hypnosis. Self-boosting of the "power-of-positive-thinking" kind has long been a feature of popular lore in many Protestant societies and has provided a market for many best sellers, such as those of Dale Carnegie and Norman Vincent Peale. However, of late the main sources of "spiritual healing" have been the various Eastern religions. Derivatives of Buddhism, especially Zen, of Hinduism, especially Krishnaism, and various concocted sects, such as the Moonies, have all provided techniques of meditation and other "mind cures." Such techniques are now an integral part of the global culture for they are prominent in many societies all over the world. They demonstrate how easy it is for techniques to pass over cultural boundaries, since even the most recherché of spiritual exercises—those that belong to mystical and other arcane religious traditions—can be easily appropriated anywhere else provided they are reduced to techniques and their original spiritual meaning is stripped away. The history of yoga in the West illustrates this very clearly.

Hatha yoga arrived in the West in the early years of the twentieth century, together with all the other Hinduizing trends, such as the theosophy of Madame Blavatsky. But it was not until much later, some time after the Second World War, that the cult of yoga began to be promoted as an autonomous exercise quite apart from religion, in the same way as karate, judo, and other Eastern physical practices. In its religious context the original aim of yoga was far from being mere bodily exercise or relaxation technique; it was intended as a means to attaining the experience of the divine through a state of contemplative bliss achieved by bodily practices, such as breath control, and through disciplines of inner concentration in order to empty out consciousness of all content. Some attempt was made by Hindu swamis during the countercultural era of the 1960s and 1970s to bring yoga back to some of its spiritual roots. But that did not take hold among

Western youth and eventually was abandoned. Now yoga is practiced in one form or another by up to twelve million people in America alone. As a result, it is being Americanized in all respects. It is becoming organized as a kind of popular mass movement with national conferences of its leadership and a publication, *Yoga Journal*, to keep everyone abreast of the latest developments. In this technified and organized form yoga is being exported to the rest of the world and is bound to become an integral part of global culture.

That America should be acting as the driving force and dynamo of technification for the whole world is only to be expected, given its penchant for know-how, effectiveness, and pragmatism. Right from the start of its history America has been the proving ground and storehouse of a variety of techniques touching on all aspects of life. Its utopian religious movements pioneered all kinds of new methods in fields ranging from social controls to mass intoxication. Its homespun inventors developed just about every available labor-saving device. Its technologists have only carried on from this native tradition to bigger and better machines. Its organizers initiated nearly all the known techniques for controlling social bodies, influencing mass opinion, eliciting a mass response, and so on. Public relations and marketing techniques, including all the methods of advertising, were usually first practiced in America. Techniques for managing small groups of all kinds were also extremely well developed there. In short, there is hardly a technical method that has not been taken further in America than anywhere else, with the possible exception of such things as methods of torture or brainwashing, which Americans are constitutionally precluded from practicing, and where, consequently, others have excelled them.

Perhaps the most successful and widespread of all American devised techniques are those of management. These are designed to achieve the business organizational goals of efficiency and productivity through a well-adjusted workforce. Numerous supposedly "scientific" methods of management were pioneered in America over the past century, and they have followed each other almost like changing fashions. The earliest were the Taylorist time-and-motion studies approaches instituted to such good effect by Henry Ford and imitated in factories all over the world, including Soviet Russia. Partly to counteract these mechanical work-efficiency driven methods there arose human-relations techniques that emphasized motivation and group cooperation. The quality-control movement, first devised by W. Edwards Deming, is one of the latest management techniques, though that has been perfected in Japan rather than America. The success of these approaches is undeniable, though whether this is due to "science" or to "magic," as Stivers maintains, is arguable. According to Stivers, "[T]he magic of human relations management is similar to that of therapy. Both function as placebos."[10] It is possible to take issue with this view, even allowing for Stivers's broad definition of "magic," by arguing that there is an empirically rational basis to both management and therapy techniques, where as there is only an irrational symbolic basis to traditional forms of magic. Modern techniques are self-correcting at least to some degree, whereas magical ones are not. But this is a debate that cannot be pursued further in this context.

The latest stage of technification is also being perfected in America and from there exported to the rest of the world—automation that takes the form of self-service. As more and more activities are automated, so people are increasingly obliged to serve themselves. Every service or function that previously required people to engage or interact with each other in some way or other in order to accomplish something is being transformed into a self-service system requiring no human contact whatsoever. Instead of buying something from someone, people are now constrained to serve themselves by selecting, ordering, paying, and receiving whatever it is they are purchasing through an automatic process in which they only operate on machines. Instead of dealing with a bank-teller they now transact their business with an automat. Instead of speaking to someone to make an inquiry over the telephone they now punch buttons and listen to a recorded message. And so it goes on, until everything becomes a mechanical matter of automation with no human engagement whatever. Every new advance in self-service, which only deepens the process of technification, is usually hailed as another step in personal liberation, freeing one from dependence on other people. But at the same time everybody's dependence on the system of technics as a whole inexorably increases. People are only made aware of this when there is a serious breakdown. But until then they are happy to serve themselves, for self-service frequently amounts to self-gratification.

The most advanced form of automation is where human agency is completely eliminated. With the aid of computer-operated systems this is now achievable to a considerable extent in many kinds of activities. By means of so-called expert systems it is now possible to automate many forms of work that previously relied on learned skills, experience, and the constant exercise of judgment. As is well known, a general process of de-skilling is now taking place throughout the workforce as types of jobs that used to depend on human talents no longer do so as the work becomes formalized, systematized, and eventually automated. Human qualities, such as practical knowledge, ingenuity, adaptability, and others, are devalued, for they are no longer of any use. Those who can operate the formalized techniques, the systems analysts and computer programmers, are the ones left to run the machinery. In general, the specific, detailed, individual, and other such context-dependent factors are discounted in favor of the abstract, universal, and impersonal. This, too, is a kind of microcosm of the global displacing the local.

The effects of automation on human relations, both in the workplace and in society in general, are by now well documented. Workers have a different sense of themselves and each other in an automated work environment. Richard Sennett speaks of a "corrosion of character" that takes place under these circumstances and illustrates this with examples drawn from many lines of work, including such seemingly unlikely things as "computerized baking." He shows that the workers in automated bakeries are no longer bakers in the old sense because they do not know how to bake: "now the bakers make no physical contact with the materials or the loaves of bread, monitoring the entire process via on-screen icons . . . few bakers actually see the loaves of bread they make . . . bread has become a screen representation."[11] These surrogate bakers no longer derive any satisfaction from their work and so it ceases to provide meaning to their lives. They no longer see each other as fellow workers engaged on a joint and mutually supporting enterprise. Consequently both the ethos and ethics of work is corrupted to the point where one can speak of a "corrosion of character."

The overall effect of automation is a gradual fraying and eventual unraveling of the fabric of human relations. People do not encounter each other anymore in ordinary everyday situations where they need to get along by saying the right things, making the familiar faces, and keeping each other in eye contact. Such personal encounters are not always pleasant for they can lead to misunderstandings, arguments, quarrels, and even fights, but at least they ensure that people engage with each other. An automated self-service and work ambience is one where people are isolated and alienated from each other. Eventually they are unable to relate even when they desire to do so for they become insensitive to each other or to the difference between people and machines. They become shut in their own loneliness.

Technification in this automated form amounts to dehumanization. In our technical civilization where there is a technique for everything—for breaking hearts as well mending broken hearts, for swelling heads as well as shrinking them, for dirtying minds as well as brainwashing—it seems as if the complete triumph of technics is at hand with all the perverse consequences that this entails. Global culture is certainly tending to this end result. Whether it succeeds in achieving it depends largely on countervailing forces, those relying on the still vital resources of local culture. In opposition to technics they must muster the symbolic meanings and values of representation and ethos. So it is to these that we turn next.

C. TECHNIFICATION OF REPRESENTATION

Representation in our culture is not immune to the trends of technification that are so dominant. Like everything else, it becomes distorted in the direction of technique and drifts ever further away from its symbolic moorings. Hence, the systems of representation in global culture are not like those of the traditional local cultures. The inroads of technics are transforming representations into something quite other, into images and models that are no longer representations in the old sense. The difference between them requires a little theoretical explanation.

Images and models need not be representations, even though they also in some sense reproduce reality. A representation is a symbolic rendering of some aspect of reality; an image or model is in itself merely a simulacrum or mechanical copy of that reality. Images produced by mere mechanical mimesis, such as photographs, cinema and television films, and computer-generated pictures, reproduce the mere visual appearance of things. There is an even older way of producing analogous images by handicraft means, such as making a picture using paint or scenic decor or by other such material devices. The material out of which an image is constituted or the activity by means of which this effect is achieved is irrelevant to its nature. And the same holds true for realistic models that are also mere copies of things. The wax figures in Madame Tussaud's in London are models of this kind—they are not representations such as a sculptor might create.

In general, representations differ from images in the way they convey symbolic meaning and significance. However, this difference is a matter of degree, for the one thing can be in some respects like an image and in others like a representation. It is also a matter of how something is seen, taken, or interpreted by those who look at or consider it, for what some people treat as a mere image others can take as also a representation. What is at issue is whether the thing in question is seen naturalistically, in the way we ordinarily look at and recognize things in our vicinity, or whether it is in some sense interpreted symbolically by reference to some cultural system of meaning, such as a scheme of values, ideas, beliefs, pictorial conventions, or whatever. Images are natural in the sense that any human being from whatever society or cultural background can see them correctly. Representations, by contrast, are cultural in that they need to be interpreted or "read" by reference to a symbolic system that only those with the relevant cultural background will possess. This is a crucial distinction that many art critics and philosophers, such as most notably the late Ernst Gombrich, have simply not understood and have most egregiously confused with very unfortunate consequences for decades of ongoing debate in this field.[12]

A photograph is usually seen purely as an image, in which case almost everyone will be able to recognize the things shown in it (e.g., that a number of men are sitting round a table). But it can also be "seen," in the sense of understood and interpreted, as a representation, in which case only those in the cultural know will be able to specify what it depicts (e.g., that it is a historic occasion when such-and-such a treaty was enacted by famous people at a designated location, etc.). The same holds true for highly realistic paintings, which can also be seen as mere images, and as such they are in principle no different from those resulting from mechanical mimesis. However, they can be, and usually must be, also treated as representations. Figurative paintings that are not realistic—and this, too, is a matter of degree depending on the style—cannot be seen as images and must inevitably be taken as representations.

As there are no sharp demarcations separating images from representations, since it is always a matter of degree and depends on the viewer's ability, disposition, and attitude, it is readily apparent how it is possible for representations gradually to be displaced by images. This has been occurring in modern society as a historical process produced by ever-increasing technification. Technification has gradually pushed representations in our culture away from symbolic meaning and value toward naturalistic simulacra. The image or model that simply and crudely re-presents reality by duplicating it takes the place of everything symbolic that represents it.

Images of all kinds have prominence in global culture and the role of representations has become recessive. Their cultural uses tend to be very different. Images are used to present things that are immediate, that are well known and close at hand, those that can achieve an impact and provoke a reaction merely by being exhibited and confronting people, especially when they least expect it. Thus advertising almost invariably relies on images; hence the development of ever-newer technologies to generate new kinds of images is always a boon to the advertisers. It is logical that advertising should work with images because imagery reflects the viewers back to themselves and shows them how they might wish to appear and so gives them a flattering version of themselves. The advertisement acts as a wish-fulfillment mirror.

All the main media of global culture evince in their imagery this mirror or echo effect of improved reflection. Viewers take great delight in seeing themselves and their ordinary lives reflected back to them through the agency of an enhancing technical medium. Hence the great emphasis on quotidian contemporary realities in television and cinema, and even in newspapers insofar as this is possible in print. So-called reality TV takes this to its ultimate extreme in presenting the daily goings-on of a chosen group of people exposed to the fascinated stares and voyeuristic gazes of masses of others, who, for all that it matters, might as well be watching themselves. Many scripted shows, especially the "soaps," offer no great advance on this format.

What this indicates is that global culture is producing a generation of people who are narcissistically obsessed with themselves. This matches evidence from other sources, such as the preoccupation with the body that we examined previously. The presentation of a personal appearance through clothes, accessories, and other consumer durables is another aspect of self-preoccupation. As colloquial terminology has it, this, too, is called creating an "image." The media are preeminent in this kind of image making, especially where it concerns politicians.

The obverse facet of this culture of the image is an inability to comprehend or deal with representations of any complexity or depth. Only the very simplest of representations can circulate in global culture. These are such as are narrowly focused on the present, because to represent the past requires more developed symbolic means. Consequently, as we shall show, the past is being lost and time stands still in a specious present with no temporal background.

Working with images to construct so-called media "texts" follows quite different principles to working with representations. The methods of montage first developed by the masters of the silent cinema, above all by D. W. Griffith and Sergei Eisenstein, are the basic techniques that have since been extended to all kinds of image "text" production. These techniques are easy to apply given the wealth of modern technological apparatus. It is no longer a matter of simple cutting and splicing, as it used to be in the early days of the cinema; now all kinds of montage effects can be achieved through computer programming. Every variety of superposition and manipulation of the image, including all its sound components, can now be achieved in the studio. Digitalization will open up even newer possibilities in this regard, for everything will be translatable into the same basic level of "information" and so alterable at will.

Montage is a technique that can also be used in conjunction with the more traditional forms of representation. The art of the cinema at its best is one such optimal combination of image and sound montage together with more symbolic representational means, such as narration, story telling, dramatic enactment, and meaningful pictorial composition. Cinema is a composite art, a *Gessamtkunstwerk*, which freely draws its resources from all artistic quarters. When it succeeds, at its very best, it achieves a unique collocation and synthesis of all its chosen components. But this is the case only when the great directors, writers, actors, and cinematographers pool their resources to best advantage, which is a very rare occurrence. Mostly filmmaking proceeds on a quasi-assembly-line basis. This is even more so the case with the production of advertisements, which clearly reveals just how far technification has ensued in the construction of such "texts."

An advertisement has to be planned on the basis of extended market research involving all kinds of information-gathering techniques, such as sampling, polling, questionnaires, and other product research. Utilizing this knowledge advertising executives plan a strategy of what kind of advertisements are to be shown in what media outlets over what period of time. It is at this point that the so-called "creative" people are called in to develop the "concept," that is, to write the script and compose catchphrases and slogans. Then the scenic designers and special effects people devise the scenario and plan the shots to be taken. Following their directions the actors and models strut their paces and the cameras roll. Finally, the cutting and editing takes place to achieve the right montage. The whole advertisement is a team effort involving many experts deploying their specialized techniques in conjunction with each other.

An advertisement is not a representation in the way that a panegyric or eulogy in praise of someone or something can be. It is a kind of complex image or at best a quasi representation of the product being advertised. It is intended to achieve an effect, to make people do or buy something. It is not a discourse in favor of something such as still takes place in courts of law, debates, or political meetings. The advertisement does not argue its case, it insinuates and suggests. We are told that a picture is worth a thousand words, but even this boast underrates the efficacy of the picture, for what it can sometimes achieve cannot be equaled by any number of words. Words pale in comparison with a vivid image. Both advertisers and propagandists have long been aware of this fact and have relied on it with startling effectiveness.

The image as an advertisement or a propaganda piece works beneath the censoring guard of conscious thought and sometimes even subliminally beneath the watchful eye of aware perception. It overwhelms by innuendo. It appeals to hidden, barely acknowledged desires, fears, and dreams. It hints at possibilities that are not realizable in ordinary life. It wards off potential criticism from the less gullible by sending itself up through a self-mocking and knowing tone. It appeals to the mutually acknowledged cynicism of advertisers and viewers. By such means it relaxes their guard in order to induce a willing suspension of disbelief while it achieves its intended effect. The seduction game between advertisers and viewers is played at ever-higher levels of sophistication, employing a barrage of changing strategies that usually succeed, for otherwise the funding would have dried up already.

Within their own terms advertisements cannot be criticized or faulted. Unlike representations, they cannot be deemed true or false. The typical claim that a product is better, brighter, cleaner, leaner, and so on cannot be refuted for these comparative terms make no comparisons with anything else. The norms of logical discourse do not apply. Advertisements do not lie because they are incapable of telling the truth. Often they merely present an image and do not make any explicit statement. Stivers quotes Daniel Boorstin to this effect: "[A]n image is a means that neither represents truth nor reality. It is an attempt to manufacture a self-fulfilling prophecy, that is, a false definition that leads one to act as if it were true, thereby making it come true."[13]

Advertising is the model for all global culture, its most refined and frequently costliest product. It has often been remarked that more effort and talent goes into the advertisements than into the programs that carry them. These programs are made much in the same way as the advertisements, following the same kinds of technified routines and employing similar teams of specialists. Programs follow a formula that is frequently devised just like a cooking recipe: so much stock adventure, a pinch of violence, a dollop of luscious creamy sex, a leavening of comedy, some sugary sentiment, some bitters for tartness, the spice of mystery, and so on to complete the farrago. But a formula cannot just be concocted, it requires an "idea," "concept," or "theme," and for that someone with some imagination is called for. That is the only point at which techniques by themselves are not adequate. But once the formula has been arrived at, it can be endlessly repeated or for as long as the ratings or attendance figures warrant it.

The greater the level of technification, the more does the representational content recede. Under intense technification even the formula is further reduced to a mere format, a stereotypical cliché. Many types of genre shows are now mostly presented in this form. Such shows are very suitable for global distribution because they require only minimal knowledge or understanding. Cultural differences hardly matter. Who now fails to grasp the bare conventions of a murder mystery, Western, sitcom, sex comedy, or soap?

Technification in all the arts has gone a long way, perhaps nowhere more so than in pop music. Producing a musical piece begins with the composition by a tunesmith of a theme or melody that must conform to a simple predetermined form, allowing for very little variation. This is followed by its arrangement, orchestration, and scoring carried out by other specialists. The performance itself is recorded by sound engineers who modulate and modify the raw material of sound into a finished product. The major recording companies are constantly at work to technify these stages still further, including the composition process itself, which they are hoping to automate and carry out by computer. Since this whole musical format is so reduced, limited, and predictable, it is well possible that in time they will succeed.

All the other arts are in lesser though analogous stages of technification. The symbolic representational element is becoming ever more attenuated. The most popular form of stage spectacle at present is the show, such as a musical or rock concert, and this is quite different in form and content to any theatrical representation. It does not involve acting so much as making an appearance, the more glamorous or outrageous the better. Success in show business depends in the first place on stars, in the second on spectacle in scenery and staging in general—namely, on techniques of production rather than on the meaning of what is produced. The more technical ingenuity expended, itself a function of the money spent, the more pleasing or thrilling the effects and consequently the more startling the show. Shows of this kind, above all musicals, fill nearly all the stages in New York, London, and many other capital cities. Only the official opera houses and out of the way theaters are left for any other performances.

The absence of regular theater in cultural life is a visible symptom of the disappearance of the theatrical aspects from ordinary life itself. As life has become more routinized and functionally segregated according to jobs, consumer habits, educational certificates, and leisure pursuits, so the range of social representations has become simplified and formalized. The roles people can enact have become standardized. They are either those of everyday working activities, which are extremely conformist, or those of leisure-time escapes, which might be as bizarre, eccentric, or flamboyant as one chooses. On holidays one can indulge in whatever escapades one likes. A consistent character part is no longer required.

The aim of self-presentation is not to express ones character but to display an "image." Such image making has become the main preoccupation of all people who want to succeed, especially in those professions, such as politics, where success depends on popularity. As Stivers puts it, "[I]mages are a major component of style—physical appearance and life-style—in a consumer directed society. Personal style is less an expression of character than of surface appearance."[14] A manifestation of this emphasis on the image in social relations is the loss of theatricality in ordinary life. The comedy of social life now runs shallow and thin. People are unable to assume roles of any sophistication or enter into really dramatic relations with each other.

The ceremonial activities of ordinary life have been much simplified, if they have not disappeared altogether. Weddings, funerals, births, and birthdays are still celebrated, but in a vestigial way. They are losing their meaning because the collective representations of religion and myth on which they depend are either not credited or not invoked at all. But this does not mean that superstitions have declined; to the contrary, like mushrooms in the dark, all kinds of irrational beliefs are now sprouting anew in the shadowy corners of everyday life. Astrology, alchemy, prognostications of all kinds, and whatever else in this vein have all revived as part of the new age lore. The prevalence and predominance of scientific representations of reality in public life coexists with the parallel prominence of antiscientific beliefs and practices. Often the very same people resort to both at once.

Perhaps the most far-reaching and pernicious effect of the transition from a culture of representation to one of the image or simulacrum is the loss of the past. As we have already noted in passing, the past is being eroded through the multiple workings of global culture, and the most salient and damaging consequences result from this transformation of symbolic meaning away from representation. For, by definition, the past is that which is no longer present and can usually only be made present through representational means. This is particularly true of the historical past, that which cannot be retained by memory alone.

An awareness of the historical past is mediated by three types of representations: those of myth and ritual; those of transmitted narratives, memorials, and commemorative ceremonies; and those of historical writings, documents, works of literature, and other such texts. All of these three types of representations are now being threatened by the inroads of technification. Techniques in themselves cannot convey the past because they cannot carry the requisite symbolic content. No number of images produced by mechanical mimesis can say anything about the past; at best they can illustrate a historical narrative, but cannot take its place. An old photograph of a person cannot express who that was, on what occasion it was taken, and what it is about its content that is significant. The photograph can act as a representation of the past only when it is "read" appropriately by someone who already understands the past context in which it was made.

The past exists as a symbolic, not a technical matter. Hence techniques that substitute for representations are making the past recede. Reliance on them in teaching reduces the capacity of students to know the past. As a result, they begin to live in a penumbra of an instantaneous and permanent present, a *nunc stans* that has no historical background. Most evident symptoms of this are apparent in all the schools and universities of the world where history is becoming a lost subject, if not yet a lost cause.

Myths, folklore, and ritual activities, which were until recently present in all local cultures, are now disappearing with the onset of global culture. They are being displaced by the animations of Disney and other such entertainment brand-name products. Children's games, rhymes, and seasonal festivities are all going the way of Halloween—a commercialized charade now current throughout the world. The past as tradition in general is suffering a similar fate. Collective representations of national traditions, which for good and ill shaped the imagination of generations past, are now becoming attenuated together with the nationalism they promoted. It is not necessary to bewail the loss of nationalism to regret the rejection of a national past and the cultural identity that it fosters. Whatever might be the future fate of nations and states, their cultural heritage should not be lightly abandoned.

Even critical history, whose main purpose has been to discredit myths and partisan national traditions, is now itself being discredited. Students are no longer willing to study it. The mocking taunt that it mainly concerns "dead white males" hides behind its apparent antiracist sneer an unwillingness to understand the past in any terms whatever. It is a foreign land peopled with foreigners speaking foreign tongues to those who have been bought up solely on global culture: all those who have been raised on nothing but computer games, technical manuals, science fiction, crime fiction, MTV, and rock-and-roll. Such people are fixated in a narrow, parochial present from which their minds cannot escape. Even something set in a distant past epoch must look and sound as if it is happening right now. A comic strip, the Flintstones, makes a cynical joke of this by projecting a modern suburban family back to the Stone Age. Those who forget the past are unable to distinguish it from the present.

For such people it is not only cultural time but also cultural space that ceases to have much reality. The cultural geography of foreign places, where one travels to experience something different to one's own land, is no longer felt to be necessary or desirable. Foreigners appear as aliens, almost as if they were people from another planet, and the difference between Mongolians and Martians is none too clear. People who have no conception of cultural differences are not too intent on cultural diversity either. Hence it matters little to them that the term "one world" assumes the far from benign connotation of a "uniform world."

The creation of one world is a worthy and perhaps necessary political goal, one enshrined in the very constitution of the United Nations. The problem is how to prevent political globalization in this sense also becoming cultural globalization. Part of the answer lies in preserving representative political institutions through which people can determine their specific cultural destiny. Whether these institutions will continue to be based on national states or on some other units of integration is of lesser importance to the more vital issue that through them people should be able to maintain their cultural integrity. Representative arrangements and institutions, whether democratically based or following some other principles of collective representation, are, therefore, of great cultural relevance.

Representation in the political sense is also now being undermined by techniques for controlling mass behavior. Such techniques permit the representatives to control the represented rather than the other way round, as it is democratically supposed to be. Those who claim to represent the people, and derive the legitimation for their authority in this way, have developed all kinds of ways of keeping themselves in power with what appears to be the consent of the electors. But frequently the voters are given little choice but to acclaim one or another contender for office where both are selected as candidates through a Byzantine process of intrigue, collusion, and complicity in secret party conclaves.

The first and foremost technique for organizing a mass electorate already emerged in Europe toward the end of the nineteenth century with the rise of the mass-party "machine." The purpose of this was to capture and hold the unthinking loyalty of a mass following and bring it out on Election Day to cast the right votes. In America, quite different Tammany Hall-type techniques of voter control were developed for the same purpose at about the same time.

This was also the time of the rise of the mass media, beginning with the press. As a result, the techniques of political propaganda were greatly improved and amplified. This became particularly crucial for political campaigns at election periods. Since then the nexus between the media and politics has drawn even closer. At a later period radio also lent its voice to the propaganda messages. This was particularly crucial in the rise of the mass totalitarian parties in Europe—both the Bolsheviks and Nazis used it to great effect—but it was also employed in the democracies. Later still, television brought about a quantum leap to an even higher level of media politics, for it permitted the cultivation of "image" politicians such as had never been seen before.

In politics, as elsewhere, the "image" displaces representation. Image making in politics is a technique closely allied to the techniques of propaganda and advertising. It is frequently undertaken by the same experts working in the same ways. Surveys, akin to those of marketing, are employed to determine what are popular and unpopular policies; campaign strategies in all their detailed particulars are tested by polling and sampling for their effectiveness; the candidate becomes an actor coached in demeanor and manner; speeches are specially scripted by expert speechwriters; prepared statements, witticisms, and jokes are learned and made to appear as impromptu utterances and bons mots; the candidate is instructed on how to address the press and especially the cameras, when to appear and with whom; and so on for the other countless ploys. In this way, through the agency of the media, the electors vote for an "image" rather than a representative who stands for them on the basis of a policy. The "image" politician, once elected, is committed to nothing and can do whatever is most opportune—until the next election.

In every state there is now a crisis of representation brought about by these techniques of voter control. Office falls into the hands of those who can afford the financial expenditures required to fund the media, the spin doctors, the speechwriters, the pollsters, the campaign managers, and all the other assorted experts necessary to win elections. The money must be sought by the candidates themselves from wealthy backers or the political party must solicit donations on their behalf. In either way, the candidates become beholden to those who pay, often business interests, sometimes also trade unions, most frequently private donors. As a result, this system approximates closer to elective oligarchy than it does to real democracy.

But even the small measure of genuine representation that is still there is not all that important in the overall political system. Authority, in its detailed particulars, is largely exercised through administration by nonelected officials who are bureaucratically organized. These cadres follow highly technified routines in decision making and implementation. They engage in expert procedures, which constitute not only their modus operandi but also their modus vivendi, for they rely on expertise as a legitimating justification. This expertise, supposedly impersonally based, is thought to be supremely rational and dependable because it only relies on scientific representations. But this is an illusion fostered by an uncritical belief in science.

In our present technological civilization, science is held to be the only source of rational and realistic representations. These are derived from theoretical explanations and models of the course of events in the natural world or of the course of history and social affairs in the human world. In the natural sciences they are most frequently mathematical equations, functional models, and abstract temporal sequences. In the human and social sciences they are evolutionary and historical progressions, social structures, economic "laws," statistical correlations, and all kinds of other measures of social reality. Where such representations are properly deployed in the hands of knowledgeable people and used with understanding—that is, with a clear awareness of their capacities and their limitations—then science works usefully and well. Culturally this can produce enlightenment where there was previously ignorance, superstition, or crude common sense. However, scientific representations are very easily misused. This happens when they are technified and transformed into rigorous formulae and rigid models; or they become a technical jargon offering pseudoexplanations for everything. In this debased form science lends itself to abuses that are conducive to mechanical dehumanization.

Applied science or engineering is particularly prone to technification, which in its proper place can be extremely useful, but extended to areas where it does not belong it is dubious and dangerous. When physical engineering becomes social engineering then it is already highly suspect, but when it goes even further and becomes "emotional engineering" then it is positively pernicious. Engineering can be another name for control and manipulation.

Science has a strong universalizing propensity because of the rationality of its representations and the ready access it provides to so many types of techniques that are universally applicable. Anyone, anywhere, can acquire the trappings of science and technology. These have become more or less identified with modernity, and through it they have become the driving force for the modernization of all societies and the constitution of "one world." Their great advantage is that they permit mutual understanding throughout all the regions of the world that transcends all cultural differences and other such divisions. At its best this trend is reflected institutionally in the United Nations and its specialized agencies. These operate on one or another vision of universality and utilize the rational representations and techniques suitable to this goal. And much has been achieved in this way. For the very first time in its long history, humanity has come together on this basis.

However, the dangers are less obvious, though ominous. Science has an ambivalent relation to culture, especially to cultural particularity or local culture and the sense of a unique historical or traditional past on which this is based. Through its universalizing, rationalizing, and technifying predispositions, science tends to erode cultural specificity and its correlative past. Such an outcome is not necessarily inherent in science as such, and one might, ideally speaking, consider it a misuse of science. Yet it is so prevalent as to be almost inevitable, part of the cultural cost of relying on science, and its technological adjuncts. Coping culturally with science and technology is as yet an unsolved problem for mankind.

In eroding local culture and its sense of the past science is only working against itself. For the loss of cultural meaning and its continuities with tradition brings on a hankering after other kinds of meaning, and these can frequently be of an irrational antiscientific kind. The antiscientific movements that now proliferate generally derive from cults and fundamentalist religions swelled by those looking for a simple faith to fill the cultural void of their lives. As a result, irrational beliefs, such as "creationism" and many others, are widespread even in such a scientifically advanced society as America. Any bizarre idea becomes believable once the barriers to credulity, built up through the culturally enlightening function of education and civility, become breached when a society is bereft of its local civilizing traditions. When that happens, then science by itself cannot counter the trend to irrationality, for the most superstitious creeds and unfounded beliefs can coexist quite happily together with the most advanced scientific knowledge—not only in the same society, but frequently also in the same mind. The nuclear physicist, rocket engineer, computer specialist, or economist who is a fundamentalist or cultist outside the narrow bounds of work is quite a familiar figure. Science exercises an enlightening function only in a culture where its fundamental values are upheld.

What matters is not scientific knowledge per se, but the whole ethos in which science is practiced. Outside a critical ethos of reasoned doubt science becomes nothing more than a congeries of working methods and techniques. Reliance on these techniques as a substitute for cultural enlightenment puts the very ethos in which science can flourish at risk. Science defeats itself once it technifies the ethos on which it depends for its meaning.

D. TECHNIFICATION OF THE ETHOS

In a scientific technological civilization the ethos is as much at risk of technification as is representation. The techniques involved in these two contrasting cultural spheres are very different, but the results are not dissimilar. In both cases, as Stivers puts it, "human technique destroys meaning."[15] With respect to the ethos, it destroys value as well. And a universal process of devaluation is what Nietzsche defined as nihilism.

Technique destroys value because it substitutes efficiency and success for all other kinds of ends. Technique aims mainly for control and power. This can be harmless where it is applied to objects, but where it involves human beings then it can irreparably damage the whole fabric of human relations on which society and the individuals within it depend. Such damage is now evident in the symptoms of social and psychological disruption that are so apparent in contemporary societies.

The techniques of the ethos are those dealing with the manipulation, regulation, and control of human behavior. Some of these involve instrumental means and make use of machines, but many do not—such are the various types of organizational, heuristic, and psychological techniques that are applied to groups as well as to individuals. Thus there are administrative, crowd-control, indoctrination, propaganda, and therapeutic techniques that require little in the way of technical apparatus. Where technology can be employed, it helps to make techniques all that much more effective. Even simple instruments, such as watches, help to impose many kinds of disciplinary techniques in the workplace, in offices, and in schools. High technologies open up new and hitherto undreamt of techniques, such as those of close monitoring and surveillance by electronic means. Other techniques of control make use of psychological means employing indoctrination backed up by drugs. The interaction between techniques and technology in respect of the ethos becomes ever tighter and more extensive.

A number of authors have already written at length on the different aspects of the technification of the ethos, among whom Lewis Mumford and Jacques Ellul are the most prominent. But they wrote before the full onset of globalization and the emergence of global culture. Both of these thinkers still allowed for a considerable degree of cultural diversity. In one of his late publications Ellul could still write that in a technological world "the greatest apparent diversity can reign provided it does not interfere with the basic fact! For, under the seeming pluralism of cultural forms, a universal and common system is crystallizing, identical in all parts of the world."[16] Now it is precisely this "apparent diversity" of a "pluralism of cultural forms" that is also disappearing. What has brought this about is the emergence of global culture made possible by new technologies whose full effects Ellul could not have taken into account. These technologies have had a great impact on the ethos of ordinary life; they have transformed our way of life on the level of everyday activities. Computing and information technologies now permit partial control, usually short of complete automation, of every kind of human activity. As we have already seen, many kinds of jobs have been thoroughly technified through computerization, and, as a result, workers become de-skilled and lose their practical competence. They no longer cooperate directly with each other in accomplishing task, but only indirectly through the machine process. Hence, they no longer personally relate to each other, which leads to all kinds of adverse effects on morale and worker solidarity.

Globalization has extended the technical impetus to every society on earth. To remain economically competitive and advanced every society has to subject its people to ever-higher levels of technification. Individuals who want to succeed under such circumstance must allow themselves to be placed under ever-tighter controls. These are mostly self-imposed and they turn people's everyday lives into a series of regulated procedures: so much time for care of the body, so much for sleep, so much for recreation, and the rest is all work. The current ethos is conducive to this kind of functionalist mentality.

Following Ellul, Stivers has further developed these insights into the technification of the ethos and studied their ethical effects as these have revealed themselves in America, the most technically advanced society in the world. He identifies two basic types of human controls, those of administration and those of psychology:

> Organizational technique refers to bureaucracy and related techniques of administration, such as human relations. Psychological technique includes advertising, propaganda, human and public relations, therapeutic techniques, and the plethora of "how-to" manuals for effective relationships (*Parental Effectiveness* and the like). Clearly there is an overlap here, for technique of administration draws upon the vast reservoir of psychological technique. Both kinds of non-material technique . . . have as their goal the *manipulation* and *control* of human beings. It is historically apparent that the more technology has been used to exploit the forces of nature, the more it was necessary to turn the same technological logic to the organization and control of the human environment.[17]

The ultimate consequence on the ethos of this overreliance on technique is that "much of the action that was traditionally motivated and regulated by ritual, manners, and social morality is now encapsulated in human technique."[18]

There are innumerable, almost patently obvious, instances of this transition from mores to technics. Walking on a footpath is still mainly governed by mores, whereas driving a car on a highway is largely a matter of technics. Pedestrians encounter and make way for each other according to the old rules of manners and forms of politeness exercised with some degree of tact; motorists must obey the inflexible code of the road and the compulsory mechanical guides, such as traffic lights, any infringement of which risks a heavy fine, if not a serious accident. The more people drive and do not walk, the more technics take over and they became less aware of public decorum and less able to follow it. Whereas until recently human interactions in public places were still subject to some customary codes allowing for all kinds of discretionary choices, now such encounters follow strict routines that are frequently mechanically regulated and permit no subjective adjustments; to break the rules is no longer an indiscretion but usually a punishable offense.

This simple example can be generalized to many other types of activities. Shopping used to involve a human interchange between a buyer and seller that would allow for all kinds of eventualities and invite conversation and intercourse, even if only to haggle and possibly to cheat or be cheated; now all this is being replaced with automated buying where the customer puts money into a machine and receives the standard item or helps herself to a range of goods which are automatically charged. The ordering, receiving, and eating of food at a fast-food establishment requires only the very minimum of human interaction. As a result of all these kinds of technifications human contact in general is being reduced to a minimum and the whole ethos governing the relations of people in public situations is gradually withering.

The ultimate triumph of technics in the ethos is automation, which we have already partially studied. The key to it is that if any pattern of activity can be reduced to a methodical series of discrete steps, then it can be automated. Once it is thus "methodized" then human discretion or guidance is no longer necessary, and, in fact, it comes to be considered as interference, for the process can proceed of its own accord. Even practical knowledge or know-how is no longer required for that, too, can be automated into one kind of expert system or another—that is, it can be reduced to "information" that can be coded and mechanically processed. Information in this sense has nothing to do with ordinary knowledge; it is a highly technified analogue that can be worked by computers.

The effect on human beings of such a high level of technification of the ethos is to render them all that much less human, for the qualities that distinguish a human way of proceeding from a machine system are deliberately diminished and repressed, and so become less relevant. Such a dehumanization has all kinds of repercussions on human beings. It isolates and alienates each individual by cutting off relations with others. At the same time, it makes them more uniform through the standardizing procedures that technification imposes. As the same processes apply to everyone, so everyone is shaped by them to become more alike. Thus the homogenization of products resulting from mass production is seconded by that of people themselves.

In a technified ethos the whole focus of personal life shifts away from relationships, and the ethical and aesthetic values that underwrite and sustain them, toward utilitarian concerns of individual success and power. This promotes an intensification of competition in every sphere of life. Competitive activities begin with the earliest years and continue throughout one's whole life: there is competition for exam results, for popularity, for jobs, for promotion, for status, for every kind of success, and so on for nearly everything. This competitive drive produces enormous psychological stresses and can result in a neglect of the emotional side of life that depends on noncompetitive relations, such as friendship, marriage, children, personal achievements, and other kinds of satisfactions apart from public success. It is precisely the most successful people who suffer from the pathologies of workaholism, obsessiveness, domineering egotism, unfeeling ruthlessness, and so on. Public success is frequently bought for the price of private privation.

The striving for success and the reliance on techniques reinforce each other, for techniques are simply the best means for instrumental ends. A means–ends mentality begins to predominate in all walks of life. Everything one has and is comes to be looked on as a potential means to a useful end. One's body is a means for sustaining the rigors of work, so it must be kept in good working order; or it is a way of attracting others, so it must be beautified; or it is a source of pleasure, so it must be indulged at certain times—and there are efficient techniques for bringing about all these results. One's brains or intellectual capacities can also be looked on as means to all kinds of success-oriented accomplishments, such as passing exams, drafting proposals, making plans, outwitting others, or anything else in which calculate intelligence is at a premium—and for these purposes there are appropriate self-improvement and study methods. One's personality can also be used effectively as a means, such as winning people over to serve one's purposes when this should prove necessary—so it must be kept flexible and made pliable by being trained in being charming and engaging. Even one's psyche, or spirit in the old language, can be treated as a means to keeping oneself in good cheer and thinking positively, so that one need never fear succumbing to boredom, depression, or despair. Everything has its uses if one can find a way of making it useful.

People, too, have their uses if one knows how to manage and manipulate them. For this purpose one needs to develop social skills, which can also be learned as techniques for handling people. These are the "how to 'win friends and influence people" techniques, which employ tactics such as being ready to listen, never openly disagreeing, encouraging others to speak of themselves and always smiling, while at the same time keeping oneself impassive and opaque. Human relations techniques of this type are the professional tools of trade of personnel managers, psychologists, counselors, and other such experts in dealing with people as impersonally as possible.

Even children are now being taught social skills rather than moral virtues. Sincerity, openness, kindness, generosity, sympathy, emotional warmth, or even good fellowship are not the qualities sought; instead it is the interpersonal techniques of management and adjustment that are inculcated. The whole ethical dimension of personal life is being lost. Mutual trust, respect, loyalty, and consideration are of no use; worse still, they are weaknesses that others can exploit; they must be extirpated, if one still has them, for they are detrimental to success. Any ties that bind too closely must be loosened for they tie one up and prevent one being free to pursue one's interests as one sees fit. Being "cool," distant, and detached is an attitude that teenagers extol and adults too cannot be averse to this for they rarely seek to admonish them.

The whole ethical tenor of the ethos in global culture is changing under the impact of technification. It is part of the same process that ethics is giving way to law, which we have examined in another book.[19] Law is a compulsory instrumental way of enforcing rules and regulations, relying ultimately on the threat of punishment. Ethics depends more on self-imposed limitations and binding norms whose breach goes against conscience and the good opinion of others. In other words, law is ultimately an issue for the police, whereas ethics is a matter of self-respect and one's standing in a community among one's fellows. Thus, to give a simple example, bigamy is a matter of law, adultery of ethics. It makes a crucial difference whether something is imposed as a matter of law or enjoined as one of ethics, even where the imperative content is identical.

The translation of ethics into law, or the process of juridification, is a form of instrumental–legal technification. The techniques of law are now increasingly being resorted to in order to make up for ethical deficiencies. In some respects this has advantages, but as a general procedure it is likely to be detrimental. In many areas of life there is an obvious and, usually, material benefit to be gained from not depending on people's fallible ethical discretion and instead relying on legal enforcement, which is far more certain and reliable. But in converting an ethical obligation into a legal compulsion much is also lost, for the spirit the laws is different from that of ethics.

An ethical principle or norm is a firm and stringent "ought," an obligation that allows of no extenuation or prevarication. One need not treat it as an unconditional Kantian categorical imperative, which must be unconditionally obeyed no matter the consequences that might ensue; yet one cannot in good conscience evade it either. A law is a much more discretionary matter. With most laws one can calculate the benefits of breaking or not fulfilling them as against the costs of the penalties of doing so. Thus, for example, an ethically binding commitment or promise cannot be reneged; however, a contract to the same effect can be broken provided one is able and willing to suffer the penalty and make the appropriate recompense. People in a highly juridified society soon come to learn when it is in their interest to break the law, even if they have to pay the fines if and when they are caught. If they can afford it, they hire clever lawyers to get them off the hook on one technicality or another that the law allows. Lawyers are also useful in instructing them how to skate near the thin edge of the law without falling foul of it. The more people act by only taking the law into account, the more ethics is discounted.

The whole regulatory trend of contemporary society is toward compulsory legal formalism and away from the personal commitments of ethics. The continuous process of bureaucratization leads to regulation by administrative fiats and arrangements, most of which have the status of law when they are promulgated by the state or other public bodies. Private bodies or organizations, such as business corporations, also set up their own internal regulatory codes, which they impose on members or employees. Thus everywhere the ethos is circumscribed by rules and regulations.

These legal arrangements have by now become so intricate and complex that only the specialized experts can know what they require and when they have been kept to or broken. Only the accountants can tell what the taxation laws demand of any citizen—what must be declared, what can be deducted, what rules govern investments, and so on. There are many other areas of life where the citizen is at a loss and has to rely on experts to interpret the law. In fact, there are so many laws, issued by so many different authorities, that inevitably even the decent law-abiding person has knowingly or not run foul of some of them. Only the good sense of the law-enforcers, police, and judges prevents everyone being charged with some breach or other. Where such good will is lacking, for whatever reason, anyone can be run in on trumped up charges. Ordinary people have become blasé and cynical about the law, which has become a technical matter far removed from ordinary ethical notions of justice and fairness. Such notions cease to be relevant or meaningful the more the law proliferates. Thus excessive legalism has a demoralizing effect.

Legalism infects all relations. Every serious arrangement entered into between people is secured by written contracts that set out the terms and conditions on which it is to proceed. Even marriage is now a contractual matter, with prenuptial agreements spelling out in advance the settlement on divorce, which, it is more or less taken for granted, is probably bound to ensue. How can this make for trust and fidelity in marriage, and what kinds of strains and constraints does it put on it right from the start? All working relations and partnerships are contractually bound and kept to the stipulated terms. How can any kind of friendship develop under these circumstances? Every profession and practice is constantly under the threat of malpractice suits or other claims for damages, real or pretended. As a result, all professionals use legal means to protect themselves, sometimes to the detriment of their clients, as, for example, when a doctor orders excessive and invasive tests just to be on the safe side that he or she has not missed something that later might be actionable at law. The law that protects people from each other also separates them by destroying the trust so necessary for amicable relations.

This kind of juridification that is spreading throughout the world is an integral part of globalization. Everywhere it occurs it brings about an erosion of the local ethos. All the major forces of globalization are behind it: the multinational companies that need a uniform legal system to invest, tourists who want the laws they are used to applying everywhere, international organizations that seek to enforce uniform standards—these and many others promote a kind of legal globalization. The drawback of this tendency toward a worldwide regime of law and order, which in itself is unimpeachable, is the effect it has on mores, manners, and morals that are invariably local. What is gained legally must be offset against what is lost ethically.

The whole tenor of public life is now beset by technical routines. Government and administration becomes a matter of the effective implementation of set techniques. There are programs for every eventuality and groups of experts are in place to manage them. Every social policy issue tends to be seen as a problem to which a technical solution is forthcoming. If traffic is a problem then motor highways are built, if slums are a problem then slum-clearance is undertaken, if unruly children are a problem then drugs are dolled out in schools, if crime is a problem then more intensive policing and harsher punishments are applied, and so on. Social problems are defined and framed in such a way as to permit a technical solution to be sought. Applied social-scientific knowledge in the hand of professional experts is utilized for this purpose. Social engineering and planning provide the methods employed.

The predisposition to resort to social science techniques has a long pre-history. It derives from nineteenth-century utopian philosophical movements, such as utilitarianism, pragmatism, positivism, and scientific socialism or Marxism. These were the idealistic precursors to many of the social science horrors of the twentieth century. They were operative throughout the world. The work techniques invented in America, such as Taylorism and Fordism, were taken up throughout all industrial societies, above all in the nascent Soviet Union. There they were vastly amplified by the techniques of collectivization and terror and all the other methods of Stalinist social engineering, and even extended to the indoctrination methods called "emotional engineering." Following the Second World War, and largely as a result of the wartime organizational practices, all kinds of systems techniques came into widespread use in the democracies as well. Later the triumphs of technology in space, medicine, computing, and so on during the 1960s and 1970s had their correlative effects on the technification of society. At the time all these developments were hailed by theorists as a move toward a postindustrial society.

The social landscape of the twentieth century is littered with the ruins of misapplied techniques resulting from a technical mentality in dealing with social problems. The former Soviet-bloc countries are a disaster area produced by the decades-long experiments of scientific socialism. But the democratic societies of the West have not escaped their share of tribulations. America is beset by the problems resulting from the failures of technification in dealing with earlier problems, or so-called second-order problems. The emergence of an underclass given to drugs and crime follows on earlier schemes to provide salubrious accommodation for poor people, especially poor blacks, in high-rise housing blocks in separate neighborhoods. Such projects, more than anything else, created ghettos where poor people, especially youth, were concentrated, segregated from the rest of society and left to rot and become demoralized. Thus an attempted technical solution to one problem gave rise to many others, some of them worse than the initial one. For in reaction to the crime and disturbances emanating from the poor areas of cities and to the slum culture that they spawn, rich people hived off into walled enclosures heavily guarded and policed. So society begins to disintegrate.

The symptoms of such a social disintegration are becoming apparent in many major cities of the world. A common civic ethos in disappearing. This will have even worse consequences in the coming generations. Further attempts at solutions through technification will only compound the problems. Under these conditions the culture that will come to predominate everywhere will be global culture for no other will be able to survive. And the effects of global culture on society are already amply evident in those places where it has become entrenched—it amplifies underlying social difficulties and transforms them into social disasters.

E. THE RETREAT FROM TECHNICS

Global culture is the triumph of technics over representation and ethos. It is not a complete triumph as yet, so far as global culture has not yet succeeded in ousting every other. But already it has made large inroads into cultural life all over the earth. And everywhere that it has spread it has introduced technified representations and a technified ethos.

Technics is by no means culturally neutral, for a culture in which techniques preponderate carries a quite different significance and orientation compared to one in which techniques are integrated into and, usually, subservient to representation and ethos. This is the case in traditional and local cultures. Thus, for instance, the techniques deployed in the traditional arts, whether at the folk, popular, or elite levels, are the means of projecting the expressive form and content determined by representational and evaluative ends. It is different in the arts of the culture industry where the technical factors, frequently based on the high technologies, are uppermost and the other aspects are secondary.

Technics is inimical to meaning and value, that is, to all the standards and norms by which representation and ethos are judged. Technique in itself is meaningless, as Stivers concludes:

[H]uman technique destroys meaning. Technique . . . is preoccupied with efficiency, with the most effective means. In other words, technique is exclusively a means of power, autonomous with respect to moral ends. In so far as meaning arises from the collective attempt to limit and symbolize power, technique thus lacks meaning. All attempts to infuse technique with meaning are futile, for technique is not integrated into the larger culture; rather it suppresses culture by rendering symbols ephemeral.[20]

The meaninglessness that is evident in highly technified societies is becoming apparent in all kinds of anomalous psychological effects. People try to habituate themselves to a lack of sense or purpose in their lives by resorting to a variety of expedients: they follow daily routines as if they were rituals, they lapse out through the use of stimulants or sex, they try to lose themselves in crowds, periodically they run away to exotic places or engage in dangerous escapades to give themselves the frisson of excitement so necessary to prove to themselves they are still alive. To some extent people can inure themselves to living in meaninglessness just as fish can become acclimatized to swimming in polluted waters. But prolonged over time, just as the fish display strange behaviors and genetic deformities, so do human beings evince unusual pathologies. Among adults and adolescents there is a continually rising level of depression—the psychological illness of our time—and accompanying incidents of suicide. Even among little children, especially those raised in crèches and reared on the "kiddy" culture of television, there are symptoms of callousness and short attention span. More such effects will no doubt reveal themselves in future generations.

Even if only for health reasons, to limit the extent of social pathologies, it will be necessary to halt the further spread of technics into areas of life where they impinge on the well-being of human beings. In many such areas, especially the cultural ones, a retreat from technics must be undertaken if there is to be a recovery of meaning and value. Such a reaction is always a possible course that can never be completely forfeited as long as society is not completely technicized and so rendered literally inhuman. This could only happen if, *per impossibile*, a "totalization of technology," as Ellul calls it, were to ensue. According to Ellul this has already happened. But his conclusion is an unwarranted extension from the partial technification of most things to the complete technification of all things: "technique has progressively mastered *all* the elements of civilization."[21] He maintains, "[F]rom the humblest to the most elevated task everything is covered by the technological process. There is a technology of reading (speed reading), as well as a technology of chewing."[22] All this might well be true, but it is inconceivable that either activity should ever become a completely technological process. Reading involves understanding what is read—how is that to be technified? Chewing involves steady movements of the jaws—what does it mean to technify those?

In fact, the main problem with Ellul's account is this tendency to exaggerate, which arises from his failure to distinguish between something involving a technique and it being fully technified or becoming an automated process. As we have established, there is a sense in which all cultural activities involve techniques and have always done so. There is a technique for all steps in composing or painting, and every musical work or picture has its technical aspects. But from this it does not follow that technique is all there is to composition or pictorial representation, or that either can be fully technified. This last possibility is precluded by the fact that these activities also touch on representation and ethos, the other crucial dimensions of culture.

Ellul's penchant for hyperbole and exaggeration accounts for his apocalyptic pessimism. When he states that "technical activity automatically eliminates every nontechnical activity or transforms it into technical activity,"[23] he does not allow for any limits to this apparently "automatic" process. But what would it take to totally technify all of culture—that is, the whole symbolic and value dimension of human life? It would mean that society would become a perfectly functioning social automatism and human life as we know it would cease to exist. Ellul seems to believe that this is not only possible, but actual. For otherwise what are we to make of statements such as these: "[N]ow it is no longer man who symbolizes nature, but technology which symbolizes itself. The mechanism of symbolization *is* technology, the means of this symbolization are the mass media of communication."[24] Technology symbolizing itself—what does symbolizing mean in this context? Perhaps what he means to say is that technology reflects itself, but reflection is not symbolization and it does not render symbolization impossible. Ellul thinks that it does: "[T]he expansion of technology is total, since technology causes and actually assimilates the symbolization that man is still capable of."[25] This is the exaggeration of moving from partiality to totality once again.

What would it mean for technology to totally assimilate symbolization? It would entail the disappearance of culture and be tantamount to the elimination of humanity. This could only happen if a "totalization of technology" were to ensue—that is, if everything was automated. For it is only the complete automation of an activity that makes it function without human input or interference. An activity that still requires human guidance and control is at most only partially technified, the extent to which it is so depending on the extent to which this human component has been reduced. As yet, few activities have been completely technified, though many have been partially so. The total technification of all activities, the automation of culture, is a utopian dream of futurologists, those who, as Ellul himself notes, assert "that in ten years, twenty years, the technological system will be 'complete' and that everything will function without human interference."[26] Ellul is rightly skeptical of "such forecasts [which] reveal the extent to which the image of [totalization] is foisting itself upon mankind."[27] And yet he himself has to rely on such prognoses in order to make statements such as "man himself is overpowered by technique and becomes its object."[28] Ellul's work should be read as a prophetic warning that we are asymptotically approaching such a zero degree of culture, and not, as he himself imagines, a prediction that we are about to reach it.

We need to take heed of these warnings and be on our guard to counter excessive technification and much more concern will need to be given to representation and ethos. This means that the standards and values of representation, such as truth, reality, validity, and authenticity, and those of the ethos, such as goodness, virtue, beauty, and expressivity, should be placed uppermost. The utilitarian and pragmatic considerations, such as efficiency, instrumental rationality, achievement, and success, should not be allowed to prevail. Above all, as we shall argue in the next chapter, utility must not be confused with value.

Every effort should be made to avoid technified forms of representation and ethos, which in essence means going against global culture, for the tendency in global culture is just the reverse, to technify everything as far as possible. It is particularly intent on technifying the whole aesthetic dimension of life. It does so by transforming art into entertainment, performance into showmanship, expression into effusion, and form into format. The retreat from technics in aesthetics must receive priority in our endeavor, for if even a little of that can be achieved then a start will have been made in rolling back excessive technification in most areas of life that are touched by aesthetic considerations.

There is an aesthetic side to representation and ethos that we need to consider in greater detail. This can be found on an ordinary everyday level; it involves such simple mundane things as a sense of humor; an imaginative use of language, rhetorical flourishes, narration, and self-expression; theatrical role playing and other forms of simple mimesis; collective ceremonies and rituals; forms of social conviviality, cultivation of a garden, decoration of a room, personal adornment, and care in self-presentation; practices of music, such as singing and playing, refinements of taste and smell, appreciation of the look of things—above all that of natural phenomena. All these can occur in the course of quotidian activities that need not require any refined cultivation and cannot even be considered art. However, if they are assiduously cultivated and refined most of these ordinary aesthetic phenomena can develop into forms of art, and, in fact, historically considered they do so in most cultures to varying degrees depending on favorable preconditions. As forms of art they can function at a folk, popular, or elite level, the three distinct ways in which art is practiced in all developed civilizations. We cannot elaborate on aesthetic theory any further in this context;[29] here we merely wish to bring to attention the importance of aesthetics in countering technification.

The general trend in our technological civilization, one dominated at present by predatory global capitalism, is for every spontaneous source of aesthetic experience to be technified and offered ready-made for free distribution or sale as a consumer product. The sum total of these products constitutes most of global culture. In this culture the differentiation between folk, popular, and elite art is elided and art is presented as mass art or, in effect, mostly as mass entertainment, which in its widest extension assumes global proportions. All that which is not entertainment takes the form of designer products—that is, especially engineered industrially produced goods intended to have an aesthetic appeal. The quality of such products usually depends on the brand label and varies with the price. Nearly everything one handles or consumes or surveys or hears of any aesthetic appeal is now the product of a highly technified system of aesthetic production, that of the so-called culture industry. This whole system of technified aesthetics, which we call global culture, has to be opposed in the name of local culture.

The retreat from technics in aesthetic life is a multifaceted process that takes numerous directions. At its simplest everyday level it calls for a changed orientation away from passive absorption and toward active engagement. What this means is that people must be encouraged to do things for themselves and ultimately to be themselves. Initially what is required is nothing elaborate or sophisticated, nothing that need even be called art, merely the ordinary aesthetic activities of the type we previously listed. Thus telling a narrative joke is in this sense an aesthetic accomplishment, of which most people brought up on global culture, with its slick comedians and comedy routines specializing in one-liners, are no longer capable. Such ordinary practices must now be relearned. The use of language for expressive purposes in general has now degenerated, especially among young people who tend to communicate with looks, grunts, and other signals, rather more than eloquently with words. The same holds true for many other aesthetic features of ordinary life, which must once again be cultivated.

The opposition of aesthetics to technics can assume a multitude of forms and can occur in every area of human life. Wherever there is a predisposition to excessive technique there can also be an antitechnical aesthetic counter. Thus the preoccupation with sport can be opposed in this way; not in any snobbish contrast of art as against sport, or, worse still, of the "arties" versus the "hearties" in the English public school sense, for what is at issue is not the playing of sport, but the sport spectatorism of the masses promoted by global culture. It is the couch potato syndrome of passive television viewing that needs to be dispelled by advising and encouraging people to get out and play or, in the spirit of Candide, to cultivate their gardens instead.

At a higher and more institutional cultural level technics can also be opposed by a recovery of art. Thus in the sphere of representation it can be shown that truth and reality are not the preserve of technified scientific representations, such as mathematical models, but can also be conveyed by means of artistic forms. Of course, it is not the same truth in both cases, but a complementary one; and both are necessary for different purposes in diverse contexts. A novel can provide as much truth about a society as a comprehensive statistical survey; the one kind of truth in no way precludes the other. This same point can be elaborated for many diverse kinds of representations. All this is of great relevance in the organization of university studies and the practices of research.

As we shall argue in the next chapter, the art that needs recovering in opposition to mass entertainment is not merely the high art of the elites, but also the popular art of the people and even the folk art of still surviving

traditional communities. Any such art will invariably be local. Artistic traditions of whatever kind are rooted in a specific milieu of time, place, and
people. And as long as these are alive, and not merely museum showpieces,
they will remain local in this sense.

Safeguarding the ethos against the excessive inroads of technification by
deploying aesthetics and art in opposition is not the only way. There are others as well, as we shall see in the next chapter, for this is an issue that touches
on all our most cherished values. It is the supreme ethical struggle of our
time. It is the striving for meaning and value as against the meaninglessness
and devaluation wrought by technics. The triumph of technics is not yet
complete, it can still be resisted and perhaps even turned back.

4

WHAT ARE THE ALTERNATIVES TO GLOBAL CULTURE?

The battle of the mind against global culture is just beginning. It will be the Kulturkampf of the coming century. Knowingly or unawares we are all living out this titanic struggle. We are all torn between fitting in with the globalizing trends in culture or resisting them, either fully conscious of what we are against or because something else still has a hold on us which we are not ready to relinquish. This struggle is as much an inner conflict in the soul as an outer one in society. For in reacting against global culture we are also acting against ourselves, since we have already been shaped by the pressures of mass culture and are continually being worked on by newer trends of global culture. This culture is inescapable, like the polluted air we must breathe for want of any other. But this does not mean that it must be complacently accepted, for just as we act against the fouling of the atmosphere, so we can also act against the degradation of our cultural ambience. Much of the damage that has been done can no longer be reversed; we can no more clean up culture than we can clean the air. What is possible is a slowing down of the polluting tendencies in both these domains. This is the sole measure of success in the desperate battle we need to wage so as to save our cultural souls as much as our societies.

The opposition to global culture must be conducted both in theory and in practice, both in the realm of ideas and that of everyday activities. As we have shown in the last chapter, we need general theories to guide our practice and we have to hold to some general standards, for otherwise everything will be compromised to the pragmatic sanctions of the moment. At the same time, a too precipitate application of theories to the complexities of reality is dangerous, as the disasters of the previous century have demonstrated. We must steer a middle course between the Scylla of radical idealism and the Charybdis of opportunism. It is particularly important not to be confused with those who attack global culture for the wrong reasons.

The worst of those who attack it and the most misguided are the religious fundamentalists, particularly the radical Islamists, who see it simply as the culture of America, the Great Satan, or even more generally, as that of the West as such. This view entails the totally mistaken assumption that America has no other culture but global culture, that which it exports abroad, or the even more erroneous idea that Western culture is global culture. Only extreme ignorance or a blind hatred of America and the West for other reasons can explain such patent misconceptions. Even an elementary knowledge of America's cultural history and of its traditions would easily dispel such wrong-headedness. Though it is sad, but true, that many Americans themselves have sometimes to be reminded that they have a more genuine culture than that which they produce for profit.

The misconception of those who attack global culture only because it is the culture of capitalism is much more understandable and vastly more sophisticated, but in the end no more plausible. And analogously so, the defense of global culture because it is the culture of capitalism—or that of the free-choice, free-market society, as its advocates like to put it more euphemistically—is not more justifiable than the contrary view. Both of these diametrically opposed positions wrongly identify capitalism—an economic system of very wide historical currency, that in some form or other has existed for thousands of years—with global culture, a contemporary cultural expression of the conjuncture of all those forces that comprise the first stage of globalization. It is true, as we have already amply demonstrated, that in the present context of globalization capitalism and global culture are symbiotically linked. But this is a particularly predatory stage of capitalism that might not persist for all that much longer. Capitalism as an economic system is not inexorably tied to global culture and will eventually do without it.

Hence, as we shall show in what follows, it is possible to act against global culture without necessarily opposing capitalism as such, merely calling on it to reform itself and abandon its present unrestricted free-market shibboleths. This course relies on distinguishing the economic formation, capitalism, from its cultural expression in the present historical context, global culture, a distinction that must be carried through both in theory and in practice. The opposition to global culture in this restricted sense has some realistic prospects of achieving something. By contrast, the revolutionary impulse to smash capitalism, which was repeated over and over again in varied situations over the course of the previous century, has not only failed miserably, but brought its exponents and their people untold miseries. To advocate it now is nothing but sterile revolutionism.

There are all kinds of other misguided grounds for attacking or defending global culture. There are those who defend it as popular culture, the demotic culture of the people, in contradistinction to the exclusive culture of the elite. There are others who see in it the only living culture as opposed to what they take to be the dead cultures of tradition. There are many who for various reasons refuse to judge it and insist on considering it as no worse than any other culture. These are the value relativists who assume various contemporary guises and disguises for they are really value nihilists. They can present themselves as poststructuralists or as deconstructivists and mouth the appropriate jargon of these esoteric theories, or more simply as postmodernists who pretend to inaugurate a new historical era. It is true that the age of modernist aesthetics is past—destroyed as much by its own avant-garde excesses as anything else—but this they confuse with the end of modernity itself. There are those among them who believe that since we now appear to live in an electronic global village—realized in practice at last thanks to the Internet—hence global culture is the only appropriate one for us. All kinds of half-baked theories and ideas circulate in the modish intellectual realm; they cross and crisscross in all kinds of ways; untangling them is the labor of a Hercules.

All we can do here to counter all this confusion is simply to affirm some fundamental truths and draw some crucial distinctions. But even these we cannot argue for as fully theoretically as necessary in this context; we can only refer to other works where this is done more adequately. This is perhaps enough for our present purpose, for here our main aim is not to expound theories but to advocate practical steps. It is not so much thinking rightly as doing rightly that is our main concern.

Our crucial practical project at hand is to defend local culture. We shall first consider this in more general terms and later with greater specificity, especially so in the field of education. Obviously, what we have to say is no party manifesto or blueprint for action, merely an advocacy of the basic cause to be pursued. It is a call to act globally but think locally—that is, to have both global scope and local roots; a call for the launching of grassroots endeavors in many localities and a worldwide movement to connect these with each other. Such a movement would be closely linked to the cognate environmentalist one. Only the two together in unison can hope to attain the eco–cultural balance so necessary to stop the world from sliding toward the industrial wasteland to which it is now heading.

But before we can even begin to defend local culture we must first uphold the very idea of cultural value as such, which is now under attack from many quarters. For without an affirmation of value there is no way of upholding any culture whatever. For ultimately every culture must stand on its values or not at all. If its values do not sustain a culture, then no other grounds will support it. Other supports of culture are but feet of clay, which in our society mainly uphold the idols of the marketplace. Culture lives or dies by value alone.

A. VALUES AND THEIR ENEMIES

Defending local culture against global culture, or even criticizing global culture in any way whatever, calls for value judgments. Once upon a time, in what now seems another age, that would have been a truism hardly worth saying; now it has become a truth that has to be upheld for it can no longer be taken for granted. Now it is necessary to defend the making of value judgments as a necessary procedure in any critical discourse, as against all those who have come to dispute the right or capacity of anyone to judge anything at all. Judgmentalism, so-called, is openly denounced in many fields, especially so in cultural matters. There are also many who declare that all cultures are equal, so by what right can anyone judge one culture to be better or worse in any respects than another. How can anyone even dare to affirm one value as superior to another, they ask rhetorically. This means that the very right to critically question global culture and to judge it inferior to other forms of culture and its values as debasing, demeaning, and debauching is strongly denied and rejected for many kinds of reasons.

Thus, to give but one out of a plethora of available examples, Ann Cvetkovich and Douglas Kellner write as follows: "In attempting to conceptualise the terms of the global and the local it is first important to divest them of normative baggage, especially conceptualisations that would positively valorize one side of the equation and denigrate the other."[1] People are, of course, free to define their terms as they choose, in line with Humpty Dumpty's adage that "a word means what I choose it to mean," but to take the step of removing the "normative baggage" equally from the global and the local, as these authors recommend, is either a willful misuse of the common meanings of these terms, or a false judgment that global culture is the equal of any local culture, namely, that it is as good as any of our cultural traditions. Very likely it is a misguided attempt to slough off "normative baggage" altogether, regarding it as merely the deadweight of the past and so an unnecessary burden to bear for those who wish to travel light in the cultural field—which suits the intellectual lightweights of our time.

Yet without normative baggage as ballast cultures are left to drift with the winds and tides of market fashion, having no firm anchor of values to hold them in place. Without value judgments one cannot discriminate, defending one culture and criticizing another, nor can one even decide where one stands in such respects. Value judgments are not, of course, demonstrable propositions or even provable theories, but they are not merely subjective expressions of personal preference either; they are defensible affirmations of critical standards that can be supported by argument. They have a rationale, even if not always an ascertainable rationality. *De gustibus non est disputandum* might apply to matters of taste or the lowest levels of preference, but it does not apply to judgments of value or evaluations, which are by definition matters of disputation; they are, in fact, the primary things to be argued about.

All this, which can here be only summarily put, requires whole treatises, particularly in ethics and aesthetics, to be theoretically established. This is, however, not the place to argue against all those who wish to deny it for all kinds of intellectual as well as sometimes political and ideological reasons. Mostly they affirm a radical cultural relativism in opposition to what they take to be no more than the elitist pretensions of a reactionary traditionalism. Such an evaluative nonjudgmentalism—an *ataraxia* reminiscent of ancient skepticism, but which is really a modern nihilism—can be derived from all kinds of modish theories and is driven by various motives. Sometimes it is a high-minded striving for cultural egalitarianism embarked on for very ideal motives; but as we know from past experience, this can very easily flip over and degenerate to cynical opportunism. We must be wary of it in both its forms.

A defense of one culture as opposed to another entails a critical exposition and affirmation of some values over against others. This does not mean that all values can always be ranked in relation to others or that some kind of absolute value hierarchy can be established. It is amply apparent that many kinds of values are incommensurable with each other and that invidious comparisons need not always be made. Furthermore, values are not absolute universal standards that have perennial validity; they are themselves changeable and subject to the flux of historical development. The values of one era need not be relevant to another. As mentalities and orientations change so do the values they subtend. But this easily provable historical fact that values are labile does not mean that values are purely relative or that value judgments are not critically defensible, anymore than the analogous fact that scientific theories are always only provisional and liable to change in the future means that science has no objective basis. All intellectual and evaluative systems are subject to change, none are absolute, but this does not make them purely subjective matters of taste.

The attack against or the disregard for value judgments, and, what comes usually with it, the explicit or implicit condoning of global culture, can at present be sheeted home to two major sources: either a misapplication of various kinds of economic theories to culture, or economism, for short; or the invocation of various types of modish theories, or postmodernism, for short. Both of these general approaches deny the autonomy and integrity of culture and attempt to discount or reduce cultural values to other kinds of considerations.

Economisms of culture come in a number of opposed variants. The most influential at present are the neoliberal or neoclassical theories and practices that subjugate cultural values to the imperatives of the market. Such views are favored by most governments intent on promoting globalization and the privatization policies that are ancillary to it. Of lesser importance, though still prominent in academia, are the surviving Marxist or really by now pseudo-Marxist approaches to culture that have adapted themselves to various other contemporary radical causes, particularly those that are in league with what they take to be popular culture, supposedly the culture of the people. Many of these advocate postmodernist philosophemes that also come in basically two modes. There are the postmodernists of the marketplace: the artists, architects, designers, and others who cater to sophisticated haut couture tastes in just about everything. These are the people who fashion the most exclusive of designer-label goods. Allied to them and frequently providing a rationale for them are the media intellectuals and academic postmodernists, those who mouth the appropriate poststructuralist and deconstructive clichés and who on this basis have launched various types of cultural studies as academic courses. We shall proceed to deal with all these overt or covert apologists for global culture seriatim in this order.

Neoclassical economic theory or economic rationalism, so-called, does not explicitly concern itself with culture. Yet it does so implicitly by default, for its unthinking application of an unrestrained free-market policy to all of global commerce and trade has had enormous cultural consequences. By treating cultural goods just like any other commodities, it has promoted the spread of global culture and blocked any resistance to this. To the exponents of this neoliberal or Friedmanite view, all goods are utilities, and the cheaper and more efficiently they can be produced the better for society in general. According to this debased variant of utilitarianism, popular preference as expressed through the mechanism of the market should be the main criterion of what is desirable and, therefore, what is good. Culture utilities, just as all others, must meet the market laws of supply and demand, they must earn their keep or go under. The discipline of the market is good for them, hence any kind of protectionism or subsidy only serves to artificially prop up undesirable tendencies and weakens natural selection and growth in culture.

This view overlooks a number of important lessons that history has to teach us about culture. Even a cursory study of the past reveals that in every society there has always existed a noncommercial culture, one that cannot earn its keep on the marketplace, one that is supported by special interest groups, those which take their culture to be more than commerce. All kinds of groups have done this for all kinds of reasons, plebeian as much as patrician groups, for secular as well as religious reasons. This is not to deny that commercial cultures, variously linked to the noncommercial, have also always been in existence. To attempt to subject all culture to the market is, therefore, historically unjustifiable, and is on historical grounds culpable. Nor is it even fair, for the cultures linked to commercial interests have enormous advantages compared to those that are not; in other words, the market for cultural goods is biased and subject to unfair competition as we have already previously demonstrated in respect of advertising. Hence, there is no choice but to protect and subsidize noncommercial culture. How this is to be done is a difficult policy issue on which there are numerous keenly debated views, and it is even desirable that different countries pursue alternative strategies in this respect. However, not to have such policies in place means to abdicate in favor of commercial culture.

Global culture wins out in market competition over every other for reasons we have already amply spelled out in chapter 2, so we will only briefly mention them here. It is the culture of commerce: its advertising and publicity departments are the propaganda arms of the business establishments, hence it can draw on almost unlimited financial, technological, and manpower resources drawn from many kinds of firms, especially the media conglomerates. Governments that follow globalization and privatization policies give it their full support in all kinds of overt and covert ways. For example, government agencies allocated the major portion of the radio bandwidth spectrum to private enterprises. At the same time, by cutting funding governments force public service media to transform themselves into business enterprises. Having no public service goals to uphold, the private media firms need only be bound by the limited ethics of the marketplace and so can set about wooing their customers by whatever means they see suitable. They need not worry about the later consequences of what they are doing now— let society take care of itself as best it can.

By pursuing such market policies and treating cultural values as utilities, governments are ensuring that every cultural sphere is eventually taken over by commerce and absorbed into global culture. We shall go on to show how this is now taking place in education. If students are considered as clients and schools and universities as suppliers of services, then what is taught and how it is taught become simply a matter of market demand. In such conditions there is no reason not to privatize the whole educational establishment and allow its component parts to be run as businesses. This is already happening to various degrees all over the world where the commodification of education has ensued. The consequences, both for teaching and research, are little short of disastrous. Whole disciplines that are considered difficult subjects by students, such as pure mathematics, theoretical physics, philosophy, classics, sociology, and literature, are slowly disappearing from the curriculum. What is taking their place are the academic adjuncts of global culture, which, as we shall show later, is a corruption of the whole educational project.

Theoretically speaking an economistic approach to culture can only be rebutted by drawing a fundamental distinction between values and commodities. This we shall undertake in the next section. Assuming that this can be successfully accomplished, it is possible to argue that values must not be treated like commodities, that things of value deserve support and funding irrespective of utilitarian considerations. Thus, for value reasons alone, even without taking account of other benefits, it is essential for every civilized society to support the discovery of mathematical and scientific truths, to cultivate literary and other creative artistic activities, to uphold religious faiths and moral traditions, to educate children and youth, and, in democratic societies, to help them become informed and aware citizens, and so on. None of these endeavors could possibly pay for themselves on the market, so they have to be funded in other ways. For the same reasons it is necessary to maintain local cultures that cannot compete on the market with global culture, but whose values are superior.

The errors of the Marxist approaches are the converse of those of the neoliberals. Whereas the latter wish to allow globalization to proceed without any let or hindrance, the former want to stop it altogether, for they consider it simply the latest form of capitalism, which they on principle oppose. This preconception against every kind of capitalism leads them into either sterile revolutionism or carping criticism without any viable alternative. At present the revolutionists are, effectively speaking, only the street protestors who think they can smash capitalism by throwing rocks through shop windows. The captious critics with no alternatives are the academic intellectuals who are fully aware that every form of socialism that was tried out in practice during the last century failed economically and could not compete with capitalism.

Thus by espousing the hopeless cause of doctrinaire anticapitalism they preclude themselves from working against those aspects of capitalism, as it operates at present under conditions of globalization, which might be opposed with some chance of success. Its treatment of culture as a utilitarian commodity is precisely one of the current practices that could be reversed. To achieve this it is not necessary, Canute-like, to try to hold back the tide of global capitalist development. To neglect the attainable for the unattainable is a self-defeating course to follow.

Marxists are prone to do this because they are ideologically and theoretically precluded from taking a differentiated and measured approach to capitalism. They must take it and condemn it holus bolus, for, unlike the curate's egg, it cannot be good in parts. They see it as a total system that embraces everything and necessarily leads to the evils of exploitation, alienation, and dehumanization, which can never be condoned. Thus the culture of capitalist societies, bourgeois culture according to the Marxist dispensation, must also be opposed in toto. But not only the culture of the bourgeois class, that of every other is also rejected, peasant folk culture as much as aristocratic high culture. Once again everything existing is condemned without allowing for any alternatives, except for the forlorn hope that the proletariat, once in power, will develop a superior culture of its own. How this is to happen, based on what values and resources, all this is not specified.

Marx's whole attitude to culture was seriously flawed in theory, though he himself was an educated bourgeois gentleman with impeccable literary tastes. He had great difficulty in squaring his cultural values with his economistic theory of culture. Thus he was genuinely puzzled how it was possible that an economically backward, slave-owning society, like that of ancient Greece, could possibly have produced the literary, artistic, and philosophical masterpieces that would be admired for all time. If culture were simply an ideological reflection of economic and social structures then this should be unlikely.

Contemporary Marxists, who no longer have any such grasp of cultural values, suffer no such *crise de conscience*. It is all too easy for them to abandon value judgments altogether and fall in with postmodernist attitudes that anything goes, or to prefer pop culture to that of the elites. Little do they realize that this is not a popular culture of the people, but a commercial culture with a mass following. Thus they become unwitting supporters of global culture, the very culture of the capitalism that they abhor.

Contrary to the tenets of classical Marxism, the main critique of capitalism should now be launched on cultural rather than on economic grounds. Contemporary global capitalism can in most respects be considered an economic success, yet it is becoming more and more of a cultural failure. As its economic stocks go up, its cultural ones are lowered, almost as if there were an inverse relation between them. For it is not the production of goods, but the creation of values that is at present the main deficit of capitalism. This is by no means a lesser fault that can be excused. On the contrary, it enables an even stronger charge to be leveled against it. Capitalism will have to reform or go under.

Contemporary Marxists, who are unaware of this, have instead gravitated to postmodernism that is a celebration of contemporary capitalist culture. Strictly speaking the term postmodernism means nothing, for taken literally it refers to something after modernism, but what that something is nobody knows. The decease of modernism is now amply evident, and in that despairing sense anyone with any artistic nous is aware that we are now after modernism or, so to speak, literally post modernist. But in that sense to declare oneself a postmodernist is really an admission of our collective cultural failure. However, this is not how the self-proclaimed postmodernists see it—they think of themselves as having gone beyond modernism to something new and unprecedented. What they have really done is gone behind modernism back to all the old styles, which they reinvoke cynically in a playful decorative manner, utilizing merely the formal and technical elements without any regard for the content and the values inherent in these features. Values are discounted in what at best has become an amusing game with satirical intent. There is some point to it when it is directed at the fashions of mass and global culture. However, this flirtation with pop art soon turns into an affirmation of it. Through these steps the postmodernists have become apologists for global culture.

The postmodernist theorists of academia openly espouse what they consider to be popular culture as against the elitist pretentions of their more conservative rivals. As we shall see, they have initiated various types of cultural, communication, and media studies in opposition to the old-style academic subjects. They consider it to be a very radical move to apply democratic principles to aesthetics, taking it for granted that what most people patronize and procure must be good. By this round about way these radicals, so-called, end up exactly where the neoliberal free-marketeers begin, with the idea that free choice expressed through the market is the criterion of value. Vox populi, vox dei, they contend applies to values just as much as to politics.

This outcome is highly ironic considering that most of these cultural, communication, and media studies began with theoretical approaches that were explicitly directed against mass culture and designed to act as critiques of it. The familiar Marxist trends derive mostly out of the Frankfurt school theories, which denounced the culture industry and through the agency of Marcuse, inspired the countercultural movements of the 1960s, especially in America. Their English counterparts of the so-called Birmingham school, led by the radical socialists Raymond Williams and Richard Hoggart, and inspired by the earlier work of the Leavises, explicitly set themselves to defend popular working class culture against the importation of pop American mass culture. The French theoretical input into the various kinds of academic studies also had Marxist credentials and was directed against every kind of bourgeois culture. Thus, for example, the semiotic work of Roland Barthes began as a Marxist critique of the press, advertising, and other mass culture strategies of distortion. How it happened that all these radical approaches which began as outright criticisms of mass culture ended up as celebrations of it is a long story of academic politics and the career pressures of advancement.

The key to this story is the effect that the study of mass cultural products had on the minds of those who preoccupied themselves with it; step-by-step what began as criticism turned to appreciation. There were numerous pressures at work in achieving this reversal of values. The pressures of the marketplace were particularly insidious. The advertisers, mediocrats, publishers, and other such were only too willing to richly reward all those who showed themselves ready to compromise. Some French media intellectuals were gradually won over, starting surreptitiously with Barthes himself when he secretly accepted a commission to advise on Renault promotion.[2] Jean-François Lyotard made common cause with the American postmodernists and adopted their anti-intellectual course in declaring all "grand narratives" over. Jean Baudrillard became cynically resigned to the domination of the electronic media. Umberto Eco, having analyzed best sellers, embarked on writing them himself. The very fact that the trash of mass culture was studied with the same degree of theoretical sophistication, using the same abstruse theoretical jargon, as works of literature set at naught any value distinctions and brought them all down to the same level.[3] Students soon learned that standards meant nothing.

Pressure from students had a great impact in the English-speaking world on the way that the special studies were conducted. In America and increasingly in England and elsewhere the very fact that students had been thoroughly immersed in mass and global culture and that they mostly knew no other made it very difficult for their teachers to openly criticize it for fear of losing their audience. Where student numbers and their approval of teachers mattered, as it did increasingly more so in the academic marketplace, this made it essential for teachers to be on side with their clientele. Out of self-protective motives, if no others, they gradually learned to admire what they might have set out to denounce.

In the English-speaking world there were also theorists who articulately upheld the products of mass culture. The most celebrated among these was Marshall McLuhan, a particular favorite with the advertising and media people. He was the first proponent of global culture, *avant la lettre*, in his conception of a global village linked by the electronic media, which only became reality much later with computers and the Internet. He espoused an extreme technological progressivism according to which new media displaced and eliminated old media. On this view books were passé because printing was an old medium that would give way to electronics. Overall, words, concepts, and ideas would be replaced by images. The practitioners of mass media, who mostly dealt in images, were only too glad to hear that they were at the forefront of intellectual progress. Students who had spent their childhood and youth immersed in these images were also happy to know that they no longer needed to bother reading any books. Their teachers were eventually also ready to comply.

Many of these teachers, who had derived from the 1968 "revolutionary" students' generation, have now become the collaborators of global culture no matter how much they might still inveigh against capitalism, racism, sexism, and whatever else is included in the contemporary litany of deadly sins. It has now become obvious to the few more honest and serious radicals that the critical thrust has evaporated from such cultural studies and these are now counterproductive to any emancipatory political project. As Nicholas Garnham puts it:

Unfortunately in my view, the educational influence of cultural studies has become potentially baleful and far from liberating because it has pursued the role of introducing popular cultural practices into the classroom indiscriminately at the expense of the wider political and emancipatory values of intellectual inquiry and teaching. . . . Whatever the reason, the tending of cultural studies to validate all and every popular cultural practice as resistance—in its desire to avoid being tarred with the elitist brush—is profoundly damaging to its political project.[4]

But not only is the radical political project crippled, so is the very effort of teaching itself. Students who are told that what they like is what is good, that standards and values mean nothing, that anything is important if it features in the media are in effect being surreptitiously taught that teaching itself is worthless.

In a postmodernist climate of "anything goes," even intellectual oppositions have been abrogated. Since consistency and integrity no longer mean anything, it is possible at once to advocate market liberalism and individual choice together with a mass-populist radicalism, to promote the seeking of pleasure as a subversive act of resistance, to maintain a cool, ironic stance at the same time as being a fan of the fashions. Attracting media attention has become a primary goal for pop intellectuals whose ultimate ambition is to become media stars themselves. This is a new kind of *trahison des clercs* more outré than anything previously envisaged: it is the ultimate betrayal of the intellectuals in making common cause with everything that militates against the intellect.

The fact that there are now no radical alternatives worth taking seriously does not mean that the present situation in culture is altogether acceptable or that there are no alternatives whatever, and that this is the best of all possible worlds. The futility of rabid anticapitalism does not mean that the victory of capitalism over socialism in the economic and political battles of the twentieth century is the triumph of freedom or the end of history. As we have seen, one of the consequences of the global spread of an unregulated predatory capitalism has been the domination of global culture over every other. It is possible and necessary to counteract this and work against it; with some chance of success. The first and most crucial step in the intellectual aspect of this struggle is to theoretically distinguish between values and commodities.

B. VALUES AND COMMODITIES

Commodities differ from things of value in that they have only a market value—that is, a price in monetary terms—whereas things of value have prizeworthy qualities that are independent of and indifferent to price. The distinction is affirmed in Oscar Wilde's definition of the cynic as the one who knows the price of everything but the value of nothing. Commodities are governed purely by economic considerations—they have no claims for regard. preservation, or maintenance other than those determined by market factors. They can be freely alienated, disposed of, or consumed at the behest of their owners. Things of value, by contrast, have claims to an extra-economic regard and safeguard based on religious, moral, legal, political, aesthetic, or any other such grounds inherent in the ethos of a society. One cannot dispose of things of value at will. Price and value are distinct also because they can vary independently of each other; something might be high-priced and have no value, or vice versa. Ideally, of course, there ought to be a close correlation between them, such that valuable things also command a high price. In our societies almost the opposite situation obtains in that shoddy high-priced goods are considered to be almost the sole things of value. According to Wilde's definition, that approximates to a cynical society.

Values are constituted by complex social and historical processes, different ones for each major category. Thus, for example moral values are the outcome of age-old religious, civic, and intellectual developments occurring in many different societies. Aesthetic values are analogously the results of age-long artistic cultivations. Similar preconditions obtain for other values. We are now the heirs of millennia of such value formations and transformations.[5] Hence for us values exist insofar as they are inherent in culture, even though they cannot be recorded in any way nor measured precisely. In particular, the values we have cannot be converted into other measurable quantities such as prices or pleasures or labor.

Marx made the futile attempt to define all kinds of value by the one unitary measure of labor power. On this basis he distinguished between intrinsic value, use value, and exchange value. The intrinsic value of anything was simply the labor power that it embodied. Thus the intrinsic value of any two disparate objects could be compared on this basis. Invoking such a unitary standard also implicitly abrogates any fundamental distinction between values and nonvalues. Since all manufactured things have an intrinsic value determined by labor power, and since there is no way of qualitatively distinguishing one kind of labor power from another, it follows that there is no way of separating the labor that goes into the creation of things of value from that which produces mere commodities. How is one to distinguish by labor power alone the work of a Michelangelo from that of a tyro painter or a house painter, for that matter? The upshot of this economistic approach is that the work of culture creation is granted no autonomy, nor can it claim any preference or priority to any other kind of work. At best it can be considered as mind-work in contrast to physical labor.

Ultimately a labor theory of value fails because values, though human creations, are not the products of labor in any obvious sense. They are the outcomes of complex social and historical interactions among multitudes of people involving countless different kinds of activities over very long periods. It is not even possible to specify separable individual contributions in such situations. Work itself differs according to the value with which it is endowed—that is, by reference to the value-context or cultural situation in which it takes place. This determines whether it is worthwhile or worthless, inspired production or mere drudgery. Of course, the price of labor or its products has no necessary relation to its value. The works of van Gogh did not command any price during his lifetime, but that does not mean that they were not aesthetically valuable even then, though few people knew this.

The distinction between commodities and values permits us to separate utilities from cultural goods, which is so crucial in regulating the operation of capitalism. Commodities and cultural goods must be treated quite differently. It is possible, for example, to maintain open markets and to practice free trade for utilitarian commodities, but not for cultural goods. The circulation of cultural goods might be restricted in all kinds of ways or encouraged depending on cultural policies designed to achieve certain desired goals. Thus trade in books need not be treated in the same way as that in steel or motorcars, for books are cultural goods and not mere commodities. Obviously, this leaves room for much disputation, especially as many things, such as books themselves, are in some respect commodities and in others cultural goods. But such complications can be left for later consideration. First it is necessary to expound things in their theoretical simplicity.

Pure commodities are all those things that only have a price and no value whatever. Most raw materials fall into that category. By contrast, pure cultural goods are all those things that have value but no price. This can be either because by definition they cannot be bought, such as love, friendship, or happiness, or because they are literally priceless since they would never be offered for sale—the Statue of Liberty or the Houses of Parliament in London are priceless in this way, as is the British monarchy itself. But, as we shall see, not everything is either a pure commodity or a pure cultural good; many things are both at once and this is what causes complications.

However, having a price is not the only criterion of a commodity. A pure commodity is also a utility that has no value apart from its price or use value. It can, therefore, be consumed in any way whatever: it can be stored or transformed or used to make something else or used up or simply destroyed. Nothing guards or protects pure commodities except the rights of ownership. Cultural goods, in direct opposition, are protected and safeguarded in all kinds of ways. There are in most societies prohibitions of legal, moral, religious, or customary kinds against abusing or damaging a cultural good. Thus, for example, buyers and owners of worthwhile paintings by recognized artists are not free to dispose of them at will or willfully damage or alter them as they please. Such are generally considered acts of vandalism, even if they are not punishable by law. Similarly so, owners of historic houses are not free to demolish them or even to remodel them to their own taste. There are all kinds of sanctions invoked against the abuse of cultural goods and none in the use of pure commodities.

However, what is treated as a commodity and what as a cultural good is by no means fixed or absolute—it is subject to historically changing conditions. Thus, for example, until very recently and in some places even now, human beings were treated as commodities and bought and sold as slaves. In fact, in Roman law the slave was the very paradigm of a commodity, an *instrumentum vocale*, and much contract law was devised for the purpose of slave trading. Now, of course, human beings are considered to have inalienable value. It is similar with crimes and other moral matters, where, for example, earlier societies commodified murder and allowed murderers to pay monetary indemnities for their crimes. By contrast, modern law has partially commodified such misdeeds as libel, slander, insult, and impugning someone's good name or honor simply by awarding monetary compensation to the injured party, whereas in earlier societies such acts could not be bought off but had to be atoned through religious rites or by offering satisfaction in a duel. Analogous changes have taken place in art, services of various kinds, personal relations, and many other areas. Thus the contrast between commodities and cultural goods has always to be considered historically, taking cultural differences into account.

It is a general historical trend in every society that commodification grows with modernity and especially so with the development of capitalism. It follows that modern societies are far more commodified than traditional ones. This whole process has taken a great leap forward with globalization and the spread of global capitalism. The correlative to this vast expansion of commodification is the steadily diminishing scope of value. This is particularly so in the realm of mass culture where there is a constant tendency to substitute price for value. A good thing is simply an expensive thing. This holds for goods, services, labor of every kind, and all the products of labor. Thus the process of commodification is one of devaluation much in line with Nietzsche's account of the onset of nihilism.

Global culture is simply the culmination of the process of commodification through its extension into the realm of culture. Every product of this culture is commodified and judged solely according to its price. Hence, any consideration of value beyond that is expunged. All that matters is the market outcome: for anything whatever, if it sells it must be good. Estimating the probable market success of any cultural product takes the place of value judgment. Thus ratings, polling, bookings at the box office, and other such measures of potential sale are now routinely used as criteria of quality. Even our language has altered to register this change in our attitude to values. Instead of using any of the old evaluative terms, we now speak of best sellers, box office hits, big-earners, and so on. Or, alternatively, such things are prospectively estimated on the amount of money invested in their production, on the usually sound market assumption that people will rate highly and be prepared to buy anything expensive to produce. Thus blockbuster movies that have cost a lot to make, records featuring high-earning performers, books whose authors are paid large advances, and so on, all these are judged good by anticipation of the probable market response. Sometimes, of course, the market outcome is disappointing and one of those embarrassing contradictions arises that people like to laugh off with terms like "dud" or "lemon." But these are the exceptions to the rule that high investments bring high returns in culture as elsewhere in the economy.

In all kinds of ways our commodified culture makes every effort to discount and dismiss judgments of value. Thus things of value that have no market success, that do not sell in the time required to accrue profits, are derided and usually destroyed. A book, record, film, or show that does not bring in quick returns is pulped, canned, withdrawn from circulation, or wound up no matter how highly critics or connoisseurs judge its merits. Everything possible is done to make sure that people who consume cultural products do not go by value judgments, either their own or that of acknowledged authorities, but instead are ruled by publicity and their own momentary impulse-buying instincts. Every form of hucksterism is employed to ensure market success, for what counts is the result, not how it was obtained in the first place. There are all kinds of marketing techniques for starting a buying surge and keeping it going until it becomes self-sustaining; some of these are of dubious morality.

Global culture is simply a sustained and far-reaching attempt to commodify the culture of the whole world. To achieve its purpose it needs to carry out a wholesale destruction of value. All of its products work toward this end. Thus, as the popular music historian Donald Clarke puts it, "today's pop-rock is a paradigm of a society with no values."[6] In particular, the values embodied in local culture must be eliminated, for these stand in the way of commodification and the rule of the market. These values are embedded in the things that people have come to honor and safeguard irrespective of price. Such people, those who do not choose to buy their culture on the mass market, are a barrier to the expansion of global culture and must be discouraged. This is usually done by deriding and discrediting them in various ways as old fogies.

To counter this we must embark on contrary policies to decommodify culture. This can be done by completely removing some things from the market and making them not saleable, as is the case with national treasures. Or it can be done by allowing such things to be bought and sold, but by placing stringent conditions on their use, as is now the case with National Trust properties or with various kinds of land environments, such as rivers, forests, and parklands. Both these methods work for things of already traditionally established value, where it is generally agreed that they ought to be protected. They do not work for things whose value is as yet uncertain or contested—that is, for the things of living culture—for these cannot be simply withdrawn from the market, or have a value assigned in advance of their free circulation.

It is essential that cultural goods currently being produced should be available on the market, for otherwise the producers of these cannot be properly recompensed for their labor. Writers, composers, painters, architects, and many other types of artists and professionals must be able to sell their goods and services. But at the same time such things cannot be simply disposed of as if they were the products of any other kinds of labor, like manufactured products in general. They must be treated at once as commodities and goods of cultural value.

Historically considered the relation between cultural value or aesthetic worth and commodity value or market price is extremely complex, and takes a quite different form in different civilizations. A study of this by Joseph Alsop, restricted to the collectible plastic arts, pictures, statues, illuminated books, and so on, occupies a very large and voluminous tome which is impossible even to summarize here. His theme, most briefly stated, is that "art collecting and art history, the art market and revaluation are intimately interlinked."[7] As Alsop shows, in only very few cultures in history can one speak of a commodification of the plastic arts, those in fact in which the above referred to phenomena have come into being, namely, in the Greco-Roman, the Chinese, the Japanese, the Islamic, and the western European from the early Renaissance onward. However, it is only in the contemporary "art scene," so-called, that commodification has reached its apogee and where "collectors and dealers, curators, critics and art historians nowadays often loom larger than creators."[8] These "creators" often now assume the role of "anti-artists," producing "anti-art" or Dada monstrosities that fetch "super-prices"—"super-prices strike me as morbid symptoms," declares Alsop.[9]

Hence, even though it is widely recognized that the present "art scene" and its associated art market are culturally pathological, it is not possible under present conditions to prescribe a cure and change it. Nevertheless, it is possible to specify an ideal relation between valuation and commodification, which should serve as a goal to be aimed for. Anything even remotely approaching this ideal relation will only be attained when the whole cultural situation is transformed for the better.

When dealing with objects and services that are both commodities and goods of cultural value it is ideally desirable that their price should be commensurate with their value. Thus, ideally, the best paintings and painters should command the highest prices and fees and the worst be very cheap. and so on for all other such activities. This ideal outcome is, of course, very rare, and at present should not be aimed at directly. However, what can be avoided is a complete disparity between value and price. This is at present the situation in the "art scene" and in many other cultural fields of endeavor. The art market works in such a corrupt way that a Warhol or even a Pollock. which are frequently valueless, command astronomical prices. whereas the works of numerous much better painters in many countries can often not be sold at all. Some meretricious writers of best sellers gain fabulous salaries. whereas most other writers cannot even earn a modest living from their efforts. This disparity between value and price can be multiplied over and over again. It is a general feature of the nihilistic state of our culture in all its domains that the most worthless things bring the highest return and the best things very little or none.

Our general task is, therefore, to reestablish some correlation, no matter how tenuous at first, between value and price. This cannot be done under the conditions of global culture. It can be attempted and perhaps partially achieved only under those of local culture. A local show directed at a smaller audience, one well short of a mass or global public, does not require large sums or high profits to be viable. People participate in it not because of publicity or mass appeal, but because they believe in it and admire or honor the artists and the experiences it embodies irrespective of price. Local culture is thus by its very nature based more on value than on price. At the same time it need not forgo price or economic considerations altogether. The popular singer who sings for a local public of devotees can still charge an admission fee, but the takings will not be such as to permit a publicity campaign to increase manifold the size of this audience, which is in any case physically limited. The writer who writes in order to genuinely communicate with like-minded people cannot produce best sellers, for almost by definition such a reading public is limited and small. These examples can be extended to many other cases.

How to bring culture back to a condition where there is a better approximation between value and price, where works of value are produced which as commodities can earn their keep, is the great task of the future. It is one that cannot be achieved as long as global culture is in the ascendancy. Hence, the main problem is weaning people away from their addiction to global culture. This cannot be done by restricting supply, as with drugs, but only by reducing demand. Educational programs starting with the earliest years of schooling are obviously in the first line of defense, and we shall return to these later. But other public activities, like those already current in nature conservation, should also be undertaken. On the principle of fighting fire with fire, even advertising campaigns—such as those against smoking—should be launched against the excessive use of electronic media, especially by children, for it has been proven that global culture taken in large doses is harmful to physical and mental health. If by such methods the demand for global culture can be reduced then the purveyors of it, the big media companies, will soon learn to adjust to local demand and might even begin to produce things with some value.

But the media proprietors are not likely to give up without a struggle any more than the tobacco companies have done so. Every tactic will be deployed by the conglomerates to retain their cultural markets. Thus any attempt to fund local alternatives will be met with cries of protectionism, protests against subsidies, and demands for a level playing field in all matters of trade. Retaliation will be threatened in other economic fields. It will be claimed that global culture is simply an aspect of globalization and that restricting it is preventing economic development in the world. These arguments are well known, for they are frequently invoked even now, and need not be further spelled out.

As against such arguments it must be firmly maintained that cultural globalization is not the same as economic or other kinds of globalization. Economic globalization has to do with trade in commodities; cultural globalization involves values. It might be poor economic policy to restrict free trade, erect tariff barriers, subsidize inefficient local products, or even to launch campaigns urging people to buy local goods out of national pride. But such measures might be necessary cultural policies where they concern values. What applies to economics need not apply to culture, and vice versa.

Obviously, it will always be a contentious issue—what is economic and what is cultural—especially as so many things are both commodities and cultural goods at once. It is also apparent that such differentiations can always be misused and purely economic interests be surreptitiously protected in the guise of cultural concern. Much international negotiation will have to go on for a long time to produce a consensus of general agreement on such issues. Thus, it will have to be decided to what extent farming communities and even farming practices are purely economic undertakings and where they begin to be of cultural significance. We will return to this issue at the end for it is also at the heart of the problem of land care and nature conservation. It is possible that in such cases and many others like them some immediate economic benefits will have to be forgone for the sake of cultural and environmental gains. But ultimately the world as a whole will be better off if both nature and culture are not left to the vagaries of the market.

Our distinction between commodities and values is the theoretical underpinning for separating the economic system from the cultural system in general. The two systems can be quite different in character even within the one society. In particular, a capitalist economic system need not entail a capitalist cultural one; and vice versa, a noncapitalist cultural system need not necessitate a noncapitalist economic one. Culture and economy are, of course, related to each other, but in very complex ways—differently so for each type of society, as Alsop's work shows.

It follows from this that an attack on global culture is not necessarily also an attack on capitalism; and, in general, opposition to global culture is not ipso facto opposition to globalization as such. Globalization in its economic form is an unavoidable development of late capitalism. The diffusion of investment and production facilities throughout the world is bound to happen if economic development is to continue. The spread of labor-intensive manufacture to low labor-cost countries has, on the whole, been to the economic benefit of those countries and mostly to the workers themselves, who would otherwise remain unemployed. However, because of the lack of international regulations about employment conditions, it has given rise to exploitative abuses, so typical of the early stages of capitalism. As happened earlier in the West and elsewhere, this will be rectified for it is not an inherent part of capitalism as such. For that to be done sooner rather than later, it is necessary for an international movement of protest to be launched to put pressure on firms and governments to institute better working conditions and labor laws to protect the workers. And this is where the antiglobalizers have a crucial role to play. All this can take place within the normal workings of capitalism and in the long run, as has already been proven in the West. it benefits it.

Something similar holds for the opposition to global culture, which is also a corrective to capitalism and is not in fundamental conflict with it. Global culture can be seen as a pathological cultural development that has arisen during this period of the growth of an unrestrained and uninhibited global capitalism. But just as the excesses of national capitalism were curbed in the past, so, too, might global capitalism be regulated in order to safeguard the values of nature and culture. Protecting the natural environment need not hurt economic output, and neither need protecting the cultural milieu. In the long run both kinds of measures are beneficial to the health and proper functioning of society and so are conducive to its productive capacity. Capitalism only stands to benefit from the restraining of its present predatory excesses.

Global culture has arisen out of the conjuncture of a number of factors: the spread of global capitalism, the weakness of local cultures, the political liberalization and democratization of the world, the spread of global media, the rise of multinational corporations, and the present power and policies of America. Such a conjuncture will not last. Sooner or later it will dissolve and global culture will lose its ascendancy. Its triumph might be short-lived, judged by any long-run historical perspective. However, the danger is that before that happens it will have done much irreparable damage. For just as our natural environment might be catastrophically affected before the necessary preventive measures are in place, so, too, might our cultural milieu. In both cases we need to do what is necessary before it is too late. Urgent measures must be taken soon to save what is still left of local culture before it is all lost, for once completely destroyed it will be irrecoverable. But if local cultures can be saved before they disappear, then eventually much more favorable conditions might arise when the present unfortunate conjunction of events is past. A future form of capitalism might be culturally much more propitious, for global culture is not an inevitable feature of every form of global capitalism.

Capitalism per se need not be destructive of culture. Marx's animadversion against it on this score was quite mistaken. Even in his own time the culture of Europe was an extraordinary civilizational achievement, as in some of his writings he recognized. This culture arose not in spite of capitalism, but because of it; the most capitalistically advanced societies were also the most culturally developed and, conversely, the least capitalist were generally backward. There was no inherent contradiction between capitalism and culture. Nor is there one now.

Capitalism is only an economic system, not the total system of society, as the Marxists have presented it. Hence, it does not determine everything else in society; it is compatible with many different kinds of social structures, political regimes, and cultural establishments. As an economic system it has many advantages over every other thus far devised. It mandates a more rational allocation of resources and is in this respect more efficient than any other economic arrangement—which does not mean that it is also more rational in any other way. As the numerous experiments with various kinds of socialist economies during the twentieth century have shown, nothing can in practice measure up on this score to capitalism.

In its historical course capitalism has evolved through a constant striving for rational efficiency, which has driven it to undergo a number of structural articulations. In its first mature phase it carried out a basic separation of ownership from production—that is, the separation of the owners of the productive resources or capitalists from those who carried out the productive process. This is what Marx bewailed as the separation of workers as proletarians from the means of production, but he failed to note that not only proletarians were separated from the means of production—so, too, were managers, technical personnel, and other high-paid specialists. Hence, this separation was not a matter of exploitation, though it was sometimes that, but rather a function of the rational investment of capital. Those productive processes that could not bring a return on capital invested, that is to say, inefficient processes, could be abrogated through the bankruptcy of the firms involved, and thereby the capital, plant, and employees freed to be redirected to more efficient enterprises. But at the same time, this also produces the callousness of the market in rendering workers inexplicably unemployed through no apparent fault of their own. This, as we now know, can only be redressed through unionism and social welfare measures.

In its second mature phase, occurring more or less during the late nineteenth and twentieth centuries, capitalism has undergone another major structural articulation: that of the separation of ownership and management. This was largely brought about by the development of the joint-stock company trading its shares freely on the stock market. The owners, formally speaking, became the shareholders and the running of the enterprise with all its decision-making functions became allocated to professional managers who were, formally speaking, employees of the company. This marked the transition from a largely entrepreneurial to a largely managerial form of capitalism; or, humanly speaking, from the robber baron to the organization man. Thus the price of shares on the stock market became the economic criterion of the productivity and efficient management of a firm. This does not mean that entrepreneurship has disappeared, for it is always necessary at the start of a new enterprise, but only that it tends to transform itself over time into orderly decision making through managerial organization. Thus the Fords of their time and the Gates of ours, who are essential in starting up new industries, are eventually displaced by boards of management and teams of directors.

At present, in the period of globalization, capitalism seems to be entering its third major structural articulation: that of the separation of production from marketing and the constitution of an impermanent work force of teams of specialists. The big multinational corporations are divesting themselves more and more of the productive process and of a stable organization of permanent employees. Either they do not themselves produce at all, merely licensing production to subordinate semi-independent local enterprises, as is typically the case in the production of consumer goods. Or they outsource and off-load the production of all the component parts and merely specialize in assembling these into the final product, as is the case with most manufactured objects, such as cars, machines, and technical devices. As we have already indicated, this is in some respects a beneficial development, for it spreads the production process and the skills involved throughout many societies in the world and provides much needed employment and technical training to impoverished masses.

However, the other aspects of this most recent articulation of capitalism are not so beneficial. The loss of secure employment has produced considerable social dislocation even in the most advanced societies. The separation of marketing and production, especially of consumer goods, has had even worse effects for it has resulted in the increased use of advertising and branding techniques, which have had such disastrous consequences for culture. Firms that produce nothing much else but brand names, fashion images, and lifestyle fictions are among the main contributors to global culture. They dominate the global media and through that give rise to the present homogeneous and unvarying cultural products that take no account of local cultural differences. As far as possible they seek to negate and wipe out local cultures. A uniform world would suit them best of all.

This is the most predatory and dangerous aspect of global capitalism, the one that needs curbing most of all. How this is to be achieved is, of course, as yet an unanswered question. Presumably many as yet untried practical measures will have to be taken to draw the teeth of this capitalist monstrosity. Capitalism must and will reform itself beyond its present predatory stage. There are already the first glimmerings of an ecologically and culturally responsible capitalism. Industry is slowly becoming aware that it must limit its impact on nature and culture or else catastrophic consequences for mankind will ensue. Most major firms now recognize that they cannot pollute the environment at will and that they must become more socially responsible. The full realization is still to come that the local cultural milieu also cannot be imposed on and insulted without serious damage to the whole social fabric of life. This is an awareness that must be furthered among media companies in particular.

What has to be encouraged is the decentralization of media production. If marketing was done at the local level then advertising would begin to adjust to local content. This would be a small step in breaking the dominant grip of global culture. But anything along this line would almost certainly require legislation mandating local content in media production. The molding of public taste through education would also have to take place before there was any shift in the policies of the media firms.

Over and above everything else there must come an acknowledgment that culture cannot be just left to the vagaries of the market. No civilization in the past has ever taken this attitude to its cultural values, the dearest possessions of its heritage. Every civilization has adopted measures of support to sustain its culture. We must now also devise such means of culture protection. In particular, to safeguard what is still left of local culture before it disappears forever.

C. CHOOSING LOCAL CULTURE

Local culture is that of a specific place, time, and people. It is what a group of people constitutes over a given time in a locality or milieu. Every such culture has a local habitation and a name, frequently the name of its tutelary genius loci. Once upon a time it would have been the name of the local god, prophet, saint, or hero. Even now in some places such a culture still flourishes. But mostly now it is a fragment of the past that has escaped the ravages of global culture.

That which a group of people participate in together might be either very old or very new. When it is old it is a tradition, when it is new it is either a fashion or an innovation that is more or less revolutionary. All of these—traditions, fashions, and innovations—are continually reacting on each other to produce orderly change when the culture is sound. Thus fashions and innovations are conditioned by existing traditions, but these in turn are recreated in keeping with the new developments. This happens at all levels of culture, but to varying degrees; in general, folk culture is more bound to tradition, popular culture to fashions, and elite culture to creative innovation. Which does not mean that tradition is absent in popular and elite culture or that fashion and innovation have no effect on folk culture. Though usually folk culture changes at a much slower pace than the others. At the same time, all the three levels of culture influence each other, such that what starts as an innovation in the one becomes a tradition in the others or even sometimes vice versa. These are, as it were, the normal patterns of cultural development.

Today, under the impact of global culture, developments do not proceed in this way anymore. Traditions, fashions, and innovations no longer influence each other in an orderly way for everything is manipulated for the sake of the market. Traditions are not respected, innovations that introduce something genuinely new are scorned, and fashions are regarded merely as styling changes required to generate demand. This is no longer a situation of normal cultural change. Rather it is a kind of stasis, an interruption of even flow and development leading to a condition of turbulence and turmoil.

In this unsettled state holding on to local culture is a way of securing the past, which would otherwise slip away and disappear. Global culture has no past in the true historical sense—like coins, it continually emerges freshly minted from the factories where its images are stamped and disappears when it is used up. Even when it alludes to the past, it only does so in a generic way such that the mythical past and the historic past are indistinguishable from each other. Disney theme parks, for example, deliberately confound any differentiated sense of the past by mixing fairy tales with literary evocations and with reconstituted historical settings drawn from all kinds of traditions. Hollywood does much the same, with even less concern for the past, which it invariably dresses up in terms of the present, so that no matter what past it is, it becomes the American way of life projected back to any other time or country. Only local culture can preserve a sense of the past specific to each locality, whether as customs and traditions, or as monuments and memorials, or as identities that depend on affiliation with something historical.

Sharing a local past is what brings people together and endows them with an identity. Without that they lose their bearings, their sense of who they are and where they belong. A common past defines a people, a nation, a religion, a distinctive group, or even a city or region. With no established practices or institutions, such as are only inherent in local culture, people drift and have nothing to motivate or move them except the desires and ambitions of the moment. Without any historic memory to maintain continuity, anything can change with no rhyme or reason except for the imperatives of the market. If it sells it must be good. What sells and what does not is largely a matter of manipulation with a large element of chance. In such a fluid situation people cannot maintain any coherence, but change their identities almost in the way they do their clothes. *Kleider machen Leute* has become literally true as people assume new identities whenever they change their outfits to conform to requirements. The contemporary fascination with spies and their need to assume a cover reflects a realization that anyone might have to become anything else on demand and that, consequently, one never knows who one is dealing with, which some people actually find exciting.

Cultural history has largely become a matter of happenstance. Hence, what is at stake in the move to global culture is not a matter of another historical transition following on the many that have already occurred. It is something totally unprecedented, a move out of cultural time into another kind of time altogether. It is a time without a past, that is, a past that consolidates the present. For just as the present is transient, so the past is continually transformed to suit the needs of the moment. What is considered the past goes in and out of fashion, as, for example, in the revivals of the pop styles of the preceding decades. This is the reason that every such change in fashion seems to its exponents and followers as if it were of major importance, for with it comes a change in everything else in their mentality. It is as if the whole world were altering, whereas in reality it is but a small variation on what went before, one that will very soon be followed by another equally inconsequential, but also seemingly earth-shaking.

It is in all these ways, some only superficial but others deep-seated, that global culture has the potential for totally changing the mode and quality of life for most people on earth in an extremely short time. Only a few more decades are all that will be required. Once this happens, once people have lost their past and assume an indefinite identity where they can be anything at all, then nothing will stand in the way of a uniform global order under which much the same conditions obtain throughout. It will matter little whether this is one of complete freedom or complete tyranny or, as seems most likely, a highly circumscribed fluidity of existence; whatever the outcome in this respect, people's lives will be prescribed and they will do what is required of them for want of any alternatives.

At present we still have some fundamental choices available, we can choose local as against global culture almost in every eventuality that confronts us in ordinary life circumstances. By innumerable such choices made every day we can still recover the past and reconnect with it in the small acts of affirming who and what we are that confirm or confer an identity. It is not a matter of credos or manifestos, of proclamations or declarations, for usually such are now spurious, but of the gestures and expressions of the moment out of which everyday life is constituted. For it is at this level of quotidian living that global culture exerts its major influence and it is on this same level that it must be confronted. For just as the looming environmental crisis calls on masses of people to develop proper daily habits of waste disposal, not to foul their rivers and nature reserves, as well as to make the countless right decisions on how to heat or cool their homes or to water their gardens and so on, so, too does the cultural crisis require people to exercise analogous small choices daily.

Global culture is not one of ideas, ideals, beliefs, or great aspirations, but one of daily habits of living and quotidian practices. It changes people's lives not through any conversions or insights, but in small incremental creeps, gradually inducing them to adjust the routines and rhythms of living to its own requirements. It seems altogether unimposing as it almost invisibly insinuates itself by degrees into the fabric of living like a virus in the body. But its overall effect can be just as deadly, for it induces habits of consumer passivity that are bad for physical, mental, and spiritual well-being. The common term "couch potato" sums up much of what is wrong with television habituation, and other such colloquial expressions will doubtlessly be coined as other ill effects of global culture become apparent. The only antidote to it, one that might almost be medically prescribed, is an active involvement in other cultural pursuits. And almost any form that such a participatory engagement takes is bound to constitute some kind of local culture no matter how minor. It is in this way that cultivating some kind of hobby in relation with others, be it pigeon racing, stamp collecting, quilt making, or whatever else in this genre, constitutes a very basic local cultural activity. Even playing sport on a regular basis, especially in a local game, is much better than watching it in stadiums or on television.

In contemporary times the issue is not one of an active versus a contemplative life, since almost everyone works; it is rather that of an active versus a passive life. It is a question of how work and leisure are to be undertaken, whether actively engaged in or passively endured. Is one's life to be filled with consumer satisfactions that consign one to solitude, or become a realization of one's abilities, preferably in joint activities with others? Other things being equal, it is usually much better to sing or play an instrument rather than listen to the radio, record, or DVD; it is better to make one's own things rather than buy them ready-made, particularly so where children are concerned; it is better to cook food and eat it at home than to buy it out, especially if it is fast food; it is better to converse with someone face to face than to exchange emails or even telephone calls; it is better to see a play or film than play a video game; it is better to wager with people than gamble against machines; and so on for all the innumerable things people do everyday. As these examples make evident, it is often culturally preferable to use the older rather than the newer technologies. The reason for this is that the newer technologies remove human contact and control and substitute for it technical mediation and automation. It is for this reason that the older photographic apparatus is artistically preferable to the newest digitalized variety. Ultimately, of course, what matters is not the quality of the photograph but its use—what role it plays in facilitating social relations.

The ultimate purpose of any cultural activity is not performance or achievement for its own sake, but for the sake of establishing human interrelatedness. "Only connect" is the watchword of culture. Consumer culture does the opposite—it disconnects and isolates. It isolates people not only within the walls of their rooms or offices, but also within the spectator crowds it promotes. As many sociologists have observed, to be alone in a crowd is the peculiar loneliness of our time.

One can exemplify the difference between isolating consumer culture and connecting local culture in studying the difference between tourism and travel. Tourism, the favorite activity of most well-off people, is an isolating experience. Tours are generally so designed that among the people of a foreign country one remains on one's own or with the group with which one came; one is cut off from the natives and their way of life by all the restrictions and barriers that the requirements of touristic comforts impose, as well as, most frequently, by linguistic and cultural incomprehension and social and economic disparities. Travel is the opposite connecting experience. A traveler behaves on the old adage "when in Rome do as the Romans"—that is, adapt yourself to the local people's way of life, familiarize yourself with their language and customs, live with them, and go out of your way to meet them. This also means do not flit from place to place, but stay as long as possible and come often to the one locality. It is to be regretted that so few people are now genuine travelers, for the vast majority are tourists.

Tourism is corrupting and destructive of all local culture, for wherever it becomes the main business activity it promotes an adjustment to its own requirements, which are those of global culture. Soon it might become impossible to be a traveler anymore because there will be nowhere to travel to—all localities will be more or less the same. Only a determined effort, launched locally but with global dimensions, can save local cultures so that intercultural exchanges are even possible. This must proceed in all spheres of culture at once, at the folk, popular, and elite levels. In what follows we can only offer some general suggestions as to how this might be furthered, which will have to be modified as circumstances require in different places.

We begin with folk culture, which is, as it were, the most fundamental and primitive, the anthropological level of any culture. It is closely akin to the original culture of primitive people, and some of it survives from these earliest ages. For the onset of civilization and later historical developments do not erase everything from the prior past, something of it remains especially among ordinary folk in rural settings. It is only now that the whole heritage of folk culture in all places is in danger of vanishing. Rural cultures are disappearing as agriculture becomes mechanized and farms are consolidated into agribusinesses. Folklore is ceasing to be a lived experience and is known only from books in libraries.

The fate of primitive people is also desperate, for their cultures are dying out faster even than anthropologists can study them. However, belated steps are now being taken all over the world to encourage them to return to their ancestral ways and recover their cultures. Obviously this cannot mean that they are to adopt a primitive lifestyle separate from modern society or that they are to fend for themselves by hunting and gathering. Maintaining primitive cultures can only be done now in a bicultural context, where the prevailing modern culture together with the indispensable professional competences are acquired by the native peoples, not only to earn their living and manage their resources, but also the better to defend their original culture. They must not only become literate, but know their rights and how to uphold them in law. This means that the traditional ways of life cannot be maintained in their original form, only adapted to modern conditions. That in itself constitutes a loss, but an unavoidable one.

Something similar holds true for all folk cultures in general. An authentic rural way of life of peasants or small town folk can no longer be practiced. However, it is still possible to recover the cultural ethos of this vanished life, the cultural traditions that it encapsulated: the festivals, feasts, ceremonies, customs, manners and mores, the charms and ritual, the old ways of cooking, preparing foods, and making all kinds of things—in short, everything that some old people remember and recall how to do can be still learned and practiced by others who wish to follow in their footsteps. As we shall see, such a way of life, linked to a duty of care of the land, can be made economically sustainable by suitable policies of recompense. It would fulfill both ecological and cultural goals in maintaining the fields, habitations, and landscape built up over countless generations that is the countryside. This humanly constituted nature is essential for the recreation and health of urban dwellers as well.

It is demographically inevitable that the vast majority of human beings will live in large cities. Among these some folkways can still be maintained, especially those associated with religion. But primarily this is the setting of popular culture. This includes all the artistic practices actively engaged in by groups of people as well as all the things made for local use and enjoyment. Much of this will involve entertainment, recreation, and objects of consumption sold commercially in local markets. Hence, though this is already a partly commodified culture, it is not one mass-produced for anonymous buyers anywhere at all. And this is what makes a crucial difference, for in culture as elsewhere "small is beautiful." People enjoying the products of local culture are not passive consumers, for they invariably do so with discernment and good taste since they are closely bound up with their production.

Popular culture is subject to relatively rapid changes of fashion. But again, what is crucial is that this not be manipulated by business entrepreneurs, but emerge spontaneously from local trends. Frequently the trendsetters are not people in authority or those with power or money; they can come from the lowest of the low, from criminal elements amid brothels and bars. Popular music and dancing, in particular, tend to come from sordid surroundings. Until recently, the circus, music hall, vaudeville, and Grand Guignol theater were not occupations for nice people. Even now spontaneous musical styles arise from such quarters. Only now such developments fall quickly into the hands of the media executives and soon lose their local character.

The problem now is how to keep popular culture away from the clutches of the mass media and their ancillary organs of cultural production. The key factor is to get people to consume mainly that which they themselves produce or, at least, in whose production they indirectly participate. Anything that comes completely ready-made should usually be shunned. Even spectators of shows take part in their production when these are designed specifically with them in mind and where they have sufficient nous as aficionados to know how to respond. But to do that they must become themselves proficient in the finer points of the art. The relationship between performers and audience in popular culture is quite different to that in mass culture, as we have already explained.

Elite culture is not for everyone. It is not even necessarily for those who constitute the social elite in terms of class, money, or power. Rather it is the culture of any exclusive grouping that defines itself by some kind of cultural refinement. This calls for special competence that is a matter of interest, schooling, practice, and even to some extent, talent. In the past such elite accomplishments were mainly open to upper classes, but not always so, for plebeian elites cultivating an exclusive culture of their own were also possible. Thus, for example, Puritan and nonconformist groups in England maintained themselves as elite cultural communities, as did the intelligentsia in Czarist Russia, even though these emerged from lower orders in society. Also, it was always possible for an exceptional individual from any class whatsoever to reach an elite cultural status. Though usually, of course, elite culture went with dominant class.

Today it is almost the reverse situation, for the rich and powerful no longer think it necessary or worthwhile to have any cultural pretentions whatsoever. Mostly such people are quite content with global culture, tending to its luxury side, of course, and the more sophisticated among them have taken to postmodernism, which in a sense is the same thing. Even the schooling of such people is no longer premised on proficiency in humanistic culture, but on professional training in legal, scientific, managerial, and other technical fields that have little cultural content. Such people do not act as artistic patrons and feel no need to display any cultural competence. If they buy paintings, it is purely for investment purposes, following not their own predilections but the advice of their dealers.

Hence, today one can no longer expect elite culture to emerge out of the elite social strata. It must be redefined as the culture of excellence pursued by self-selected groups who come together out of common interest. Such groups will now be small gatherings of artists, connoisseurs, devotees, intellectuals, and other like-minded individuals usually specializing in one or another narrow cultural field. They are not broadly cultivated, all-rounded types any more. Yet they deserve unstinted encouragement and support for they are the ones who still uphold what is left of elite culture. This is no disservice to others, provided that access to such groups is not restricted to the privileged, but open to anyone with the necessary competence.

It is interesting to note that elitism—which is condoned by everyone where it concerns technical, sporting, or any other pragmatic pursuits, as the cult of the expert so clearly demonstrates—arouses intense indignation and hostility as soon as it is referred to culture. This is itself an expression of the disappearance of values in the dominant nihilistic ethos purveyed by global culture. To counteract it one must confront it openly and affirm the claims of excellence in culture whenever this is challenged. It must be shown that elite culture is essential for society in general in that it establishes standards and norms that can percolate throughout the whole cultural milieu. Popular and even folk culture are leavened and quickened by it. One only has to recall the Romantic movement, which began in small elite groups that were not socially elevated, but eventually transformed the whole culture of Western societies. Today such a movement is inconceivable, yet not all is lost.

Today, unfortunately, elite culture is commonly identified with the traditional cultures of the past; it has become an antiquarian preoccupation. Performing, studying, storing, restoring, and transporting the remains of these cultures has become the main concern of the official elite institutions, such as museums, galleries, theaters, concert halls, libraries, and universities. Hence this is now a mostly petrified culture; it is no longer part of any living traditions. How and why this petrification of the past ensued we have already adverted to previously and cannot expound here any further. What is to be done about it is the major problem of elite culture at present.

Here we have the opposite predicament to that presented by global culture: not how to hold on to the past, but how to free oneself from the burden of a dead past. And the only way this can be achieved is to make this past alive by bringing it into closer relation with the present. This cannot be done through scholarship or research alone. For it is not the past as recorded history or historical record that matters, but the past as living tradition providing a sense of belonging and a source of identity. Such a past will not emerge out of the official cultural institutions, only out of elite groups of self-selected individuals in pursuit of the highest standards in their endeavor. Such, for example, are groups of poets who cannot hope to sell their work or secure sinecure appointments, yet publish slim volumes or little magazines that are mainly read by those who write for them. Such, too, are groups of intellectuals less intent on careers or media appearances and more on grappling with important issues. There are analogous groups of religious thinkers who are trying to redefine the nature of faith, both in terms of theological speculation and in life practices. These and many such others are elite cultural groups still active. Now they work in isolation, cut off from each other and without much social backing, so they lack the concerted effort and critical mass to be able to launch large-scale cultural movements. But they all deserve support for they keep alive the elite idea of cultural excellence.

Under present circumstances it would be foolish and presumptuous to expect any kind of cultural renaissance. But it would be equally mistaken and needlessly despairing to believe that everything is lost and that global culture will inevitably destroy every other alternative. It is within our power to prevent this happening; all that is necessary is to resist the steady intrusion of global culture into local culture.

All over the world global culture is infiltrating into every local culture and transforming it in its own image. This is particularly pronounced in the arts. Every type of "native" music is losing its authenticity as local musicians adopt the latest electronic instruments and adapt their local styles to the pop-rock forms in rhythm, melody, and harmony. Local staging and performing practices are drifting in the direction of film techniques or toward musicals, the two major theatrical forms of global culture. Narrative conventions are also tending toward film scripts. The works of plastic art, those which are not simply mass-produced accessories of the tourist trade, are being traded as collectors' items like rare stamps or anything else unusual.

This infiltration is particularly dangerous when it occurs in education, for then it destroys every other culture at the source, in the minds of children and young people. Once imbued with global culture in youth it becomes very difficult to outgrow it and reach out to anything else. Hence it is in education that the decisive stand against global culture must be made. There would indeed be cause to despair if total failure ensued in this regard.

D. RESISTING GLOBAL CULTURE

Until very recently it could have been safely assumed that education was the one sphere of society fairly free of global culture. Now this is no longer so. In fact, education at all levels, from preschool to postgraduate studies, has become an arena of cultural contestation. This is so because the merchants of cultural death have been invading all educational establishments and infusing their wares into the learning process itself. Together with the drug pushers, they have now gained a sure foothold in all schools at all levels.

The hucksters of mass culture have always targeted children and adolescent youth with their sales pitch, on the proven assumption that if they succeed in habituating people at an early age then they have gained consumers for life. But until recently this could only be done outside school hours and outside school gates. Now they have gained entry into the very classrooms, so they can all the more effectively solicit cultural customers. They are all the more emboldened by the fact that they have been invited in by the educational authorities themselves. Hence the classroom has become a crucial battleground against global culture.

Even before formal schooling begins, there is already taking place a struggle for the hearts and minds of little children, for these hold the keys to the purses of their parents. The seduction of the innocents proceeds by way of the usual temptations of childish things. At this early stage the main responsibility for resisting falls on parents, who are usually too preoccupied to realize what is going on and unsuspectingly make use of the electronic child-minding facilities that the media provide. Few understand what this involves, and fewer still have grasped that bringing up children should take place with as little recourse to commercial culture as possible. Those who sense this are often intimidated by the shibboleths of libertarian childrearing pedagogies that denounce as authoritarian any attempt by parents to supervise and if necessary censor their children's access to the media or the Internet. It is precisely at this early age that the local culture should be used to counter the global. Children should be brought up as far as possible in their local traditions, whatever these might be, whether religious or secular, rural or urban, popular or elite; without, at the same time, neglecting intercultural understanding and the necessary universalist norms of toleration for living at peace with others in a global society.

After parents, the main responsibility for bringing up children and youth lies with educators. It is they who have to ensure that the classroom is safe from commercial cultural influences. If they fail to do this then they are derelict in their primary duty of care. Teenagers and youth in general are most vulnerable in this respect—they are most susceptible to the blandishments of the commercial ads, most fascinated by technological gimmickry, and most responsive to peer pressure and the urge to worship the market-place idols. If global products and practices are allowed to become part of their earliest memories, how can they ever detach themselves from this influence? They constitute a large market with disposable money to spare, so they have become the focus of much promotional propaganda. Their youthful insecurities and unsure identities are played and preyed on for this purpose. They are made to feel inadequate in all kinds of ways and are urged to compensate by buying the recommended products. As most of this takes place outside school, there is little that teachers can do about it, but they must not elicit attitudes that in any way condone it.

However, what takes place in school should be of concern to teachers, for schools were until recently among the few refuges from intrusion by commercial culture. Now the cultural salesmen and their collaborators within the educational system are beginning to impose their wares on the educational process itself, and thereby to subvert whatever traditional cultural values are left. Large sums of money are routinely expended for this purpose in the form of gifts of equipment, grants for research, prizes, and awards that amount to little more than bribery by another name.

Commerce in various guises is invading educational institutions at all levels. Advertising is now allowed in many schools in the primary and secondary grades, and even in kindergartens. Klein reports that in the United States, Channel One, and in Canada, Youth News Network, are beaming advertising to 12,000 schools reaching nearly eight million students; advertising that is, in effect, compulsory viewing for students and teachers, since the ads cannot be turned off or muted.[10] Direct sponsorship of commercial products with an appeal to children, such as Coke, Pepsi, Nike, and so on, is now commonplace in schools, and brand-name fast-food outlets are taking the place of all older tuck-shops and cafeterias and are being patronized by the more affluent students. The utilization of video equipment and computers with built-in Internet browsers is itself a technification of education that serves the interests of information technology companies and is a beachhead for further commercially sponsored technified learnings to follow later.

The computer has proven itself to be a veritable Trojan horse in schools—once taken in it brings with itself all kinds of other hidden invaders. The sheer technical wizardry of the machine and the relentless sales pitch from the computer companies have swept away all opposition and even doubt or hesitation as to its educational utility. School authorities, who should have known better, were pressured from all quarters—parents, children, businesses, the media, and politicians—into a frenzy of computer purchases, which they carried out as long as the funds lasted. What they bought they had to find a use for; they consequently applied computing to everything and so transformed the whole curriculum into a series of technical competencies. This precipitate drive for computer literacy has frequently come at the expense of real literacy or numeracy, for many among the screen gazing generation of students are no longer able to read books.[11] Instead of immersing themselves in real texts and making use of libraries in doing research for their assignments—and thus exercising their own judgment about what is relevant and interesting—they are now content to key in search words and receive prepackaged and predigested extracts. Not only does this teach bad learning habits, but it is also morally dubious because it blurs the line between composing and copying-out and leads to what amounts to cheating with a good conscience.

Instead of this wholesale surrender to the computer—and all that comes with it, from computer games to pornography—schools should be teaching sensible attitudes to technology and a proper use of machines, including computers themselves. The basic principle of instrumental use is a version of Occam's razor: never multiply technologies beyond necessity. This means that one should always match the technology to its intended purpose or use appropriate technology, as it is commonly called. One should not use a high-technology instrument where a low-technology tool is just as good and more convenient. For the higher technologies one employs the more one makes oneself dependent on a whole complex technological system, which can easily become subject to malfunctions and even catastrophic breakdowns. The problem with computer viruses is only a small case in point. Low technologies tend to be generally safer and often cheaper.

Computer literacy is only the technical facet of an even more general tendency to promote global culture in schools and universities that goes under the name of media literacy and is taught in various faculties under the rubric of culture studies, communications studies, and numerous other such studies. Initially such courses were begun with the laudable aims of informing students about the culture of their everyday lives and prophylactically forearming them with the necessary critical theories so as to be able to confront and deflect the messages of the media. We previously mentioned a number of the philosophical schools that were enlisted for this purpose, such as the Frankfurt school, the Birmingham school, and the school of Paris, with their well-known major thinkers. As always, the road to hell is paved with good intentions. Like the prophet Balaam, teachers came to curse but stayed to praise: what began as criticism of the media ended up as appreciation of it.

What turned all the critical theories on their head in the classroom was the very demand from students for such courses. As the student numbers grew it became increasingly more difficult for their teachers to tell them that the only culture most of them knew was really no good. It would have taken very brave teachers indeed to stand up against the ingrained tastes of so many students. So teachers generally succumbed and began to see virtue in necessity, in pop music and all the other products of global culture. Thus the net effect of such courses was to legitimate the trash of the media. The very fact that students could see such "texts" studied with all the critical acumen of major theories, utilizing a barely understood jargon of technical expressions, was in itself extremely reassuring for their prejudices, showing them that what they thought they had liked instinctively was being treated with utmost seriousness, and even if not wholeheartedly approved of, at least taken to be of major significance. And in any case, it was much easier for them to study materials they already knew than launch into texts they were barely able to read and whose very titles they had hardly heard of. Those teachers who wished to attract and hold a large student clientele could easily do so by telling them what they wanted to hear.

As always in such academic "revolutions," the publishing industry was waiting in the wings to capitalize on the situation. Very soon hundreds of books were issued in all these studies. Pushy editors and academics came to the fore by commissioning and writing texts about texts, which were not real texts in any ordinary sense, but pictures, songs, films, television shows, or whatever. The production of these books easily outpaced and outnumbered publications in the old disciplines, such as literature, history, politics, sociology, or philosophy. If this keeps up at the present rate the old disciplines will be swamped before too long and disappear. Most of these are already sadly depleted, and their hold is very tenuous except in the few oldest and best-established universities. Everywhere else new subjects that concern themselves primarily with the products of global culture are displacing the old disciplines.

It is not to be denied that the products of global culture are suitable subjects for academic research. Given their role in society it is important that they should be investigated. What matters is the manner and spirit in which it is done. It can be done more or less critically or objectively, but it is in all cases crucial that proper value judgments inform the inquiry. However, the fact that these are possible subjects of research does not mean that they also constitute suitable "texts" for teaching purposes, especially of young undergraduates. Thus, for example, it is undeniable that gambling should be researched, but it does not follow from this that gambling should be taught. Analogously so, "soaps," best-seller novels, crossword puzzles, or whatever else that occupies the time and attention of masses of people and is undoubtedly sociologically and economically important, should be researched. But these are not appropriate or fitting "texts" for teaching and neither is hip-hop.[12]

It goes without saying that curriculum design and the choice of proper texts at various levels of education is a very difficult and contentious undertaking about which there can be rational disagreement. It is not necessary to follow Matthew Arnold's dictum to teach only "the best that is known and thought in the world." Quality is not the sole criterion for choosing teaching material; relevance to students' lives and interests, crucial national issues and political problems, even questions of identity can all play a part. But whatever considerations enter they should not involve a surrender to commercial interests.

Commercial interests are more than ever involved in education because with the onset of globalization education has become a lucrative export business for many countries, especially those in the English-speaking world. Prepackaged learning courses are now being devised by universities in partnership with media conglomerates and electronically delivered to masses of anonymous students all over the world. The best that can be said for this is that it enables such students to receive a form of technical training that they might not otherwise get. But it is far from any real education. In fact, it undermines this by eroding any relation between teachers and students and substituting for it a purely impersonal process of intellectual management. The teacher is now no more than a facilitator or supervisor of instrumental techniques, in which even assessment is being increasingly done by machines.

Where teaching no longer matters, education itself goes by default. What is emerging in its stead is pure training, which is the learning complement of the triumph of technics. Technics does not require any education and militates against it. As Ellul puts it, "humanism is antiquated because the environment in which the student is immersed is, first of all, no longer a human, but a technological environment."[13] And not only is humanism antiquated, so is any other educational project. For any such endeavor must have a cultural basis which is more than that offered by "cultural studies," so-called. Without that it soon degenerates to mere training. The prevalence of cultural studies is only speeding up this process, which is taking place anyway for the weightier reasons that Ellul notes.

Education must always be counterposed to training. Training is the attainment of proficiency in some set of techniques, either those of a technological system or those of the various professions. Education, by contrast, is an enculturation process, the immersion in the representation and ethos of a specific culture. One is trained to do useful work; one is educated to lead a cultured and decent life. Training has a utilitarian function and concerns itself only with the acquisition of the knowledge and skills necessary to carry out that function. Education has no such specific aim in view but seeks to produce a certain kind of individual character, one able to exercise judgment in any of the major activities of the social life in which that person will be engaged. Obviously what are such major activities varies from society to society. So it is not possible to prescribe the one optimal educational course for everyone. However, in a contemporary modern context education should prepare people to take part in communal, political, public-spirited, investigative, artistic, convivial, and generally also religious concerns of their societies.

Thus education has above all to do with culture, which does not really matter for training. Insofar as learning any subject or field of knowledge and expertise—such as science, engineering, economics, social studies, business studies, law, or anything else in this line—only involves training, it has nothing to do with culture. Hence, all the confused debate on the so-called "two cultures" that C. P. Snow initiated forty years ago was largely vitiated by a failure to distinguish between education and training in both these fields. It is possible to be educated in science, though this is normally a very rare occurrence, just as it is possible to be trained in a humanistic discipline, which is becoming more and more the case as cultural studies proliferate.

The intrusion of global culture into the schools and universities subverts education in favor of training. Education in a specific local culture, with its particular standards and values, is displaced by expertise in the products of the culture industry. No genuine education is possible on this basis alone. But this is not to deny that knowledge of global culture can be fitted into an educational program as part of an awareness of the state of the world. In fact, such knowledge is necessary if there is to be any intelligent reaction against it.

In our commercialized world, not only teaching but research as well is being preempted by business interests. The firms that are involved in providing global culture fund research that is designed to make them more acceptable, on the model of the research supported by the tobacco industry. Some of them now have such a controlling hold in some universities that research that runs counter to their interests can be stopped from proceeding or discounted even when published. Professors who engage in it can be threatened with loss of funding or even dismissal in some cases. In all these ways global culture is assuming an unassailable position in schools and universities. Even the best of these are becoming corrupted and turning into mere training facilities.

The struggle for education goes beyond schools and universities and concerns society as a whole, for an informed and aware citizenry is crucial to democratic political life. This inevitably involves a battle for the media, for it is crucial to this that there be some media outlets dedicated to public service goals. Real democracy is not possible where all the media are controlled by a handful of moguls who are rarely publicly minded and not chary of deploying their oligopolistic advantage for their own political and commercial interests. Politicians, even those in the highest positions, become dependent on and beholden to these media proprietors who are in a position to promote or damage their image, particularly during elections. The cultivation of image means that no real public debate can take place focused on issues and instead it is diverted into the trivialities of personality. Politicians are packaged by advertisers seconded to run election campaigns just like any other lines of consumer goods. These campaign-management techniques are international in scope. Thus local political culture becomes everywhere subverted by global political culture.

It is doubtful whether much of any democratic political culture can be sustained unless there are some independent public service media. It is for this reason particularly crucial for citizens in democracies to keep their public service media from falling into the hands of commercial interests or becoming themselves commercialized. In Britain and the other European countries there is a steady corruption of the public service media taking place, and everything possible should be done to redress this. Where such media barely exist, as in America, it should be developed with public funding. The laudable example set by Australia in publicly funding a special channel devoted to international programming in all languages, SBS, should be followed by all countries.

At present only public service broadcasting can be relied on to counter global culture in the electronic media. Given that mass media are unavoidable in all mass societies the question still remains who is to control these media and for what purposes are they to function. Privately owned media that are primarily run for profit must largely depend on promotion and publicity for their income and so they become tools of commercial interests, which in a global context means becoming purveyors of global culture. Only media outlets that are free of these pressures can be relied on to oppose this. They might, of course, do so in the name of national culture and lend themselves to the arousal of nationalist feelings. But in the contemporary historical and political context that is a lesser danger, one that is no worse than the propensity for chauvinism in the privately owned media. One need only remember the behavior of the Murdoch-owned press in Britain during the Falklands war, which was certainly far worse than that of the BBC, to be persuaded on that score. Unfortunately, of late the BBC seems to have evened the score by going too far the other way in its reporting of the conflicts in the Middle East.

Advocating local culture does increase the risk of nationalistic and other xenophobic reactions if this were done without the necessary counterbalancing internationalist corrections. As we have argued before, this can be achieved by cultivating the potential complementarity between localism and cosmopolitanism. The one can be used to promote the other, for a full grasp of one's own local culture requires a reaching out to others. In many societies some kind of bilingual and bicultural solution is the only possible recourse for many citizens. Hence, the proper course to follow lies somewhere between globalism and xenophobia; in this Aristotelian mean are located the sensible reactions against global culture and the soundest actions in defense of local culture.

E. TOWARD AN ECO-CULTURAL BALANCE

We must not imagine that global culture can be overcome or that it will somehow presently disappear. Given its role and function in the present world economy and all the forces that promote it, one must expect it to remain for the foreseeable future. But it need not be dominant and it must not be allowed to expand at the expense of local culture. If it were kept in its place alongside local culture then it would not constitute the danger it is at present. For global culture has a kind of inverse Midas-effect—it turns to dross all the gold it touches. All that it has taken over from local culture it has transformed into commercial trash. This is particularly evident in America where so many of the treasures of local culture have been melted down and converted into tinsel, and so effectively destroyed. A similar fate awaits local culture everywhere else.

We can now see this process at work even in the very lowliest of milieus, in culinary culture. McDonaldization is seizing hold of all local cooking and food preparation methods all over the world. This began in America with hamburgers and fried chicken, but it has spread so fast and so far that the Japanese are now complaining of a McDonaldization of sushi. In this, as in all such cases, the name and some of the basic ingredients remain the same, but the taste has inevitably altered. And not taste alone—all the cultural traditions associated with the preparing and consuming of food and drink are now disappearing. This has far-reaching consequences for such things as family togetherness and the rites of friendship and conviviality all over the world.

These changes in culinary culture come together with and even promote further a thoroughgoing rationalization of farming practices toward specialization in a limited number of crops mechanically harvested and animal species that are factory-farmed. As is well known, this is ecologically and genetically dangerous; it is not so well understood that it is also culturally impoverishing. For where farming is industrialized, the whole rural way of life is destroyed, as well as the landscape itself. To maintain a variety of produce it is essential to keep up a variety of farming practices, most of them traditional in origin and peculiar to each major region. And for this to happen, something like a traditional rural way of life will need to be maintained, for both cultural and ecological reasons at once.

A sound eco-cultural balance between humanity and the natural environment must be focused on agriculture, or the way in which we produce our food. Agriculture and culture are closely integrated, for sound agricultural practices call for a total care of the land undertaken by farming communities that are devoted to this task. The farmers must become the first line of conservationists, custodians of the land and the whole environment of which it is part. To achieve such a land-care program will require a complete redefinition of the nature of farming. It cannot just be a matter of production, but must be one of conservation as well.

Already this is starting to happen among enlightened rural circles all over the world. It is also starting to be promoted by the agricultural policies of some governments. In Europe a new policy called multifunctionality has been introduced to pay farmers for a whole range of rural tasks, and not just for output, as was the case with the old policy. Thus farmers are encouraged to undertake ecological protection measures as well as to maintain the historic and cultural landscape. This is also a means of preventing rural depopulation, which had nearly emptied the countryside during the course of the last century. The encouragement of organic farming after the recent health scares in Europe is another indication that attitudes in this respect are changing.

Only a transformed farming life can provide a basis for any kind of rural culture whatsoever. This will have to be a culture that incorporates many of the old folkways that are traditional in different localities. The old and the new will have to join hands to save the land and its people: old traditions must come together with the latest, most up-to-date farming techniques based on a scientific awareness of ecological interrelationships. There is, of course, no question of returning to primitive methods of farming. Even if this were humanly feasible—and given the back-breaking labor it requires, it no longer is so—it would not be practically possible, for it could not feed humanity. Industrializing agriculture even further is not the answer to this problem. A solution based on better cultural premises has to be sought.

The preservation of nature on our planet in general has now become a cultural issue. Nature can no longer be seen as a force independent of humanity, and hence able to repair and renovate itself no matter what damage is wrought by puny Man. Nature is now under our control and we can make it or mar it as much as we choose. It is our culture that will determine what happens to nature. Hence we must develop a culture that is respectful of and caring for nature. This cannot be global culture, with its incessant drive for consumption. It will have to be a culture with local roots that knows the land on which it grows.

This basic point is still not properly appreciated by the followers of the environmentalist movement. They tend to be indifferent to cultural considerations, and many of them are exponents and even practitioners of global culture. They have to be made aware that nature conservation and culture preservation are linked, not only in rural environments, but throughout. Such an awareness is beginning to arise among some young people who are equating culture pollution with nature pollution and are engaging in minor acts of cultural sabotage called "jamming," such as wittily defacing advertising billboards and interfering with the transmission of TV commercials. This is an anarchistic "propaganda of the deed" of a somewhat jejune kind, though it could develop into something more serious. The cultural environment movement launched in America is another example of a laudable desire to extend the ecological movement from nature to culture. On a global level of action there are cognate moves, such as that propounded by Jeremy Rifkin to set up a World Cultural Organization on the model of the World Trade Organization, in order to gather and publish statistics as to the world's cultural state. It is important, for example, to record the extinction of languages just as it is that of species. All these developments, like daffodils in early spring, are but uncertain premonitions of what might come.

The biggest and most concerted struggles for culture will take place not in the country, where only a small proportion of the population will continue to live, but in the burgeoning cities where the bulk of humanity will reside. In the huge conurbations, which are growing all over the world, more and more poor people are becoming squeezed in ever more tightly and becoming ever more culturally deracinated and impoverished, even if their material conditions might be slightly improving. For them, if they are lucky, a modernized version of *panem et circenses* will be developed: part-time work or the dole, and TV or videos leavened with drugs. But this new entertainment is no occasional gladiatorial performance, it flows unceasingly from the cornucopias of the media, spewing out the wish-fulfillment dreams of consumption.

Under these circumstances, weaning the masses away from the blandishments of global culture will be a Herculean social undertaking. It would be presumptuous and foolish to prescribe simple solutions to problems of this dimension. But it must be recognized that these are as much cultural problems as economic ones. Cultural deracination is as much responsible for people's condition of helplessness as sheer poverty. Hence it is essential to foster some kind of cultural self-respect. It is difficult to see how else this can be attempted except through a recovery of local culture based on a revival of communal life. That this is at least part of the solution is clear from those societies where the people coming in to the cities have kept some of their local traditions, for invariably they have also maintained a better social cohesion. The symptoms of alienation and demoralization are less evident in such cases. Where there is no such counterweight to global culture the degeneration that ensues is even worse.

The cultural problems at the other end of the social scale, among the rich, are no less pronounced than among the poor, except that wealth hides the seriousness of their shortcomings. An affluent lifestyle based on conspicuous consumption is in its own way as corrupting as sheer want. The model for this kind of a lifestyle is provided by global culture. Since the rich are the ones who spend most, it is to them and their aspirations that the global media address themselves. The same images of wealth and indulgence are continually being beamed to all the people of the world. Those who can afford to live up to them consider themselves superior to all others. Hence the affluent way of life is becoming more or less the same wherever it is encountered. It is what we previously described as flight-culture, that to be found in airliners and in airports.

Redirecting the rich away from this culture of the air toward an earthier kind of cultural engagement is perhaps the most crucial of all cultural transformations. It is the rich who in most societies have the means, the abilities, and the energy to establish other ways of life. The problem is one of convincing them that this is worthwhile and that they need to attempt to do so. It is a matter of getting them to take time off work and assume a leadership role in their local communities and in local cultural affairs. For this to happen they will have to rediscover self-worth in working for others rather than just for themselves and their own advancement. The organizational capacities they have usually demonstrated in gaining their fortunes might then assume a wider scope and be applied to the cultural problems of their societies. A precondition of any moves in this direction is that the dominating influence of global culture, which teaches the opposite course to follow, must somehow be contained and muted.

One start to this would be to encourage more people to become travelers rather than tourists, which would also have a salutary side effect in curtailing the culture of the air. If people visited other countries as travelers and mingled with the local population, then modes of cultural interchange could be established based on a mutual cultural respect. If those coming from so-called advanced societies did not look down on the native cultures of under-developed societies, but sought to understand and even temporarily to share in them, the dignity of these would be much enhanced. For this kind of rela-tionship to be possible it is essential to travel many times to the same place and build up a familiarity with it and a real concern for it. This is the oppo-site of being a tourist globe-trotter just so as to see the sights, which is what global culture and the tourist industry promote.

At present it is the intrepid young who constitute the bulk of travelers. These are also generally the ones who show most concern for local cultures in faraway places, for the ecology of endangered habitats, and some of them are also in the forefront of the antiglobalization struggles. They tend to be less concerned with the ravages of global culture in their own societies and they do not fully understand what it is that they are opposing in the name of antiglobalization. This catchall term has impelled activists in many places to engage in violent demonstrations with considerable displays of vandalism. The net effect has tended to be counterproductive, for it is all too easy for the supporters of globalization to present themselves as the exponents of reason and rebut as irrational the accusations of the activists.

On both sides there is confusion as to what is meant by globalization. The antiglobalizers simply take it to mean a capitalism that has now assumed global dimensions. They trot out all the old anticapitalist arguments and im-plicitly invoke some of the old socialistic and anarchistic causes, which they cannot explicitly advocate since these have already been forfeited during the struggles of the previous century. Hence they appear as an unruly assortment of rebels without a cause, whose slogans can easily be refuted. Globalization can be shown to be economically beneficial for all those poor countries that can take advantage of it, despite temporary setbacks and recessions. Those that cannot do so are far worse off. It is developing all over the globe, much in the way that capitalism did during the nineteenth century in the West, with some of the same brutal exploitative practices, which one might expect will in time be overcome. Opposing it in the name of anticapitalism is short-sighted and futile, giving rise only to sterile revolutionism.

To this extent the supporters of globalization are quite right. However, they overlook the harmful cultural consequences of these economic devel-opments, just as they previously did not see the destructive ecological ones.

By now, largely thanks to the earlier generation of youthful activists, everyone is aware of the ecological damage that unrestrained capitalist exploitation of sensitive environments, such as tropical jungles, can bring about. But few have taken in that cultures are also prone to irreversible damage, with all the adverse consequences that we have here explored. On both these counts, the cultural and ecological, the unrestrained course of a predatory capitalism must be curbed and controlled. This, as we have shown, can be done without unduly disturbing capitalist production itself or forgoing its economic benefits.

It follows from this that the activists must be shown the right targets for their protests and taught better tactics that will work. They must learn to be discriminating in what they are against. They must avoid the mistakes of their parents' generation, the rebels and countercultural student activists of the late 1960s and early 1970s, who sought to confront the "system" as a whole and smash it with one blow. Their demonstrations, billed as revolutions, soon degenerated to street carnivals. The history of revolution, as Marx unwittingly predicted, repeated itself twice: the first time as tragedy, the second as farce. When the farce was over then disappointment, disillusionment, and utter cynicism set in. Those who undertook a Maoist "long march" through the institutions only served their own careers, frequently much better than anyone else for, blinded by self-righteousness, they were totally without scruple. They are now often in positions of power and so maintaining the very system they originally set out to destroy. This is particularly so in the media.

Will the same history repeat itself yet once again with the current generation of activists? Will this new crop of antiglobalizers end up as hucksters of global culture? Or will they come to realize that global culture is the real problem not globalization in itself? Will they be capable of acting against their own formative cultural experience and so against themselves? Is that kind of self-criticism possible for them?

Only the future will provide answers to these questions. The difficulties are immense. Acting against global culture will not be as simple or easy as demonstrating against Third World debt or child labor or sweatshop conditions. It will be more like acting against the spread of AIDS, which calls for a long-term effort of self-discipline to change ordinary people's assumptions and habits. The environmentalist campaigns also provide many models for action. Analogous such culturalist campaigns will also require organizations made up of diverse groups and interests. Strange partnerships and peculiar bedfellows will have to be envisaged between those deriving from radical and conservative sources. Culturalist politics, which transcends the usual Right–Left divide, will be different from any hitherto undertaken.

Such culturalist campaigns must keep an ideal goal in the forefront of their vision, that of a multicultural world where many local cultures bloom. This is also the vision of a cosmopolitan world where many people are travelers well versed in two or more cultures. In each society itself there will be diaspora communities practicing their own cultures in a bicultural setting of toleration and understanding. Within this ideal vision allowance can be made for global culture, which will also be there, but as one among many other cultures, not the dominant one. Those who are drawn to its charms and amenities might indulge themselves to a limited extent, but turn to other values when something more serious is at stake. Thus reduced to acceptable proportions global culture would not be the threat it is now.

Our quest is not to slay the dragon of global culture, only to draw its teeth and render it harmless. Once toothless this monster would no longer prey on people and could be left to graze in the financial pastures where there was money to be made. Those people who wish to watch advertising or buy silly entertainments or tasteless pap might still to do so to their hearts content. It would be none of our concern. But before we can reach this point there is a long journey and difficult struggle ahead, and many a fierce dragon to be confronted on the way.

This then is our ideal vision, one that constitutes a fairy-tale ending to our story. It is a wish-fulfillment dream born of frustration and fear. In the cold light of waking reality the apprehension that things will not turn out as well as we might wish makes one shudder and gives one pause. But that must not deflect us from acting now to the best of our foresight and ability. We must summon up the resolution to cope with the demands of the coming day. What the ultimate outcome of our efforts will be is not for us to say.

EPILOGUE

The fairy-tale ending of our story is obviously not the last word on the subject. The more realistic prospect is for a long and protracted period of struggle, strife, and stress as humanity gradually learns to adjust to living in a technological civilization. What is in store for the immediate future, when global culture is in the ascendancy, is likely to be a period of cultural disruption and dislocation. During this time there might be all kinds of desultory reactions against this domination, but mostly they will be futile. Those that are purely reactive have little chance of success, as is already proving to be the case with the fundamentalist Islamic movements at present. Others might be more enduring provided they have a better sense of what they are up against and how they must confront the challenge. A culturalist movement, such as is being advocated here, might have a better chance if it is based on a firm understanding of the basic principles at stake. These can provisionally be outlined in very general terms even now.

The basic all-embracing problem is how technology can be made compatible with nature and with culture. That means, how can we deploy our technological tools and systems in developing a technological civilization without destroying nature and culture in the process, and so, in effect, destroying ourselves? Technifying nature and culture, as we have shown, has produced unforeseen consequences that have proved difficult to manage. Our attempts to do so by imposing still further technical controls have themselves threatened to spin out of control.

The problem is clearly one to do with technology. Since technology is unavoidable, so is the problem. We cannot retreat to a pretechnological age. Mankind has ineluctably entered into a technological phase just as it had previously in its history entered first, about ten thousand years ago, into a sedentary agricultural and then, about five thousand years ago, into an urban civilizational one. There is a strong element of historical inevitability in this progression, which must not naively be equated with progress. Nevertheless, not everything in it is determined, and even though we cannot avoid entry into a technological civilization it is up to us to manage this transition with least harm to nature and culture. We have considerable scope for deciding how far we allow technology to dominate the various aspects of society. We can be critically discriminating between the technologies we utilize and those we reject. As Ellul, the foremost modern critic of technology, puts it, we must "live *in* technology and at the same time against technology."[1] This involves a difficult balancing act that no doubt some societies will manage better than others. It is not always the case that those who implement technologies first will be the most successful because they are the most advanced. Rather, it is those societies that deploy technologies with the least adverse consequences on nature and culture that will in the long run come out best.

Those countries that do least to poison their soil and avoid all the other identifiable ecological problems have gained for themselves the prospect of a sustainable agricultural future. Obviously no society can go back to "natural" farming and abandon all agricultural technologies, but these can be used more sparingly, more selectively, and more carefully. Anything that causes immediate harmful effects, such as noxious pesticides, must be eliminated; anything that causes long-term damage, yet cannot be avoided—such as burning fossil fuels—must be reduced to bare necessity; anything that is going to be difficult to reverse if it should go wrong, such as genetically engineered crops, should be applied very sparingly and cautiously. These, then, are some general principles in guarding against the technification of nature.

Guarding against the technification of culture follows analogous principles. Anything that is an immediate danger to well-being or has an obvious corrupting effect, such as the access of children to pornographic and violent forms of entertainment, should be banned. Anything that is highly technified and purely mechanistic, such as computer games and engineered music, should as far as possible be reduced. Anything that has little human content and no relation to reality, such as the various genres of fantasy literature and the films based on them, which are often no better than computer games, should only be indulged in with great care. If these principles of elimination, reduction, and caution are applied to all the products of global culture, then much would be achieved in limiting its damaging effects.

The ultimate principle at stake is to refuse to allow technics to dominate representation and ethos, the meaning and value endowing functions of culture. In the sphere of representation we should be committed to the fundamental standards of truth, reality, and objectivity. In our ethos we should take a stand for basic norms of morality and aesthetic and political values. Obviously there are no absolutes in these respects and no humanly optimal way of achieving any of these ends. Each society will have to develop its own unique forms of representation and ethos and shape its standards accordingly. But as long as there is a free and unforced exchange between societies, and discourse and argument proceed unhindered, as is bound to be the case in a global world, then some agreements will be reached and the differences that remain will be more in the nature of dialectical oppositions. The aim is not to reach consensus in everything, as theorists such as Jürgen Habermas suppose, but only to make disagreements comprehensible and so acceptable, and, above all, not to try to settle them by resort to violence.

In the sphere of representation the striving for consensus can lead to the current wrong-headed search for a unanimity of discourse. This, in a scientific context, amounts to the demand that truth should only be established by technified methodical procedure. Thus, on this basis, the typical method in the search for truth in our technological civilization becomes restricted to quantified measurement of variables, preferably of such things as instruments can record. Positivism is its rationalizing philosophy. This is one of the most limited and culturally impoverished criteria of verity that humanity has ever devised. It is the truth of bare material matter of fact, a truth bereft of most of the qualities that make something worth knowing. It can explain happenings, but not account for actions. For example, it can register and describe the earth's tremors and quakes, but not make meaningful the emotional tremblings and shudders of a single human body. It lacks the illuminating powers that answer to human curiosity and the need to understand.

If scientific representation is not to be reduced to the unanimity of instrumental measurement, it must cultivate alternative forms of description and explanation. Such possibilities have been explored in previous publications, above all in *The Ends of Science* and *A New Science of Representation.*[2] There it was argued that there can be no single, uniform mode of representation of complex phenomena. Even an ordinary ecosystem can be described and explained in different and even opposed ways. Obviously, any social system is of an exponentially higher order of complexity, and that greatly increases the possible alternate modes of representation. The fact that there are distinct social sciences and humanities and that these contain diverse types of theories and methods is not a weakness or a symptom of intellectual backwardness, as is assumed by those, such as Thomas Kuhn, who see physics as the supreme paradigm of all scientific endeavor, rather it exemplifies the level of complexity of the phenomena involved. The present dominance of physics in the sciences is itself a disturbing phenomenon.

The recognition of the multiplicity of sciences and approaches is in itself the basis of some degree of cultural difference. Science practiced in different ways in various types of institutions and social contexts provides an intellectual rationale for other cultural alternatives. If there can be no single unified science of Man, but always contending human sciences, then there can also be no one uniform conception of human nature or of human possibility. There must always be different visions of humanity and opposed views of human excellence. These will, in turn, promote cultural differences; or, putting it the other way, where cultural differences already existed, then these will fasten onto scientific alternatives in articulating themselves in opposition to each other. If it were ever the case that unanimity was attained in all the sciences, then this would be a sure proof of the onset of cultural homogeneity.

The prevalence of homogenization in the ethos reveals itself most prominently in the loss of stylistic diversity in the arts. In aesthetics it is the opposite of consensus that must be aimed for. Historically it was distinctiveness of style expressive of cultural uniqueness that was sought. Every culture had its style that embodied the worldview and values of that particular society. And every major grouping within it had its own forms and genres. This was especially true for the great universal styles, such as the Greco-Roman classical, the Byzantine, the Gothic and Renaissance of medieval Europe, the

Chinese-Japanese, the Buddhist, and the Islamic. Remnants of all of these still survive, but now in a highly debilitated state. The inroad of global culture into all the formerly independent civilizational areas is wiping out the last vestiges of their traditional styles and destroying their unique values. This is what Alsop in his book on art referred to as "a mass massacre of independent art traditions in every inhabited region of the globe."[3]

What is peculiar about global culture is that it has no style in this sense, for in it every art is reduced to technically manipulated stereotypes. It expresses no fundamental truths or values—not even the simplest ones, such as those of the old-time religions. But it seems equally set in its ways. In popular music there is the rock of the age, which has been around for nearly half a century; in pulp literature there are the gospels of adventure constituting various types of fiction, which have been around even longer; in films there are the constantly recycled quasi-comic book formats of crude mystery and morality plays; and so on for all the other arts. What this amounts to is not merely a loss of variety and diversity but a dulling of the mind, a dumbing-down that signifies a diminution of all the basic aesthetic qualities and critical faculties. Everything is converging to a common level of stupefaction. And that in itself is an index of the homogenization that has already taken place, and an indication of where the striving for aesthetic consensus can lead.

If there is to be any recovery in the arts and the critical sense in general then the preponderant aim must be a revival of distinctiveness of style and of stylistic integrity. Only a coherent style can embody the uniqueness of a culture. Where cultural differences exist these will inevitably reveal themselves in opposed worldviews and values, which will generate different styles of art. The emergence of stylistic diversity will, thus, be an indication that cultural homogenization has been overcome. How to attain a style is our main artistic problem, one which we will have to consider in a separate work on aesthetics. We cannot here foreshadow all the conclusions of that work, but one point of relevance will clearly reveal itself: the starting point for any stylistic departures is to be found in local cultures and their historic traditions. Going back to one's own roots and developing from there in a free and modern spirit is a possible course for artists even now. But obviously no single artist can forge a style alone. That will have to be the joint endeavor of groups of artists and communities of connoisseurs, as well as other aesthetically supportive parties.

What we need to demonstrate in different fields of representation and ethos is that the onset of a technological civilization does not mandate cultural uniformity. Such a civilization is, at least in theory, compatible with cultural diversity. The success or failure of mankind's transition to this new civilizational basis is premised on this possibility. If this is not so, then mankind faces a grim future, indeed. But if it is true, then the technological revolution that we are now undergoing might in time prove as providential as the Neolithic revolution of mankind's distant past—provided, of course, that none of the many immediately threatening catastrophes eventuate. How this will play itself out cannot be foreseen; there is no science of futurology that amounts to more than science fiction.

The crucial thing for us in the present is not to foreclose the future by shutting off the past. Conserving cultures now means preserving the heritage of the past for the sake of future generations, so that they might make use of it in ways that we cannot do or even imagine. What we can do is to safeguard such future possibilities. This is the supreme task of our generation according to which we shall be judged by those generations to come.

ENDNOTES

INTRODUCUTION

1. Joseph Alsop, *The Rare Art Tradition: The History of Art Collecting and Its Linked Phenomena* (London: Thames and Hudson, 1982), 20-21.
2. Richard Stivers, *Technology as Magic: The Triumph of the Irrational* (New York: Continuum Press, 2001), 24.
3. Stivers, *Technology as Magic.*
4. Stivers, *Technology as Magic*, 23.

CHAPTER 1

1. Thomas Friedman, *The Lexus and the Olive Tree* (London: HarperCollins, 1999), 23, 278.
2. Norman Lebrecht, *When the Music Stops . . . Managers, Maestros and the Corporate Murder of Classical Music* (London: Simon and Schuster, 1996), 35.
3. Zygmunt Bauman, *Globalization: The Human Consequences* (Cambridge: Polity Press, 1998), 3.

CHAPTER 2

1. Robert McChesney, *Rich Media, Poor Democracy* (Urbana, Ill.: University of Illinois Press, 1999), 39, 85.

2. See Jacques Ellul, *Propaganda: The Formation of Men's Attitudes*, trans. Konrad Keller and Jean Lerner (New York: Vintage Books, 1973).

3. Naomi Klein, *No Logo* (London: HarperCollins, 2000).

4. Stivers, *Technology as Magic*, 114.

5. Nicholas Baker, *Double-Fold: Libraries and the Assault on Paper* (New York: Random House, 2000).

6. Christopher Allen, *Art in Australia* (London: Thames and Hudson, 1997), 188.

7. Shakespeare, *Measure for Measure* (Act III, scene 1, lines 32–34). From Harry Levine, ed., *The Riverside Shakespeare* (Atlanta: Houghton Mifflin, 1974), 565.

CHAPTER 3

1. Harry Redner, *A New Science of Representation: Towards an Integrated Theory of Representation in Science, Politics and Art* (Boulder, Colo.: Westview Press, 1994); Harry Redner, *Ethical Life: The Past and Present of Ethical Cultures* (Lanham, Md.: Rowman & Littlefield, 2001).

2. Harry Redner, *In the Beginning Was the Deed: Reflections on the Passage of Faust* (Berkeley, Calif.: University of California Press, 1982).

3. Charles Hartshorne and Paul Weiss, eds., *C. S. Peirce: Collected Papers* (Cambridge, Mass.: Harvard University Press, 1960), 155.

4. Jacques Ellul, *The Technological Society,* trans. John Wilkinson (London: Jonathan Cape, 1965), xxxiii.

5. Jacques Ellul, *The Technological System*, trans. Joachim Neugroschel (New York: Continuum Press, 1980).

6. Ellul, *The Technological Society*, 66–77.

7. Joseph Needham, *Science and Civilization in China* (Cambridge: Cambridge University Press, 1959).

8. George Ritzer, *The McDonaldization of Society* (Thousand Oaks, Calif.: Pine Forge Press, 1993).

9. Lebrecht, *When the Music Stops*, 399.

10. Stivers, *Technology as Magic*, 196.

11. Richard Sennett, *The Corrosion of Character: The Consequences of Work in the New Capitalism* (New York: Norton, 1998), 68.

12. Ernst Gombrich, *Art and Illusion* (Oxford: Phaidon Press, 1960).

13. Richard Stivers, *The Culture of Cynicism* (Oxford: Blackwell, 1994), 132.

14. Stivers, *The Culture of Cynicism*, 133.

15. Stivers, *The Culture of Cynicism*, 73.
16. Ellul, *The Technological System*, 191.
17. Stivers, *The Culture of Cynicism*, 72–73.
18. Stivers, *The Culture of Cynicism*, 73.
19. Redner, *Ethical Life*.
20. Stivers, *The Culture of Cynicism*, 73.
21. Ellul, *The Technological Society*, 127.
22. Ellul, *The Technological System*, 170.
23. Ellul, *The Technological Society*, 83.
24. Ellul, *The Technological System*, 177.
25. Ellul, *The Technological System*, 177–178.
26. Ellul, *The Technological System*, 200.
27. Ellul, *The Technological System*, 200.
28. Ellul, *The Technological System*, 127.
29. Redner, *Aesthetic Life*, forthcoming.

CHAPTER 4

1. Ann Cvetkovich and Douglas Kellner, *Articulating the Global and the Local* (Boulder, Colo.: Westview Press, 1997), 13.

2. According to Louis-Jean Calvert, in 1964,

[Barthes] was offered a contract to study the semiology of the state-owned Renault company; starting from images, a few sets of photos and posters he had been given, Barthes produced an analysis of the advertising strategies used to sell the car. Gradually, the semioclastic aim of *Mythologies* was becoming endorsed by professional advertisers. . . . The fact that Barthes had accepted the Renault contract, that he used his scientific or intuitive skills, albeit momentarily, to improve car sales might lead to the conclusion that he was fascinated by a world which elsewhere he criticized.

From Louis-Jean Calvert, *Roland Barthes: A Biography*, trans. Sara Wykes (Cambridge: Polity Press, 1994), 143.

The conclusion that Calvert draws from this apparently "momentary" episode (how long can "momentary" be?) is not the only one; there is the even more obvious conclusion that Barthes could be bought. He is by no means an exceptional case in the realm of higher learning. Just recently it was alleged that the highly regarded conservative English moral philosopher and aesthetician, Roger Scruton, was secretly in the pay of Japanese tobacco companies to promote the virtues of cigarettes by planting articles and "news" in the British press. (Report by Kevin Maguire and Julian Borger, in *The Guardian Weekend*, February 2002.)

3. Once again Barthes was in the lead in showing himself very appreciative of pulp fiction. He analysed aspects of the James Bond novel *Goldfinger* in highly theoretic terms. See Roland Barthes, "Structural Analysis of Narratives," in Stephen Heath, ed., *Roland Barthes: Image-Music-Text* (Glasgow: Fontana, 1977). This practice is now commonplace as many other critics have followed in his lead.

4. Nicholas Garnham, "Political Economy and Cultural Studies," in Simon During (ed.), *The Cultural Studies Reader* (London: Routledge, 1993), 500.

5. Redner, *Ethical Life*.

6. Donald Clarke, *The Rise and Fall of Popular Music* (New York: Viking-Penguin, 1995), 492.

7. Alsop, *The Rare Art Traditions*, 15.

8. Alsop, *The Rare Art Traditions*, 19.

9. Alsop, *The Rare Art Traditions*, 19.

10. Klein, *No Logo*, 201.

11. The latest evidence in education research is that computers have had an adverse effect on maths learning, the one subject where one might have expected them to do some good. See Joshua D. Angrist and Victor Lavy, "New Evidence on Classroom Computers and Pupil Learning," in *The Economic Journal* 112 (October 2002): 735–765.

12. Undergraduate courses in hip-hop are now offered in many leading American universities, such as Stanford, Michigan, and Penn State.

13. Ellul, *The Technological System*, 312.

EPILOGUE

1. Jacques Ellul, *Perspectives on Our Age*, ed. William H. Vandenberg, trans. Joachim Neugroschel (New York: Seabury Press, 1981), 83.

2. Harry Redner, *The Ends of Science: An Essay on Scientific Authority* (Boulder, Colo.: Westview Press, 1987); Redner, *A New Science of Representation* (Boulder, Colo.: Westview Press, 1994).

3. Alsop, *The Rare Art Traditions*, 20.

INDEX

ABOUT THE AUTHOR

Harry Redner is an Australian and peripatetic academic who spent the major portion of his career at Monash University in Melbourne, but has also lived and worked in many other countries: England, Italy, Israel, Germany, France, and the United States, where he was a Senior Fulbright Fellow and held visiting appointments in a number of universities. He is the author of eight other books on many subjects, ranging from literature and philosophy to sociology and science. His next work will be on aesthetics and art in general.

MORE
evidence
that
demands a
verdict

historical evidences
for the Christian Scriptures

**compiled
by
Josh
McDowell**

Traveling Representative for
Campus Crusade for Christ International